burnt bridges

Hodder & Stoughton

LONDON SYDNEY AUCKLAND TORONTO

a souvenir of the swinging sixties and beyond

burnt bridges

Charles Marowitz

A John Curtis Book

British Library Cataloguing in Publication Data

Marowitz, Charles
  Burnt bridges: a London souvenir
  1. Theatre
  I. Title
  792

  ISBN 0-340-49659-2

First published in Great Britain 1990

Published by Hodder and Stoughton,
a division of Hodder and Stoughton Ltd,
Mill Road, Dunton Green, Sevenoaks, Kent TN13 2YA
Editorial Office: 47 Bedford Square, London WC1B 3DP

Photoset by Rowland Phototypesetting Ltd,
Bury St Edmunds, Suffolk

Printed in Great Britain by
St Edmundsbury Press Ltd, Bury St Edmunds, Suffolk

for

Susan K.
Gypsie K.
Inge-Margrete S.
Rachel S.
Gillian W.
Lesley F.W.
Diane S.
Lisa T.
Sian H.
Nancy T.
Jill D.
Penny I.
Margaret R.
Clovissa N.
Fenella F.
Chris F.
Linda H.
Anne-Helene G.
Claudia vA.
Karin S.
Belinda H.
Annie L.
Ashley H.
Hopi S.
Liz K.
Karyn M.
Anne F.
Susan P.
Linda R.
Aideen M.
Liz B.
Kari O.
Ann L.
Caroline H.
Claudia A.
Zoe P.
Michelle V.
Pola C.
Karen F.
Jean G.
Anniker H.
Alexandra B.
Mo D.
Giesele H.

contents

acknowledgements

The author acknowledges kind permission to quote copyright material from the following sources: the Literary Estate of Kenneth Tynan, the *Observer* (for the review by Alan Pryce-Jones), the William Saroyan Foundation, Peter Brook and Mark Boyle.

illustrations

Introduction

In New York City, in the mid-Fifties, the spirit of Senator Joe McCarthy lay heavy on the land. If you advocated recognition of Red China, you were a 'red'; if you opposed the Cold War, you were a 'pinko'; if you approved of Judge William O. Douglas or the editorial sentiments of *The Nation*, you were a 'radical'; and, if you had a good word to say for Soviet culture, you were a 'fellow traveller'. Accordingly, I was considered a red-pinko-liberal-fellow-traveller.

At seventeen, I had founded an acting company on the lower East side of New York and, when the *Village Voice* started up in Greenwich Village, I was their youngest and most intolerant critic, but I was stultifying in New York. American life was dominated by plasticity and conformity – the twin curses of the 1950s – and each day I found myself bristling with contempt for what was happening in my society and the craven politicians who were allowing it to happen.

Having experienced the civilizing influence of France during a two-year stint with the US Army, I began to fantasize a different, more meaningful life in Europe and, being eligible for the GI Bill of Rights, which subsidized education for veterans, I tried to organize myself back to France. There were no approved theatre academies in Paris, whereas in England there was one in Glasgow and another in London. I rationalized the abandonment of France and opted for London, convincing myself that I would be hopping across the Channel almost every week.

When I arrived in London in 1956, I was only dimly aware of the social ferment. CND marches, assorted demos and plays like *Look Back in Anger* were opening shots in a battle that would rage for the next fifteen years. People read the *New Statesman* and talked about 'the new Left' as if determined to reorder the past three decades of British history. But everywhere I was conscious of the rigidities of the British heritage. People were obsessed with 'class', but that was merely a code word: it really meant working-class discontent and a growing impatience with middle-class privilege; it was an ensign of envy raised as if it were the Union Jack. The vast majority of the British were essentially a horde of poverty-stricken workers in drab green attire living in terraced houses and bedsits, still reeling from the blight of Clement Attlee's austerity programme, and determined to redress the social imbalance. The political leaders seemed unequipped to deal with the social changes. All of them, Tory *and* Labour, seemed to have been fashioned in another age and fit only for past crises. It was as if Harold Macmillan had been created for the sole purpose of having the mickey taken out of him by Peter Cook. When Harold Wilson ushered in his watered down brand of British Socialism, it was as if *he* had been tailor made for John Bird and the satirists of *That Was The Week That Was*. There was an unreal theatricality about British political life; as if the sets of a new play had suddenly flown in behind them, but all the actors were still in the costumes of the previous show.

Dissent, anti-Establishment fervour, social polarity, rock, pop, poetry and jazz, sexual audacity, artistic innovation, the underground press, mini-skirts and pot all swirled together in a bubbling stew. New icons appeared almost monthly: McLuhan, Dylan, the Stones, the Beatles, Marcuse, Laing – the avalanche of new writers, thinkers and artists made it impossible to keep up. There were so many new ideas, artifacts, trends to assimilate; so many new places to go to, cuisine to sample, people to meet. It was as if a small but dynamic segment of the population had invited the entire nation to a party and, because it was noisy and precluded the possibility of getting any sleep, neighbours felt obliged to leave the sedateness of their own homes and join in. Those who participated got an enormous charge out of the Sixties; the po-faced grumps who shut their windows and pulled down their blinds never quite realized what they missed.

The convulsions produced by the counter-culture and its youthful insurrectionists were, morally, politically, culturally, and quintessentially un-British. The fashion for long hair flouted the icons of City respectability; mini-skirts were a sexual abomination (especially for middle-aged British women, who never had good legs to begin with); and bright colours in clothing and design were instinctively perceived as 'bad taste'. The American influence was all-pervasive, often masking more deep-rooted British hang-ups. Rock 'n' roll, for instance, enabled frustrated English kids to let off steam under the pretext of musical emulation. Vietnam protest was a metaphor for the abuses of a rigidified Establishment and the deadly stodginess of middle-class suburbanity. Smoking pot and shooting up on acid was a form of decadence so diametrically opposed to the cosy British notion of 'a good pipeful of tobacco' or 'a nice cuppa tea' that it turned the Heaven of genteel recreation into a Hell of satanic satiety. Although the most vociferous proponents of the new consciousness were on the whole politically *un*conscious, what they unleashed was a rebellion the social tendencies of which were thought to be dangerously subversive.

It is a great compliment to the British character that between 1960 and, say, 1973 to be *English* was to be thought of as being swinging, loose, innovative, experimental, freaky, uninhibited, idealistic, transcendental, off beat and trendy – words which would have been unthinkable in 1950 and incomprehensible a century earlier. But, despite the prominence of these social characteristics, they really applied to only a tiny percentage of the population; the vast majority of Britons not only frowned upon these departures from tradition, many held them in contempt.

A good deal of the time cultural life in London felt like one of those typical 1960s symposia which had got out of hand – rattled by hecklers and sabotaged by strident 'happeners' whose subversive private agendas trashed all prearranged schedules. It was a time when the intimidating pressure of novelty and trendiness was felt everywhere. To be 'up' on the latest theory was far more important than being able to understand it. It was a time when *reference to* rather than *immersion in* ideas was at a premium. The babble was incessant and vigorously encouraged by the Sunday newspapers, which were constantly on the look out for new culture heroes or fringe weirdos wayward enough to divert the rubberneck readers of the *Mail*, the *Express* and the *Sunday Times*. To be 'elected' to esoteric talk shows such as *Late Night Line-Up* or magazine programmes like *Tempo* and *Omnibus* meant achieving a certain artistic credibility which needed no further validation. From such a perch it almost didn't matter what one said or, indeed, if one said anything at all. The implications of the iconography were sufficient to insure celebrity. At social occasions (and they were both ubiquitous and inescapable) what one needed most was a few glib phrases which implied an understanding of theories such as R. D. Laing's on schizophrenia, Bertolt Brecht's *Verfremdung*, Antonin Artaud's Theatre of Cruelty, Marshall McLuhan's 'global village', Wilhelm Reich's orgone therapy or Marcuse's extrapolations from Marx and Freud.

Most publications were rooted in that same sense of 'intellectual quick fix' which infected their readership. To have lingered too long over any of those theories, to have actually begun in-depth research into their deeper significance, was considered intellectually non-U (to use a term from a generation earlier) and indicated a condition dangerously close to being 'not with it' – that is, losing the alacrity to flit, butterfly-like, between subjects, ideas and disciplines which, because they actually required years of study to grasp fully, had to be winged in private conversations so as not to blow anyone's cover. Ideas themselves were the equivalent of body paintings or macrobiotic food, and the more they came daubed in psychedelic colours, the more attractive they were. That stretch of fascinating ambiguity which we call 'the grey zone' was extremely unfashionable. 'Black', of course, was 'beautiful' and white – particularly in art, wall furnishing and theatre design – *à la mode*. Rainbows were decidedly 'in' – the more psychedelic the better. Everything, in short, that conspired to be flashy, fashionable, immediately communicable and easily convertible to journalistic shorthand tended to confirm one's favoured position in the hierarchies of the Now Generation.

There was a certain aesthetic stance (the artistic equivalent of a mass-produced T-shirt) that automatically inspired admiration because it connected with postures we instinctively found sympathetic. In an era sensitively attuned to body language, we were particularly responsive to that stance. It confirmed our shibboleths, helped identify our enemies and define our own position versus our malevolent antagonists: the Establishment, the Politicians and the Avatars of Good Taste. With the passage of time we had to pay the price for being blinkeredly partisan, and much of the intellectual book-keeping of the 1980s was taken up with painful reappraisals of what we once took to be *chefs d'oeuvres* or the *summum bonum*.

Behind much of the euphoria of the 1960s was an irrepressible desire to manufacture experience which didn't come naturally to the celebrants. When I recollect the most effusive jamborees of the 1960s, at places such as Alexandra Palace, the Royal Albert Hall, the Round House or almost any protracted and ear-splitting night at UFO, I can distinctly recall the despair that smouldered behind all that superficial frivolity: the vain hope that external stimuli would touch, shake up and possibly transform the inner lives of kids who dreaded the idea that, sooner or later, the ear-shattering bands would pack up their monolithic speakers and the psychedelic slides would be extinguished, that pot, hash, booze, itinerant sex and multi-media stimulations would eventually wind down and that the drab reality which all those things temporarily obliterated would return. 'Fun' was essentially a negative concept: it meant the removal of deadening tedium and the annihilation of predictable regimentation. Novelty, that much-prized 1960s virtue, was so prized precisely because, in breathlessly pursuing the new, the mundane could be fleetingly denied, although never permanently transmuted. After highly touted media events their 'myth' would achieve massive pro-portions. It was 'a blast' – 'too much' – 'far out' – 'mindblowing'. It was almost never a recollection of mediocre music, bad poetry or puerile happenings. Because it was romanticized going in, it was mythologized coming out. In one sense, the artifacts them-selves didn't really matter. Good poetry and brilliant music would not have appreciably affected the nature of those experiences since they were predicated not on the artifacts themselves, but on the philosophic notion of what they stood for. To be 'far out' was not a critical mien that needed to be proven by argument or analysis; it was enough that it was happening in the appropriate milieu and being sopped up by people wildly predisposed to it. At the *International Times* inaugural at the Round House little white cubes of sugar were given out at the door and lots of people got high on them. In a placebo culture the 'real thing' almost violates the spirit of the occasion.

Beneath the flamboyant gentleness of the period, within the hearts of those blossoming quietly on the idea of flower power, lay an iron dogma: to be 'square', conformist, materialistic or solemn was to be a sworn enemy of the loose, the free, the adventurous and the fun-loving. I remember a public event held at the Institute of Contemporary Arts and a platform on which sat representatives of the New Consciousness – in their jeans and Afghan jackets, beads jangling round their necks, their unruly locks swirling round their shoulders. Beside them sat two gentlemen in three-piece suits radiating the well-coiffed look of middle-class affluence. The iconography was immediately apparent and the opinions expressed entirely irrelevant. The dominantly youthful audience had immediately distinguished their role models and, no matter how pathetic their reasoning or vapid their views, they were already triumphant because they were 'on the right side'. As regards image, the men in three-piece suits never stood a chance.

After a particularly blistering review of Paul Foster's *Tom Paine* which I'd written for the *New York Times*, Kevin O'Connor, one of the lead actors in that off-beat farrago, encountered me in a corridor at the BBC and cried agonizingly: 'How could you write such a review! I thought you were one of us!' – Clearly 'one of us' freely translated meant: with all critical judgement suspended and mindlessly in favour of the dogma contained in a simplistic, pseudo-experimental mish-mash directed by trendy Tom O'Horgan of *Hair* fame. I smiled and was evasive, and will never forgive myself for not scalding him with the lava-like contempt I felt for the boorishness of artists who believe that ideological partisanship condones every banality. In that heady, indiscriminate, everything goes time of cultural matyness, how one burned with loathing for the gormless excrescences of those up-beat, off-beat deadbeats whose allegiance to woolly-minded anti-Establishment convictions unquestioningly justified execrable art. To be 'one of them' would have inspired as much self-loathing as to be counted among the stalwarts of the National Front or the founding members of the Monday Club.

Nourished in the afterglow of the Twenties, loosely modelled after the Dadaists, the Transcendentalists, the Aesthetes, the Pataphysicians and archetypical fun couples like Oscar and

'Bosey', Gertrude and Alice, Scott and Zelda, the 1960s may well have been the last Age of Innocence. For the writers, poets, musicians and artists that dedicated themselves to the events, edited the journals and poured their lifeblood into the social credos it was a time without a bottom line. No one counted the cost because cost accounting was alien to hippie philosophy. What the intellectuals, the poets and the journalists did was to engender an idealism to which a large number of people, many of them young and impressionable, dynamically responded. If it was naïveté, there was something liberating and constructive about its energy. If it was simplistic, it served as a useful corrective to the cynicism bequeathed by previous generations. If it dealt with the grand generalizations of human life, how people should try to live with one another, how spirituality should be returned to a world that had become gruellingly materialistic, it elevated social debate by addressing fundamental issues.

Driven by unquenchable desires to commune and to celebrate (the rock star being the High Priest, the rock concert the Mass), there were legions of kids between the ages of sixteen and thirty-five who really did influence the perceptions of an age. They did it by trying to implement the image of a society derived from inspirations as various as Rousseau, Paine, Thoreau, Reich, Fanon, McLuhan, Marcuse, Millet, Malcolm X, the lyrics of Bob Dylan and John Lennon – and they were motivated by the complacency of an unventilated political system which, in terms of the inner violence it inflicted, was comparable to the Reign of Terror. The demos, the marches, the idealization of cult heroes such as The Who, Joan Baez, the Stones and the Beatles were all part of a cultural dissent which was sixty years in the making and thirty years overdue. 'Revolutionaries' only in the sense that they had Che Guevara posters on their walls and accepted the risk of overnight lock-up for attending sit-ins in Grosvenor Square, the young instinctively realized that the way to make revolution work was to change the interaction between individuals and by questioning the bedrock values which had produced the stasis.

I always recoil from people who blandly dismiss the impact of the 1960s with epithets such as 'naïve' and 'mindless', assuming that its mores, its passions, its priorities no longer apply, have, in fact, been superseded by the social and economic advances of the 1980s and 90s. Nothing could be further from the truth. It is not only in the baby-boomers that much of the 1960s idealism lives on, it is also in the intellectual vestiges which continue to influence contemporary behaviour, both private and public. It is not for nothing that the period is being so vigorously researched and so relentlessly reconstructed in books, exhibitions and retrospectives of all kinds. The zealots of the 1960s made similar cultural forays into the Transcendentalists, the Pre-Raphaelites and the cult heroes of the Twenties. Whenever a new epoch announces itself, it speaks in accents redolent of the times on which its strongest passions have been modelled. Despite the callowness and innocence of the ideals that stirred the Sixties, I believe a return to some of those ideals would do much to improve the quality of contemporary life. Indeed, the fervour that toppled state Communism in countries such as Poland, Czechoslovakia, East Germany and Romania is kindred to the spirit which swept through that politically destabilizing decade. (In Czechoslovakia, for instance, it was students and artists who actually brought about the downfall of the regime and an underground playwright who was elected President of the new government.)

If the communal instinct produced the excesses of Charles Manson and his murderous psychopaths, what can one say about the avaricious egocentricity of the 1980s, when insider traders and brokers without consciences looked no further than their bank accounts, their new Porsches and their giant City holdings. The 'we' generation was naïve, but the 'me' generation is ruthless and contemptible. At least in the 1960s a collective passion against social and political injustice produced spontaneous attempts at direct action. The notion that change was possible was not only in the air but also embedded in the entrails of young men and women who huddled beside each other, ritualistically singing folksongs while being unceremoniously lifted into black marias. A social action was connected to an intellectual passion and people held the belief that the heartfelt sentiment of many people banded together to speak their mind could influence the larger issues.

Today an overriding cynicism has squelched that belief. 'Change' is produced by pulling the right strings, knowing the right people, infiltrating the media or mounting an opposition as cynical and insidious as the evil one is trying to overthrow. This may be the fruits of a greater maturity – but it is frazzling the threads which keep together the fabric of our lives. Thirty years ago standing in the cold in a public square and blowing clouds of vapour from one's nostrils was a small price to pay for a sense of lively engagement in vital issues. Today there is almost nothing so chaffing that we feel the need to 'demonstrate' our opposition. Opposition itself has become inner directed and we are much more likely to sublimate our social and political hostility into family feuds, interpersonal abuse or irrational acts of urban violence. Today we not only do not 'fight city hall', we disdain those who obstreperously criticise its *raison d'être*. We have become a society of pawns and cowards – too sophisticated to dirty our hands with causes 'which are bound to fail anyway'. The tumult of dissent is subdued by the muzak of our self-complacency. Our 'donations' are there to support the worthy causes – so long as they don't become so pressing they demand personal intercession. We are too clever not to realize that in all important matters we are impotent and, to avoid the egregious implications of that impotence, we convert that depressing insight into proofs of our maturity. In the 1960s we didn't know 'it didn't matter' – that 'every protest was doomed to failure' – we were preposterous enough to assume that the exercise of national will could change the law, stop a war, topple a leader, demolish an attitude, instil a new value. We were foolish enough to believe that passion could change the world.

Autobiography is predicated on the false assumption that there is a coherence in a person's life which can be chronologically recollected and, once transcribed, represent a true picture of past events. But if we know anything about our lives, we know they are an admixture of accident, happenstance, miscalculation and pure fluke. We also know, if we are honest with ourselves, that, out of the teeming cascade of events and non-events which make up our lives, there are at best only a few dozen moments that have any durable meaning.

Proceeding on that assumption, I have included here only the peaks of my reminiscence: those moments, incidents, people and sensations which, if I had my life to live over, I would reprise for the pleasure they bestowed or the agony they conferred.

I am concerned here with only a portion of my life – my London life, as it were – which began roughly in 1956 and ended (even more roughly) in 1980 – the twenty-four years in which the blandness of the Fifties gave way to the tumult of the Sixties, the contradictions of the Seventies and the retrenchment of the Eighties.

Because I was regularly lodging reports throughout this period for the *Village Voice*, the *New York Times*, *Encore* and *Plays & Players* magazine, my articles and reviews have in some ways fulfilled the role of a diary. Where the memories grow faint, I acknowledge the fact; where they are vivid, I try to render them as I recall them; but throughout I am conscious of the fact that distortion, myth, fabrication and self-delusion are so much part of our lives that it is impossible to extirpate them entirely from our recollections. In that sense, autobiography is merely a form (some would contend the highest form) of fiction.

C. M.
March 1990

I Arrival in Wonderland

On the boat that brought me to England in 1956, I struck up an acquaintance with a young Iranian musicologist named Adi, who, miraculously, was able to identify by name and Köchel listing any Mozartian piece I would hum or whistle. For someone who had only just begun to discover the vast treasure trove of classical music, this struck me as an astounding magical power tantamount to that of Blackstone or Houdini.

From the day we docked in Southampton and took the train into London, Adi, short, tubby, swarthy, constantly sucking imaginary mouthfuls of succotash, was my constant companion. Together, we experienced London for the first time, making the obligatory pilgrimages to Piccadilly Circus, Soho and Trafalgar Square. In those days, as I suppose is still the case today, the fountain where Eros stands was a kind of unofficial club house. On humid evenings you could find emigrés from almost every country in the world sprawling on its black, granite steps, basking in the (usually) wet incandescence of the Piccadilly lights, making obeisance to the God of Love balletically poised above the fountain by studiously chatting up au pairs from Sweden or knapsacked students en route to hostels in Earl's Court.

After an evening crammed with (for us) spectacular sights (theatres, strip joints and skiffle clubs), we found ourselves standing at a bus-stop unaware that the transportation, like heating or plumbing, was still in its embryonic stage in Britain and that, in fact, the last bus had come and gone about half an hour before. We were given this information by a pert, auburn haired girl who, like ourselves, had also missed her connection. Since, as it turned out, we were all heading to roughly the same part of town (Earl's Court), we cavalierly offered the girl a lift in our cab and, during the course of the ride, discovered her name was Heather and her personality flighty and outgoing. She briefly but conscientiously orientated us to London, its pitfalls and its splendours, and so enchanted were we with the briefing

– purred out in a soft Scot's burr – that we offered her a nocturnal night-cap in our hotel room, if she were possibly that way inclined, which, as it turned out, she was.

I can no longer remember the sequence of events once we got into the room, all I do know is that within what felt like five or ten minutes all three of us were in the same bed and Heather was suggesting an inexhaustible number of elaborate positions by means of which we could all remain equally occupied and pleasurably pass the time. Needless to say, my relationship with Adi deepened immeasurably as neither he nor I had ever found ourselves in a situation of such triangular intimacy. Heather, as it turned out, was more predisposed to white caucasians than 'Arabic gentlemen' and therefore conspicuously favoured me in the days to come. However, outside the exhilarating confines of our Earl's Court hotel, her blunt, practical approach to life and dull-as-dust personality left much to be desired. After a particularly barren night following a showing of Ingmar Bergman's *Smiles of a Summer Night* at the Academy Cinema, which I loved and she loathed, our brief liaison – to use the appropriate verb – petered out and that was the end of the episode. As for Adi, he vanished forever like the genie he may well have been.

I recount this vignette not to titillate but because it was my novitiate London experience, a harbinger of what my life in London was to be. The city, I learned quickly and emotionally, was a place for unexpected encounters with unpredictable people, a place where sensibility and sensuality would always be in tandem, and where the most mundane people and commonplace events could suddenly transform into adventures redolent of the *Arabian Nights* or the tales of Boccaccio.

Once classes began at the London Academy of Music and Dramatic Art, the institution in which I had been enrolled thanks to the magnanimity of the GI Bill, the splendours and miseries of British life started to come in fast profusion. The principal of LAMDA in 1956 was Michael MacOwan, a short, bespectacled, reformed alcoholic director who was potty about Shakespeare and used to direct the Bard with a copy of the folio spread on his lap, his gaze averted from the stage and his finger beating out the iambic pentameter. When an actor stressed the wrong syllable, neglected an ellision or ignored an *enjambement*, he would stop the rehearsal, point out the error and then, the speech corrected, return to his folio and, with his gaze still averted, continue to audit the performance.

The staff at LAMDA were quite respectable, consisting at various times of Catherine Lacey, Peter Coe, Michael Warre and the legendary voice coach, Iris Warren – with much ballyhoo'd appearances from luminaries such as J. B. Priestley and Christopher Fry. It was Fry himself who directed a student production of *The Firstborn*, in which I played Aaron, one of the more unspeakable performances I essayed at LAMDA – almost as execrable as my Lord Foppington in *The Country Wife*, my spastic and inaudible *King John* or my dandified and round-shouldered Ludovico in *Othello*. Genial, avuncular, soft-spoken, with the abstracted manner of a beatific nun, Fry used to imply that, despite the dispassionate air, he was, spiritually speaking, 'getting it regularly'.

As a director, he was almost invisibly 'laid back', making arcane literary allusions through a smokescreen of pipe tobacco. He had a passion for run-throughs and I remember one dress rehearsal night when, having once trotted through the whole goddam biblical epic, his only 'note' was that we trot through the whole damn thing again.

Fry's emergence as a playwright was late in coming. Although he felt it was something he was destined to do, he kept trying to avert his fate. He succeeded until he was well into middle age and then, as if keeping an appointment made years before, it all began to flow out. *The Firstborn*, for instance, was started in 1938, but not actually completed until 1945. In America, works such as *The Lady's Not For Burning* and *Venus Observed* created the impression that he was merely a fancy word-spinner. Despite a grudging appreciation of his dramatic and poetic gifts, that impression persisted throughout his life. According to a mildewed notepad from that period, during a rehearsal, he said: 'You'll remember in the beginning was the Word, and it's always been the Word. Each new piece of writing has tried to articulate the inexpressible. It is because a thing ceases to be true as soon as it is said that people continue writing, hoping the next word may have the permanence and irreversibility the last one lacked.'

Unlike his mellifluent characters, Fry always spoke haltingly and with great caution. No sooner had he verbalized a thought than he began to qualify it, reroute it or completely reject it. Often during rehearsals, trying to explain himself, he would throw up his hands in exasperation and cry: 'Words, words – how difficult it all is!' He was a member in good standing of the E. Martin Browne Society (Browne had been T. S. Eliot's mentor), which equated poetry with piety and, as one actor put it, 'often seemed like a visiting angel in between earthly and heavenly stops'. I remember when I once questioned him about foreign locales, he replied: 'I don't do much actual travelling. I'm very much a mental tourist.' In the late Fifties, despite serious misgivings by many critics, he was riding high, but, even with regular revivals of *The Lady's Not For Burning*, his reputation seems not to have survived into the 1970s or 1980s. He was very much part of that amateur gentleman tradition which was rife in England in the late 1950s: writers and artists who could just as easily sink without trace into the middle-class gentility from which they sprang as leap forward into commercial success.

At LAMDA I became aware for the first time of what the British, as opposed to the American, approach to acting was. According to the general perception, it was somewhat weighted towards technique and strong on voice and movement. In fact, it was exclusively concerned with externals and thoroughly oblivious to the concept of inner technique. Stanislavsky was given mindless lip service, but the only class which theoretically touched on his ideas, a bi-weekly improvisation session conducted by Brian May (an instructor with one lung who, it was rumoured, was subsidized by Dorothy L. Sayers), was a travesty of Method work. The improvisations consisted of little playlets worked up by the students under the instructor's watchful eye, invariably followed by the question, 'Well, how did it feel?' A question which regularly elicited vague and confused rejoinders from people who, having no objectivity of their own, were hungering after authoritative critiques. A rough kind of consensus more or less determined the success or failure of each playlet and, when some of the American students, who were versed in the Method, ventured to suggest the work was devoid of appropriate 'actions', sub-text or palpable 'contact', the instructor merely blinked at this new terminology and went on to mount newer and more diverting playlets. Bitterly disillusioned, two of the more talented Americans resigned early in the term and, although I had an overwhelming urge to follow suit, my GI Bill subsidy was all I possessed and, had I foregone that, I would have had to leave England and return to America – which was by far the worse fate. So, I soldiered on, gradually becoming the thorn in everyone's flesh, just as the school itself became an irremovable one in my own.

The situation at LAMDA was complicated by two contradictory facts. On the whole, apart from some interesting work on verse technique and exposure to classical habits of thought from people like Warre, Coe and MacOwan, the training was puerile and backward – as ignorant of Stanislavsky as it was of Brecht or Artaud. Acting was thought to be merely a mode for projecting language, and 'physical technique' meant deportment almost exclusively. Despite an innovative vocal approach by Iris Warren (later perpetuated by her disciple, Kristin Linklater), the school's overriding philosophy was 'Have a bash!' Everyone was encouraged just to get on stage and do something. 'Exercise that modicum of talent which the staff acknowledged by accepting you in the first place,' they seemed to say. (Of course, having enrolled in America without an audition, the rancour against me was entirely justified. I had, as it were, 'snuck in' to LAMDA, as even the most perfunctory examination would have revealed such a moiety of acting talent that I would probably have been requested to cut short the audition-speech.) Intellectually and artistically, the school was a kind of British bulwark for the boulevard theatre, which was just beginning to crumble and which, in five years, would be in disarray. But its poisonous mole and most outspoken critic was an inept and gormless young man with a goatee who could not act, was unapologetically anti-social and seemed to spend most of his time seducing the female students. The paradox was we were both right: it *was* a ghastly institution and, from an acting standpoint, I was its most lustreless fixture.

Gradually it dawned upon me that, given the breadth of my physical and vocal inadequacies, I was not intended for a berth in the professional theatre, but it had never occurred to me how implicitly this view was already held by the staff. It was dramatically brought home to me during a rehearsal of *Othello* conducted by André van Gyseghem, an old-styled Leftist married to a permanently inebriated Jean Forbes-Robertson (daughter of the great old classical actor) who had latterly become a traditionalist director. I was Ludovico at the time and had just performed the speech 'O Spartan dog/More fell than anguish, hunger or the sea!/Look on the tragic loading of this bed,' which, in previous rehearsals, used to saunter by in stony silence, although my private antennae regularly picked up a tiny tremor emitted by the director. On this occasion, as I sailed into the speech, Van Gyseghem leapt from his stool, threw down the prompt book and screeched in a tone that brought the plaster peeling from the ceilings: 'It's not Spartan *dawg*, it's Spartan *dog* – Spartan DOG!' His fury at my New York pronunciation was quite the most Shakespearian moment I ever experienced at LAMDA, made even more memorable by the intensity of its volume and the falling shrapnel impact of its rhetorical flourish. Being a breech of student-teacher protocol, Van Gyseghem was very apologetic afterward – although I was more regaled by the theatricality of the outburst than I was by its critical implications. A year or so later, by then sponging off the US Government at the Central School of Speech and Drama, I can remember incidents when Clifford Turner, the doyen of British speech teachers, loosed a similar barrage of invective against certain American students' 'lazy speech' and 'gutter diphthongs'. In academies such as LAMDA and the Central School, desecration of the Queen's English was a serious transgression for Tory diehards trying to civilize the natives. When the floodgates opened and drama schools actually encouraged the preservation of regional accents, North Country growls, marmoset drawls and even Cockney glottal stops, it was a sure sign the Empire was sinking into the sea and a new and terrible age dawning for the British theatre.

Although very little drama training was absorbed, it was a period during which I was soaking up British culture like the hungry sponge I was. One of my earliest niches in London was the Unity Theatre (having confused it in my mind with the

Mercury Theatre, where Auden and Isherwood had premièred their verse plays). The Unity was a Left-wing amateur theatre manned almost entirely by lower working-class men and women with a strong Communist bent. Very early in my perambulations there, a middle-class lawyer by the name of Bram Bootman adopted me and before long I was directing my first British production, my own adaptation of Gogol's comedy *Marriage*, which, because it garnered a favourable notice in *The Times*, turned me into a mini-celebrity at the Unity. I was then asked to work on a show which was being devised collectively on the subject of Suez. I dutifully attended the meetings and sat around with old Lefties and a couple of television hacks hashing together a revue about Anthony Eden's recent foreign policy fiasco. During the heat of the collaboration, one of the older members of the team kept saying, 'Yes, but what about the line? What about the line?' I had no idea what he was talking about and nothing the others said ever seemed to elucidate what this mysterious 'line' was. It wasn't until after the opening that I came to realize that he was referring to the Communist Party 'line', which, in the hurly burly of collaboration, seemed to have become obscured. Shortly after the show, again encouraged by my sponsor Bootman, I started a Method workshop at the theatre and began the fascinating process of indoctrinating English actors into the arcane mysteries of Stanislavsky – but instead of testing them out on the theatre's favourite writers like Odets, Gorky and Miller, I inclined them towards Shakespeare, Marlowe and Webster. After the GI Bill subsidy ran out and I found myself penniless in England, the Method workshop became my mainstay. I began collecting outrageous fees from actors and actresses enthralled by the recent notoriety of Lee Strasberg and the Method, who believed that my peculiar brand of Stanislavsky-cum-classical work, being American, was in some way part of the same New York mystique that produced Brando, Dean, Newman and Steiger. That being the case, I made it a point to immerse myself in Method researches and quickly discovered that Strasberg's bastardization of Stanislavsky, although it turned out facile behaviourists for films and television, was worse than useless for the challenging texts of Shakespeare and Marlowe and that the further Strasberg had gone into the Method, the more he had veered away from those sound Stanislavskyian practices enshrined in the System.

When I finally left LAMDA, the sigh of relief was so immense you could have used it to power sailboats up the Thames. And when, only weeks later, the teachers became aware that their most grotesque and inadequate graduate was actually conducting an acting workshop for professional British actors, hilarity swept through the corridors like a monsoon. It was a thoroughly justifiable whoop of derision. The teachers at LAMDA had no way of knowing that the kind of theatre I had been elaborating in my imagination bore no relation whatsoever to the musty drawing-room frolics they were methodically embalming in their syllabus. A theatre radically re-routed by Brechtian theory or pulverized by Artaudian notions of stagecraft was totally beyond their imagination, and if anyone had told them that, within five years, playwrights like John Osborne, John Arden, Brendan Behan and Arnold Wesker were going to up-root middle-class icons such as Terence Rattigan, Noël Coward, J. B. Priestley and Charles Morgan, they would have evidenced just as much hilarity. In 1956 the world that had become memorialized in places like LAMDA was essentially the world of the 1930s. There were virtually no glimmers of what was about to come flashing round the corner.

As much as I felt myself ideologically opposed to it, the Method was the label by which I had become identified in London and it was in disseminating the Method that I first came to public attention. During the course of my Method workshop, I was exposed to a variety of British actors – many of them talented and more knowledgeable in day-to-day acting technique than myself. In devising and assessing improvisations, analysing scenes and adjusting the basic theories to the variety of individuals with whom I was working, it would be true to say my students taught me almost as much as I taught them. Mainly I learned about the constituents of the British character – how English men and women expressed fear or love or joy or cunning, or rather how they used social gambits and camouflage language to avoid the expression of such basic emotions. It was a little crash course on the English disguised as a workshop in American acting technique and it made me profoundly aware of the differences between the two cultures.

In 1958 I persuaded Peter Carpenter of the British Drama League to allow me to convert his minuscule rooftop studio at Fitzroy Square into an experimental theatre. It was a rickety little room that seated about fifty and, with adorable stalwarts such as Gillian Watt, we set about creating In-Stage, the first of the many fringe theatres I was sure would soon sprout throughout London. (The fringe phenomenon didn't actually arrive until ten years later – so you could say we were a fairly early harbinger.)

Beckett and Ionesco were then the dominating influences in London, and so, in their honour, we put together an off-beat revue entitled *Under the Influence*, which shamelessly recycled the style of their works in four or five derivative spin-offs. At that time I suffered from the American weakness for fancy nomenclatures, naïvely believing that creating a new label was tantamount to establishing a new artistic tendency. The subject of those early researches was something called 'Hi Style' – a puerile classification which attempted to define the non-naturalistic tendencies of the early Absurdists and the general drift towards surrealism which was one of my own personal predilections. The unfortunate term was picked up by Alan Pryce-Jones in an *Observer* notice of our inaugural production in which he wrote: 'Hi Style is likely to be badly needed, if, as Marowitz has himself written, language is to go on serving "as functional a purpose as a gauze curtain on the stage – existing in order to reveal something behind it in a diffused and more interesting light". This is paring down language as far as possible, and leaving correspondingly more to the actors. It needs awareness of half-meanings, asides of thought, tropes; a variety of humour; a grasp of what things are rather than what they seem; which has filtered into the theatre only during the last few years. Hi Style means no more than a careful coordination of responses so that what may roughly be called the post-Pirandello play is given its full value. It runs in parallel to the classical and the commercial theatre. But it needs just the same careful and affectionate watching as any other manifestation of vitality in the theatre today.'

Mr Pryce-Jones was being very sweet and probably intending to give a new group a boost, but the fact is he was responding in a scholarly and po-faced way to an invention which was entirely arbitrary and not a little pretentious. In the vast, swirling, grandiose chamber of my artistic imagination I was probably trying to create a methodology similar to Brecht's or Artaud's which would enshrine my name for generations to come. Were I writing criticism at the time, I think I would have gunned myself down for the pretentious twat I was. Yes, there was an anti-verbal, non-naturalistic, slightly surreal trend in the air, and yes, we were very much part of it, but we should have just done our work and resisted the temptation to codify and label something in the hope that it might become fashionable.

In-Stage went on to produce a murky but enthralling little play by J. B. Lynne called *The Trigon*, which boasted two splendid performances by Timothy West and Prunella Scales, and which transferred to Brighton before re-emerging at the Arts Theatre Club. We also mounted the British première of Beckett's *Act Without Words II*, Arthur Miller's *The Man Who Had All The Luck*, William Saroyan's *The Cave Dwellers* and a number of evenings devoted to bizarre entertainments the memories of which make me cringe.

Round about 1960, Jerry Tallmer, my Features Editor at the *Village Voice* (to which I was still a regular contributor), sent me a playwright named Murray Schisgal, who had about a dozen short plays tucked under his arm. They all had a highly distinctive tone of voice and tended to telescope action in such a way that, after thirty or forty minutes, you felt the character had lived through a lifetime. I chose three of them *The Tiger*, *The Typists* and *A Simple Kind of Love Story*, for a programme which for reasons I no longer remember was titled 'Schrecks'. They proved highly successful on Fitzroy Square and were subsequently picked up by Eli Wallach and Anne Bancroft for production in New York. Schisgal was a troubled but relentlessly jokey American schoolteacher whose cynical and self-deprecating New York sense of humour was similar to my own. He seemed to be genuinely astonished when I told him we would mount his plays and right up to the start of rehearsals would blink disbelievingly at the preparations being made.

Once rehearsals began, however, he was thrown into agonies because of what actors (and probably the director) were doing to his work. He would roam around the back of the auditorium as if anticipating crucifixion, shaking his head and audibly groaning. It froze the actors, who were made to feel they were methodically strangulating his newborn baby, so I asked him to discontinue his visits. He took this badly and I felt badly about barring him, but I realized that no useful work would be done with that semi-audible Jewish drone running like a Talmudic undercurrent behind the actors' efforts. When the plays opened to positive notices and commercial managements started expressing interest in the writer, I automatically assumed he would let us produce his next plays, *Ducks and Lovers* and *Luv*, but that was not to be. *Ducks and Lovers* was ineffectually staged at the Arts Theatre Club and *Luv*, directed by Mike Nichols, became a smash hit on Broadway. We were too young and naïve to concern ourselves with contracts and options. What interested us in Schisgal was the tenor of his subject matter and the flapdoodle liveliness of his style. It wasn't until many years later that I learned that you don't take gratitude and loyalty for granted in the theatre; that a contract is a straitjacket which you lovingly fasten around the trunk of a new writer so as to insure that you will be the main beneficiary of his later work.

The In-Stage evenings at Fitzroy Square glow fondly in my memory. As spectators lined up in the congested ante-room below the rooftop studio, they would be offered tea and biscuits by the pert and lovely Gillian Watt. When the show was about to start, they would move in single file up the narrow staircase that led to the tiny platform stage. More often than not, I was wedged into a burrow backstage working the lights or the sound tape. After the performance, as they filed out, Gillian would be standing at the bottom of the stairs holding a wicker basket into which the members of the audience would drop coins and sometimes notes – on good nights an occasional fiver; on one memorable occasion a fifty-pound note. There was a whiff of church hall dramatics about the place. The actors received no wages, the audience paid no admission, the fare was remorselessly off-beat and highbrow; and before long it became known throughout London that a night at In-Stage would be oddball, idiosyncratic and different. Our audiences were likewise. Many of them were readers of the *New Statesman*, the only publication in which we could afford to advertise, and consequently independent, intellectual and Left-wing. There was a shared awareness that what we were doing was unconventional – a little freaky – not what theatre is supposed to be in London. In retrospect, I realize that those regulars at Fitzroy Square were the beginnings of that new public which would eventually invade the Round House, UFO, the Ambiance, the Jeannetta Cochrane, the King's Head, the Soho Poly and the Open Space. They were the front runners of what would eventually be 'the fringe'. But ten years before the advent of hippies or 'beautiful people', there were no distinguishing characteristics and I am sure neither we nor they would have been able to predict the social upheavals that were only a half a decade down the pike.

2   *Dunked in the* New Wave

The theatrical *Zeitgeist* and I arrived in London at exactly the same moment: the summer of 1956. John Osborne's *Look Back in Anger*, the salvationary play by the recently established, but still wobbly, English Stage Company, had just opened at the Royal Court and the emanations of the New Left were reverberating everywhere. The rambunctious offerings of Joan Littlewood's Theatre Workshop (specifically, in 1956, Brendan Behan's *The Hostage*) were beginning to make themselves felt and shortly Joan's working-class musicals would make that fateful (some would say fatal) odyssey from the East End to Shaftesbury Avenue. In the same year, Bertolt Brecht's Berliner Ensemble paid a visit to London, giving the exponents of 'committed theatre' a jubilant rallying point. The Theatre of the Absurd, Martin Esslin's inaccurate nomenclature for a variety of styles as different as Ionesco's *The Bald Prima Donna* and Beckett's *Waiting for Godot*, had become a talking point from Chelsea to Hampstead and the air was thick with polemical fumes from those who felt the theatre should serve an overt political purpose and those, like Ionesco, who believed it should eschew politics and pursue surreal ambitions, dreams and magic.

To my overstimulated imagination, the fulcrum for all these events was the colourful, acerbic, brilliantly deflationary drama critic of the *Observer*, Kenneth Tynan.

When I was seventeen, I had started writing drama criticism for a short-lived American periodical called *International Theater Magazine*, following this precocious leap with a stint as off-Broadway reviewer on the newly created *Village Voice*, the weekly begun by Daniel Wolf, Ed Fancher and Norman Mailer soon to become the flagship of the cultural revolution which was about five years down the line. Through the rose-coloured spectacles with which I was beginning to get my bead on British culture, Tynan quickly became both my Plato and my Socrates.

To a large extent his passions were already mine. I had come from America a convert to the Stanislavsky system and believed, as did every good radical of the period, that any theatre which didn't essay the social and political verities of those troubled, Cold War, Suez-haunted times was not worth the newsprint it took to trash it. Tynan's reviews assailed his readers with a pronged sense of social purpose; his advocacy of Brecht was converted into a hammer with which he regularly bopped all West End trivia on the head. Unimpressed by Ionesco, Beckett or their leading British disciple Harold Pinter, he counterd Ionesco's internalized view of theatre in a series of dashing *Observer* pieces. There were fistfights in the foyer of the Royal Court theatre between proponents of differing views and a profound sense that what one felt, thought or wrote about the theatre was in some inexplicable way crucial to the future of mankind.

The period was awash with revolutionary imagery. Writers were forever being urged to 'take to the barricades', 'rally round the flag', 'invade enemy territory', assert the Left-wing perceptions of ideologues such as Jean-Paul Sartre and Albert Camus, and the Marxist ideology that underpinned the works of Bertolt Brecht. Even Trotsky had made a startling comeback and within a few years, under Vanessa Redgrave's strident advocacy, would inspire the Workers Revolutionary Party to try and subvert British Actors' Equity. To appeal to the 'workers' was considered the height of chic. I remember a mawkish interview with John Osborne in which he informed a tabloid journalist that the glowing approbation of the stage-hands in the theatre where his play was being performed meant more to him than any media or critical approval. It was a climate which persuaded numerous members of the intelligentsia (many of whom had never worked a day in their lives) that art based on Socialist principles and informed with the shibboleths of the New Left were valid in a way that somehow required no artistic validation.

Tynan was, in many ways, the most colourful exponent of this view – although, to be fair to him, he never grew so ideologically soppy as to praise playwrights merely because they wore the right pins. On Sundays one looked forward to those *Observer* reviews as to an assignation with a glamorous woman who came out of hiding only once a week. One came to know that whatever semi-literate moonshine might issue from the other critics, there was bound to be a spray of brisk coherence and

refreshing good sense from that particular nozzle, and so fatuousness, though pervasive, would not prevail. Tynan was the custo-
dian of our finer sensibilities in those days. With him at his post
one felt one could fend off the most imbecilic assaults of the
intellectual gutter press. Here was a voice dry, laconic, acerbic,
witty, punitive, provocative and exhortatory which made events
on stage seem as exciting as a western and as nationally relevant
as the fluctuations of the stock market; a voice demanding
excellence of an art form which, when it lagged behind the other
arts or the best of which it was itself capable, deserved to be
ferociously savaged. It was in the intensity of Tynan's indignation
that one could measure the esteem in which he held the theatre.
You don't rail, hector, fulminate and grow apoplectic over plays
and players unless you care deeply. Behind Tynan's attacks on
mediocrity, complacency and middle-class pretentiousness was
an obsession with *latent* quality to be badgered out of the
fecklessness and insubstantiality of current offerings, castigations
for the sake of what could emerge if the *shlock* and *kitsch* were
summarily swept out of the passageways in preparation for its
arrival. Perhaps it is this quality of imminence which distinguishes the great from the commonplace critic: the tacit assumption that behind the inadequate, the extraordinary is raging to
get out.

It was common in the Sixties to applaud him as a stylist and
to deplore his intellect: 'A great writer but no great shakes as a
thinker.' How asinine this attitude seems in retrospect. A great
critic doesn't need to be a deep philosopher. The Shaw who
wrote critiques for the *Saturday Review* was not the Shaw of the
Prefaces. George Jean Nathan, Stark Young and James Agate
were not intellectual giants, but they were all stimulating and
pertinent critics. The critic's basic equipment consists of a finely
tuned aesthetic sense, a responsive temperament and an even
mixture of passions and prejudices. Tynan had all these virtues
and they crackled through his reviews. It is true he had stars in
his eyes and it probably meant more to him to attend an opening
night with Marlene Dietrich on his arm than to receive a knight-
hood, but there are worse things than to have stars in your eyes.
Without them, he could never have mustered the boyish idolatry
that fuelled his enthusiasms. He could be neglectful and obtuse,

as he was in the case of Pinter's and Beckett's early work, but I can think of no critic who confessed his shortcomings so openly and was quite so free of rancour.

What further endeared him to my burgeoning zeal for all things British was the fact that he could also enthuse over comedy and music-hall performers. No po-faced longhair, he! Champion of British satire (instrumental in fostering the Oxbridge quartet that produced *Beyond the Fringe*) and iconoclastic stand-up comedy (fan of Max Miller, Mort Sahl and Lenny Bruce), Method proselytizer extraordinaire (he emceed one of the most widely seen television programmes about the much maligned Actors' Studio), drum-beater for John Osborne, Arnold Wesker and other Royal Court ground-breakers, here was a critic with fire in his belly who regularly inflamed the tempers of those stodgy defenders of the *status quo*. The sparkle of his prose and the romance of his convictions combined to create a personality of glittering charisma. What Tynan said on a Sunday morning was as close to a Royal proclamation as the New Left would ever get. There were many imitators who tried to emulate the devil-may-care insouciance of his style and the crackle of political dissent behind his opinions, but ultimately there was only one Tynan and, looking back almost thirty years later, the dialectical frivolity of his writing is one of the few permanent legacies of the Sixties.

I was introduced to him by Mary Holland, the pert, Irish journalist and sometime critic, at a luncheon in Stratford-upon-Avon and was immediately rendered tongue-tied and mawkish. What I wanted to say was: I share almost all of your enthusiasms and think you're one of the greatest prose stylists of our generation. What I wound up saying was an inarticulate rehash of my views about permanent companies and the future trend of the British theatre, trying, in a few inchoate phrases, to distil the essence of about twenty-five years of theatrical convictions, and radiating the crabbed gaucheness of someone having so much to say that he virtually winds up saying nothing. As for Tynan, he spent most of the lunch regaling us with Green Room anecdotes and knocking off caustic verbal doodles of people I had never heard of. I was young and vulnerable enough to be so dazzled in his presence that all my forthrightness uncharacteristically disappeared.

I was not alone in having been simultaneously mesmerized and paralysed by the Tynanic charm. It was a common condition among aspiring writers of the time. In a review of one of Tynan's collections Irving Wardle, long-time critic of *The Times* and a one-time second stringer for Tynan at the *Observer* asked: 'I wonder if anyone was quite as badly bitten as I was with the Tynan bug – a curious disease: a mixture of envy, fascination and fear characterized by fantasies of his glamorously satanic private life and nightmares in which I was turned to stone looking at his head crawling with snakes.' Although close proximity in the offices of the *Observer* gradually diminished the obsession, Wardle admitted: 'He had only to walk into a room for me to turn into a tongue-tied idiot.'

What possessed many of us in the late 1950s and 1960s was the myth of Tynan being manifest in our own time. We knew, as no doubt the coterie around Shaw in the Nineties knew, that we were in the presence of someone who, day by day, was assembling the lineaments of his legend. The fact that we saw him consciously working at it in no way diminished its fascination.

In subsequent encounters, after I had established my own reputation as a critic and budding director, my aplomb was restored, and in 1964, when he had become Literary Manager of the National Theatre, we even had a mini controversy in the pages of the *Transatlantic Review*.

In a previous issue, in an ostentatious 'Interview with Myself', I had made some disparaging remarks about the National Theatre's repertoire and Tynan, as its newly appointed Literary Manager, had stoutly come to its defence. (In order not to handicap my departed opponent with self-serving extracts, I give the full exchange in an appendix; also because its polemical vivacity is characteristic of the times.) Despite the snideness of the exchange, I have to confess I loved the idea of being baited by Tynan and experienced a high charge of adrenalin in locking horns with such a fire-snorting bull. The issues on which we disagreed were, to my mind, secondary to the passion we both felt for the subjects in contention. In retrospect, I find his letter unconvincingly defensive – the kind of rejoinder a Literary Manager with a brief to resist all hecklers is obliged to make. As for my own tone, it is callow and overblown, and, though I stand by its definition of the *avant garde*, it was conjured up mainly to retaliate for real or imagined blows to the ego. But, again, this was very characteristic of the times. We *were* what we were alleged to stand for and once our 'position' was taken, our convictions proclaimed, it was *de rigueur* to defend them to the death. With the rise of the New Left and the depiction of the Establishment as some kind of sinister, middle-class ogre we were all honour bound to resist; factionalism seemed to be a way of life in the mid-Sixties. I see now that divisions were never really that clear cut and that some of the rhetoric of my Left-wing allies was intellectually preposterous in its extremity. The irony was that, as we slithered from the Sixties into the Seventies, nothing made my hackles rise faster than the Pavlovian slurp of parlour radicals mindlessly reiterating New Left shibboleths. Ultimately I came to see no difference at all between Right-wing and Left-wing clichés. It was the dull thud of the made-up mind that came to be the real enemy, the empty clang of partisanship, no matter what its political complexion, that had to be guarded against. But in the late Fifties and early Sixties there was still a romantic *frisson* in the idea that one was a guerrilla fighter in the war against middle-class complacency.

After Stratford, Tynan and I met on numerous occasions, and I was even persuaded into producing a play by one of his relations at the Open Space, a calculatedly crafted cod nineteenth-century comedy which wasn't fully recognized for the contrivance it was because it had come swathed in Tynan's recommendation. As Kathleen Tynan's biography clearly brings out, the great thing about Tynan was that he always made you smarter, brighter and more pertinent than you would ever be outside his company. He had that rare ability to raise lesser spirits to his own level and nothing pleased him more than an evenly matched intellectual punch-up. In the presence of bores or meat-heads he disengaged shamelessly. If you couldn't breathe in his higher stratospheres, you were reduced to asphyxia. He made enemies the way the incontinent make water, but even to encounter people who detested Tynan was a salutary experience. It immediately defined one's own standards and, in almost every case, those who were against Tynan eventually earned your opprobrium by revealing other, more contemptible prejudices.

Ken's stutter seemed to be the reflex action of someone so infuriated by life's grossness that his desire to fulminate against it caused him to become tongue-tied. He always spoke as if he were on a raiding mission against the imbeciles that benetted him on every side. He'd leave the bunker of his superior sensibility just long enough to pitch a grenade, then hightail it back and bolt the doors. His mind was like a munitions factory, constantly manufacturing incendiary devices in his war against the commonplace. He could also be furtive and studied. To those who appreciated his penchant for the sound of cathedral glass being shattered by brickbats, his nationally disseminated 'fuck' on a television programme called *BBC-3* in November 1965 was not so much a refusal to edit himself (as he explained it) as it was a conscious ploy to stir the shit. It was the sly, exhibitionist Oxford undergrad in him which equated such actions with meaningful revolutionary gestures. Although they were never that, they did charge the atmosphere and increase the flow of national adrenalin, and in a country where torpor was so often the order of the day that alone was commendable.

When Tynan, in his position as Literary Manager at the National, persuaded Olivier to proceed with a production of *Soldiers*, a play by Rolf Hochuth which alleged that Winston Churchill was associated with a wartime plot to murder General Wladyslaw Sikorski, it was a foregone conclusion that Lord Chandos, Chairman of the National Theatre Board, and the other Tory worthies who stood at the helm of the National would turn their fire upon him. The play was a humourless piece of docu-drama inflated with artificially lit moral indignation, but it projected a reasonable argument and dramatically explored the lengths to which statesmen might go in achieving political ends. For Tynan it became a *cause célèbre*, mainly because he loved *les causes célèbres* and, unconsciously, because it was yet another way of pissing in the tea of that smug and self-satisfied class which, in Tynan's view, was strangling dissent and restricting 'the free play of the mind' in British life.

To understand Tynan fully one has to understand that the inveterate and ubiquitous enemy in Britain, against whom every artist has to struggle, is that well-scrubbed, immaculately dressed, upper-middle-class ghoul who is secretly betrothed to the twin monsters of Good Taste and Inoffensiveness. This ghoul, well educated and highly articulate, can be found in the well-upholstered meeting-rooms of theatre boards, local councils, civic groups, grants panels, government bodies – anywhere and everywhere that public money, private investment or corporate grants are disbursed to the Arts. He has the pale, sensitive complexion of the helpless vampire – the Living Undead – and can unhesitatingly advance half a dozen impressive arguments why it would be 'better not to take the risk', 'defer decisions to a later date', 'establish a fact-finding committee to study the matter', 'avoid the danger of giving offence', 'not make exceptions for fear of setting a precedent' and a thousand and one other rationalizations which bust the kneecaps of progress, demoralize innovation and dampen down those divine sparks which, if ignited, might fire new ideas and provoke change. These are the ghouls that run England and are solidly entrenched in its cultural establishment. They blossom like deadly nightshade on television councils, theatrical planning committees and in every aggregation of sober citizens where considerations of practicality and expedience soundly trounce the fresh, the untried and the potentially astonishing. Tynan despised them and they him, and had he lived, his tangles with them would certainly have proliferated. If his life and writing have any special social distinction, it is that they helped identify the coagulated scum that, in the 1960s and 1970s, settled on every creative and original endeavour causing it to be stillborn. They helped identify the enemy.

Peter Hall, who took over the National Theatre after the Olivier regime, was intensely disliked by Tynan; Hall was the living antithesis of everything Tynan stood for. Hall's supreme talent has always been for committee work and 'politickeering'. He began as a protégé of Glen Byam Shaw at Stratford and learned very early the art of infiltrating charmed circles. His greatest gift was, perhaps, inspiring a middle-class camaraderie among men of power and influence, at the same time flattering them into the belief they were in some sense 'functioning artistically'.

As a director, he was always riding piggy-back on playwrights such as Harold Pinter (who, before the Hall–Pinter axis was formed, was already a known quantity on the British stage) or firmly established acting personalities who, to a large extent were accustomed to directing themselves. The intellect was always eclectic, which is to say he tended to absorb different ideas from the gifted people with whom he surrounded himself and fused these into his productions. His highly praised productions of Harold Pinter (a playwright with whom he was conspicuously associated until their break after the publication of the Peter Hall Diaries) consisted of little more than creating stagecraft which duplicated the strict economy of Pinter's writing. By the late 1960s and 1970s, when Pinter's style and aesthetic had become thoroughly familiar, it was the easiest thing in the world to mount Pinter 'faithfully', especially when the author – an actor and director himself – was sitting perched on the director's shoulder. During Hall's reign at the RSC, morale was apparently always at rock-bottom because many of the actors felt that they were sometimes nothing more than the victims of Hall's concern with his own ambitions.

Tynan, with that laser-like perception that discommoded all his enemies, saw through Hall and, if he had lived, Sir Peter would not have had a single night's sleep – constantly fearful that his limitations and his motives might be glaringly revealed in print. But despite swingeing newspaper articles about personal profits and mounting criticism of his directorship of the National, he was tucked cosily into the Establishment fold and the ranks closed around him.

In the late Fifties, when I was mounting my first production in England, William Saroyan's *The Cave Dwellers*, a semi-professional effort with jumped-up amateurs in the leads, Tynan was in the audience along with his then girl friend, Penelope Gilliatt. They chuffed out during the interval never to return, an exodus I might well have made myself had I been in their place. That, more than anything else, defined the event for me and caused me to brand it as contemptible. About ten years later, when I ran into him during the interval of Peter Brook's *King Lear*, on which I was assistant director, he puckered his lips and rolled his eyes in admiration of what he had just seen and, in my soul, some small reparation was made for *The Cave Dwellers*. My great disappointment was that he almost never came to the Open Space and so never saw the productions of which I was proudest. For a long time I felt that, when he thought of me, it was almost always in relation to that execrable first act of the Saroyan and, on the basis of that, considered me more a critic or journalist than a director. When, some fifteen years later, I was living in California and he dying of emphysema in Santa Monica, I tried to seek him out, but was told he was too ill to receive visitors. He died on 26 July 1980, by which time I was residing in Los Angeles. For years afterward, kicking myself for my lack of perseverance, I would scan the houses around Santa Monica, wondering in which one he might have expired.

Tynan's is the only memorial service I have ever attended. It was held the following September in St Paul's Church, Covent Garden. I wasn't quite sure what it was that compelled me to attend, although on the morning of the service I found myself bustling to Covent Garden as if preordained. Tom Stoppard made a poignant address to Tynan's children perched in the front rows, and George Axelrod conjured up some hilarious anecdotes. The clatter of laughter in that august church seemed to me terribly out of place. In the courtyard afterwards, in what struck me as a contemptible show of disloyalty, I saw Peter Brook chatting and smiling with Peter Hall. Knowing how sincerely Ken had loathed Hall, it struck me as a traitorous liaison. Many of the obituaries were snide; I can recall one by lustreless playwright Ronald Duncan being particularly nasty. (The mediocrity's revenge, I thought to myself. It *would* be people like Duncan who would smugly eke out the last bitchy word.) For months afterward I found myself mourning Ken, fulminating against the waste, dreaming about him with distressing regularity, remembering how that rich, archival mind flew like an arrow to the paradox or contradiction in any play or a performance, and lamenting that spry, quicksilver, unique intelligence prematurely laid to rest and survived by serried ranks of second-raters.

I realize now that I had constructed a rather massive identification with Tynan and the most distressing part of that psychological mirroring was the fact that, in the final analysis, Tynan had not really changed very much and his influence had been minimal. He had left a zealous cult behind him which would always rhapsodize his talents and dramatize his personality, but, ultimately, the Establishment against which he raged so eloquently had closed ranks and retained all its smug, impenetrable affluence and power. Part of the distress occasioned by that realization was the suspicion that my own life, poised as it was against so many of the same enemies, would be likewise impotent, a few reams of hot copy for the delectation of radicals and Left-wingers, but, when all the final audits were in, of no real consequence in the crucial power struggles.

One of Ken's great friends was Clive Goodwin, a fly, sardonic, lightweight actor who became a television executive and eventually a literary agent. Clive, with Owen Hale and Tom Milne, created *Encore* magazine when Clive was still a student at the Central School of Speech and Drama. When I arrived in London, I made a bee-line to Goodwin and started writing for *Encore* almost immediately and became one of its editors.

Our editorial meetings, usually held in coffee bars or bistros around Soho or the British Museum, were stimulating learning experiences. Not only did I discover what was thought to be 'in' or *chic* in the London theatre but I also learned how quick, irreverent and brilliantly co-ordinated the English mind could be. For an American, it was truly edifying to hear Goodwin or Milne (later on Michael Kustow), tapping deep reserves of radical sentiment and class bitterness, douse the work of a commercial playwright in a spray of withering critical analysis. Kustow was particularly illuminating and I can remember leaving many such meetings with a profound sense of envy for his erudition. Penelope Gilliatt attended some of those meetings and I recall being struck by her grasp of literary politics. She knew precisely who was in, who was out and who was on the way up. Radical theatre may have been one of her avowed interests, but a more abiding passion was her own upward mobility. One felt that every one of her opinions, before being released to the world, was first put through the wringer of a highly objective sense of political protocol, as if what she actually thought was secondary to the impact it might make compared to what everyone else was thinking at the time. (Alan Brien, the drama critic, suffered from very much the same syndrome. His Sunday pieces were calculated to supplement or vary the prevailing views of most of the daily critics – as if aesthetic response was as arbitrary an element as floral design.)

Vanessa Redgrave, who had gone to drama school with Clive and was a staunch supporter of the magazine, was something of a hanger-on in those days. On one occasion, when she was appearing in Robert Bolt's *Flowering Cherry*, I was summoned to her West End dressing-room by a breathless and obviously impressed Clive. She had read one of my *Encore* articles and wanted to meet the surly and cerebral Yank. When we got there, a small crowd of well-wishers had already been steered into the 'royal presence' and since it meant hanging around in a draughty hallway for what might be an interminable length of time, I declined the honour and went off for a hamburger and a milk-shake. Even then the Redgrave aura had begun to elevate young Vanessa into the higher stratospheres she would shortly inhabit and I remember it struck me as somewhat incongruous that Clive, who was such a fiery Left-winger, should instinctively defer to the upper-middle-class ring of the Redgrave name. I found among many of the British New Left of that time a curious conditioned reflex when confronted with upper-middle-class celebrities. They seemed to be aware, as much as anyone else, that their signal reactions in such cases belied their social convictions, but the instinct seemed too deeply embedded to shift. As an untutored American, of course, I had very little knowledge of whom I might be snubbing. At the time I remember thinking that the little I'd seen Vanessa Redgrave do was pulsating and grossly over the top and, if I thought of her at all, it was as an actress who had to scale down feelings which, because they seemed out of proportion to the character's, invariably diverted attention to the actress and away from the play. As time went on I found myself progressively unimpressed by her work and when I got to know the combination of oddballness and fanaticism that underpinned her political beliefs, I began to understand what it was that repelled me about her as an actress. She constantly dispensed the fulsome energy of the unenlightened. They were performances which had all the tremulousness and blind intensity of someone locked in a false intellectual position. In debates you often find people who, to make up for fallacious reasoning, come on too strong. Their passion is unconsciously proffered as compensation for their sophistry and is often persuasive to people who have a weakness for unbridled feelings rather than judicious ratiocination. The ricketyness of Redgrave's positions on various topics always made it impossible for me to accept the alleged subtlety and sensitivity of her performances. I saw them always as finely contoured plastic spaceships monitored from a command-station that was totally unmanned. I know you can have 'vacant great actresses' – god knows, history is full of examples – but in the case of Vanessa this pre-knowledge always prevented me from seeing her as anything other than an actress whose soulfulness was falsely construed as 'moving' by a public more swayed by moodiness than mindfulness. She exemplified the worst of Bernhardt's faults, possessing none of the discriminating intelligence that characterized Duse and made critics such as Shaw prefer the Italian to the empty bluster of the Divine Sarah.

Although a great advocate of *Encore*, I don't believe Vanessa ever contributed anything very telling to its pages – other than the charisma of her name – and when she fell in love with Trotsky and came to believe that the injustices suffered by the Palestinians justified anti-Israeli terrorism, she moved off into even more fanatical realms. Like many undiscriminating zealots, her proclivity to give herself to a cause is what remained constant, while the objects of her commitment would vary according to political fashion and personal idiosyncracy. Recalling her performances, those large, mooselike and mindless eyes are two of the most appalling souvenirs I have of the Sixties.

Encore was read by no more than 3,000 hard-nut subscribers and yet, between 1956 and 1965, it was the most influential theatre magazine in England. This wasn't because its articles were particularly pithy or its writers more enlightened than those who wrote for the Establishment press, but because it was temperamentally embroiled in what was then the ideological ferment of the time. With naïveté, unqualified zeal and gross (often maddening) oversimplifications, it was nudging the theatre out of the stasis of the post-war years. Its contributors were a widely varied bunch, but they were all united by exasperation with the social stonewalling that characterized the British theatre in the late 1940s and early 1950s. When they warmed to writers such as Osborne and Pinter (*Encore* first published *The Birthday Party* despite its calamitous opening, and continued to champion Pinter for several years before his breakthrough), they were instinctively backing the dark horses that seemed to them could go the full distance. It was fuelled by a powerful *animus* against the *status quo* and, in the case of some contributors, a doctrinaire Marxist bias which was often as windy as the Toryism it regularly fulminated against. Pugnacious, vituperative, derisory, sophomoric, it was the flag of the New Wave's disposition, and we would have understood less of Brecht, Stanislavsky, Artaud, Brook and Grotowski without it. It had the adorable adolescent quality of feeling strongly about subjects without realizing that, in the eyes of more sophisticated readers, such undocumented enthusiasm could sometimes look foolish. It never cared about looking foolish and, if it did, it could always justify itself by pointing out that five years after its demise, all of its dark horses had come in. The British theatre had changed radically and almost exactly along the lines it had been espousing. Osborne, Pinter, Wesker, Arden, Bond, Mercer, Wood, Stoppard were its chief hobbyhorses. Brechtian consciousness, a National Theatre, an open door policy for new writers, the advent of satire and encouragement of experimentation were only some of its chosen causes.

When cultural changes take place, historians invariably attribute them to a 'change of climate', which they usually find hard to pin down. Criticism, in the form of agitational journals and polemical magazines, is often what makes that 'changing climate' conscious of itself. By articulating the changes taking place in people's thinking about art and society, it defines things that are nebulously in the air. *Encore*, like the *Criterion*, *Scrutiny*, the *Partisan Review* or the *Nouvelle Revue Française*, bantered the ideas and constructed the vernacular with which theatre in the Sixties and Seventies defined its newly evolving character. It may be pushing it somewhat to argue that a bi-monthly magazine with a readership of barely 3,000 could achieve such formidable results, but, if you consult its passions and compare them to the events that followed, the proofs are incontrovertible.

In retrospect, what was 'new' about the New Wave was its willingness to face down the Establishment powers which had ruled British theatre since before the war. There was a wilful, driven pertinacity about the writers, critics and artists of that period which seemed to suggest they knew their time had come. The old style managers (H. M. Tennent, Prince Littler, the Stoll group), the old style critics (W. A. Darlington, Beverley Baxter, Ivor Brown) were quite content for the theatre to go on with business as usual, but the narky Socialists from the redbrick universities and the canny radicals down from Oxford and Cambridge were steeled for change. It is pointless to consider the changes in the British theatre in the late 1950s and early 1960s outside the context of the New Left movement, of which the theatre was an integral part. Something which had begun to burgeon in the 1930s got sidetracked during the Second World War; it then came back with irrepressible vigour in the 1950s and eventually took hold of the theatre and gave it a good throttling. Whatever its artistic limitations (and from the vantage point of the 1990s they are glaringly obvious), it was an upsurge that realigned the cultural forces of the time and, in so doing, created a lot of genuine excitement in a society that, for almost half a century, had prided itself on being imperturbable.

3 A *short sprint with* Lenny Bruce

On the day that Lenny Bruce held his press conference at Nicholas Luard and Peter Cook's club the Establishment, I made sure I was present. I really had no business there since *Encore* never reviewed comedians or night-club performances, but the legend of Bruce had gathered enormous momentum from San Francisco to New York and I was fascinated by reports of the inspired obscenity and madcap insolence which had preceded his arrival.

Bruce was wearing his black Nehru jacket buttoned to the neck, clinging black trousers and a pair of high-heeled cricket boots. He had broody, dark eyes and the kind of casually coiffed, 'sharpie' hairstyle I associated with heroes from my high school days. He seemed ill at ease in the midst of the British journalists and, wanting to demystify the culture of the land into which he had just landed, tended to ply them with almost as many questions as they did him. He was being neither funny nor provocative, not quite sure which part of his reputation he was expected to live up to. I stood silently at the back beside a pillar, wanting nothing more than to take in the phenomenon. As he roamed around the room pursuing his crash course on British *mores*, his eye caught mine and he gave that sudden halt of recognition which happens when someone picks out a familiar face in a crowd of strangers. I couldn't help noticing the look, although I could not explain it. I had never seen or met Bruce before and, having been in London for over six years, it was highly unlikely he would ever have met me. After several more fugitive answers to half-hearted questions, the reporters dispersed for drinks and snacks, and Bruce gravitated towards me.

'I know you, right?' he said.

'I don't think so,' I replied.

'You're American, right?'

'Yes, but I don't think we've ever met.'

'New York City, right?'

'That's right.'

With that he gulped down what he'd been sipping and said, 'Let's split.'

I found myself shuffling down the stairs behind him and heading out through Soho towards Oxford Street. Bruce was talking a mile a minute, as if to an old friend, although he had now stopped trying to place me.

'Everybody's so polite here. I mean, even if they shit in their pants, it's, "So sorry. Hope the smell doesn't inconvenience you. Rather clumsy of me, I *am* sorry."'

After only hours in the country he seemed to have caught both the lilt of the language and the special talent the English have for making disagreeable realities magically disappear by simply pretending they don't exist.

We stopped at a fruit stall and Lenny bought a bunch of green grapes then, still uncertain about the exchange rate, tossed a fistful of £5 notes on to the cart. I returned all the fivers but one, and got the vendor to give the correct change.

'Do you know where the New Victoria Theatre is?' Lenny suddenly asked me.

'Yes, in Victoria. Not too far away.'

'I gotta see an old girl friend there. Let's hop a cab.'

We took a taxi to the stage door of the New Victoria Theatre, where Annie Ross was appearing. In the cab I began asking him about his routines: how much was improvised, how much prepared.

'I do about twenty minutes of new stuff every show,' said Bruce, not boasting, but merely stating facts. 'In a week or so I have about two hours of new material – that's every week. But it all goes. I forget it. The thing is not to hold on to the material, but to the mechanism that keeps pumping it out. That's the goose that lays the golden eggs. When I'm hot, I'm shitting gold bricks.'

'What about the highs and lows? Everybody who improvises experiences those, don't they?'

'If I go like clockwork, bang, one, two, three, four – I know I'm bad. Nobody's rhythm is like that. It's gotta be one, two –

miss – pick up – three, four, otherwise it's not really there – on *that* night – for *that* audience.'

'What happens when you feel yourself bombing?'

'I bare my soul – as far as I can – and, through a kind of catharsis, I become funny. The thing is, when you're not being funny, it's because of the flak between you and the audience, so you have to manoeuvre around that flak without letting the shit get into your eyes.'

'Is there anything you personally find offensive?'

'Mother-in-law jokes! Once there was an Irishman, an Italian and a Jew kind of jokes. The only thing that's really offensive is what's trite.'

As we left the cab, Lenny handed the taxi driver another clump of £5 and £10 notes. I deftly removed them from the driver's paw, paid the appropriate fare and told Lenny he'd better get a handle on the exchange rate or he'd come out of this engagement a big loser.

'I'm already losing! Do you know what they're paying me for this gig?'

It turned out to be far below his usual whack, as he was hoping London would open up a whole range of European engagements, although I couldn't really imagine Lenny's machine-gun rapid Brooklynese going down a treat in Paris or Rome.

Once in the theatre, he asked me to come down with him to meet Annie Ross but, if she were there, to leave them alone together. As it turned out, it was between shows and the singer was sitting in her dressing-room. When Bruce knocked and walked in, she looked as if she had seen a ghost. There was no big reunion. Lenny's sudden appearance had triggered off a rather guarded, uneasy atmosphere – like people instinctively registering gladness at meeting one another and then, in the next moment, remembering the grim circumstances of their parting. We exchanged a few pleasantries – or rather I did – Annie herself remaining wary and even morose. Lenny gave me a high sign, I excused myself and left the dressing-room. I cooled my heels in the corridor. Inside I could just make out the muted tones of serious, even grave conversation taking place. A stage manager rapped on the door and a very up-tight Annie Ross called out,

'Okay'. In a moment Lenny re-emerged and we were shuffling up the stairs and back into the street.

'Did you see her hands – oh, Christ, did you see her hands?' he asked me in a pitiable tone of voice.

In fact, I hadn't.

'Oh, Christ,' he kept moaning, 'what's happened to her hands?'

We hopped into another cab and headed to Lenny's hotel. On the way, now entirely recovered from the shock of Annie's hands, he was praising the intellectual level of British culture, although I don't think he had experienced any more of it than the press conference. At the hotel I started to excuse myself, but he said, 'No, no, come on up.' I followed, experiencing a vague sense of obligation to an American newly arrived on foreign shores, but really just quietly delighted and flattered that, for reasons I could not fathom, I had been, as it were, 'chosen'.

Once in the room, Lenny pulled the shades and wheeled into the bathroom without closing the door. There he began fishing out a hypodermic needle and some small vials. I had always been queasy about hypodermic needles. During my Army physical in New York the sight of my own blood emptying into a test tube strapped to my arm had caused me to faint dead away – almost, but not quite, getting me exemption from military service. As Lenny started rolling up his sleeve and fuelling the hypo, I began to make consternated exit noises.

'It's just enzymes,' he said, holding up one of the vials. 'My doctor prescribed them. I've got a vitamin deficiency. I need to take enzymes to build me up – that's all.'

It was all said so disarmingly one couldn't disbelieve it. But, whether enzymes or coke or doses of ambrosia, I knew that if I saw the hypo go in I'd be sick.

'I'll see you at the club tomorrow, Lenny. Good luck with the opening.' And I scooted out of the hotel, trying to restore my aplomb. (Years later I discovered they actually were enzymes. It was that period when Lenny was on a drug substitute therapy.)

When I actually caught his act at the Establishment, I was bowled over. It wasn't only the sharpness of the comedy, it was the fact that the diction, the frame of reference, even the dialect was everything I had grown up with. It was my own New York background, resolutely forsaken in the mid-Fifties, returned with a vengeance. Lenny was serving up sly, coruscating insights and withering flashes of irony on subjects about which I had been only half-conscious growing up on the lower East side. He had missiled me back to my adolescence – what my adolescence would have been if it had been articulate, probing, unhypocritical and revelatory.

The following day the *People*'s headline read, 'He makes us sick', and the *Daily Sketch* wrote, 'It stinks'. Bruce always seemed to inspire short, nauseous epithets – and of course, if one is billed as a 'sick comic', it goes without saying that the 'healthy reaction' is to register nausea at his performance. Although these kinds of reactions were quite predictable, neither he nor anyone else was prepared for the tenor of the up-beat reviews. George Melly in *New Statesman* hailed him as 'the evangelist of the new morality' and compared him to Jonathan Swift. Ken Tynan and others followed suit and in most quarters the foul-mouthed, dirty minded Lenny Bruce was vaunted as a moral crusader and front runner of the New Consciousness.

'Did you read that guy in the *Statesman*?' he asked, trying to jibe his own conception of himself with the perceived image. 'I'm not just a *dreck* and a *trumbanick*, I'm a "moralist",' and he laughed his fiendish, Lamont Cranston-Shadow laugh.

Lenny's opening was a walloping great success, playing, as it did, to a hand-picked, largely show-biz crowd. After that, the 'real people' came to the club and were, on the whole, bored or outraged, occasionally both. There were constant walk-outs – which cut up Lenny terribly as he couldn't bear flagrant proofs of rejection. As the run progressed, reactions became more vituperative. The Establishment was an intimate club and its close confines tended to encourage audience participation. Lots of people got into Lenny's act – hurling first insults then pennies, glasses and eventually bottles. This was no longer the idealized British public which Lenny had romanticized when he first arrived nor was it the carefully selected *cognoscenti* that Peter Cook and Nicholas Luard, the club's backer, had gathered for the première. This was the stiff-backed, toffee-nosed British public drawn from the City and the suburbs – the posh, anglicized version of American rednecks – and they found in Lenny the personification of that same free-ranging Sixties spirit which they had come to fear and loathe. Fist fights were not uncommon. Before leaving the theatre in a huff that would eventually make headlines, actress Siobhan McKenna's escort, resenting slurs on the Irish, bopped Peter Cook on the nose.

'These are Irish hands', wailed Ms McKenna, 'and they are clean.'

'This is a British face', retorted Cook, 'and it's bleeding.'

Since everything was grist for Lenny's mill, he took to recording the reactions of the hostile houses and playing them back to subsequent audiences. Expecting 'live entertainment', they grew similarly hostile at being exposed to endless reams of tape-recordings. Lenny (like Krapp, whom he came to resemble in the final days) was an obsessive recordist. On one occasion, a 'nice Jewish couple' from the suburbs came backstage to compliment him on his act. Though they themselves were sympathetic, they had to point out 'with all due respect' that Lenny was giving offence to certain Jewish members of the audience. Lenny was so regaled by the couple's hypocrisy that he cruelly played the conversation back to the following house which, he naïvely assumed, would be more liberated than the previous one – which of course, it wasn't.

Lenny was fascinated by the British legislation on narcotics which allowed addicts to 'sign on' with certain doctors and receive prescribed doses. He once fantasized for me a British GP's typical prescription: 'Take two aspirins, a hot bath, half a glass of Epsom salts, fifty grammes of coke and an acid suppository.' He was forcibly ejected from two London hotels, once for stopping up the toilet with used spikes and another time for conducting a nocturnal trio of blondes in an original composition, the chorus of which ran, 'Please fuck me, Lenny', in three-part harmony. In one of his temporary abodes he threatened the chambermaids that, if they reported the presence of his pharmaceutical storehouse, he'd get them fired, and genuinely seemed to believe this threat would safeguard him and his larder. Often, in his private life, Lenny was not only naïve and simplistic, but downright imbecilic. I was always amazed at the transformation which took place when he stepped on stage. Those petty, small-scale life aggravations that seemed to occupy all his energy suddenly gave way to a soaring imagination, as if the real world were only a pathetic suburban airport from which Lenny's shambly little monoplane, once airborne, turned into a Lear jet.

Although flattered by his more admiring critics, Bruce never allowed their eulogies to muddy the clear-cut perception he had of himself. He was a 'pro' – no more and no less, someone who had zealously worked himself up from third-rate stand-up dates in the Catskills to the point where he could command large fees and the attention of a sophisticated 'room' in San Francisco, New York or London.

'I don't read enough books,' he once told me, 'so I guess I'm pretty shallow. I'm a lot into the physical. With me, first attraction is never intellectual,' and he proceeded to give me chapter and verse on how, on the road, he would make a bee-line for the biggest 'jugs' and roundest bum in the chorus line and not relent until he'd 'shtupped it'. Even in the midst of a fatal car crash, he once quipped in one of his routines, with only one male and one female survivor, horniness still rears its ugly head. Like Boccaccio or Rabelais, Bruce was always reminding us of our animality and, like de Sade, urging us to celebrate it. Even blue films, he often pointed out, were preferable for children than violent flicks which gloried in blood and gore. 'Nobody ever dies in blue movies,' he pointed out – although only a few years down the line the 'snuff' films might make us all question that one.

A few days before he left England (never to return, in fact, because, once his narcotic riots had become known, the Home Office barred his re-entry), I asked him what lay ahead for him.

'The same,' he said, 'ballbusting and brickbats.'

However he didn't say it sadly, but with a wily, almost eager smile on his face as if, for him, battle was the quotidian and he would no sooner avoid it than expect to be awarded an Oscar for outstanding services to family entertainment. In fact, he had been consulting with Stanley Kubrick and was eager to write a film they had been discussing – yet another ambition that was doomed to fizzle out in the endless array of drug busts and court appearances that would torment him for the remaining four years of his life.

Lenny was the closest thing we had to a Zen comic in that age when Zen was being vigorously rediscovered and regularly proselytized, a direct descendant of those mad monks whose lunacy is depicted in the early Zen drawings. Out of an astonishing relaxation such as we find only in the finest jazz musicians, Bruce pursued his riff to the furthest borders of rationalism and then winged across. Without warning, he could thrust us into a world no longer confined by logical positivism or dulled with conventional associations, true Zen country where new frames were added to the mind and the third eye not only opened, but popped, rolled, swivelled and hung out on a stalk. I remember one session when he stepped out on to the stage of the Establishment and addressed the bass fiddle, which had been placed on its side and turned to the wall.

'Aw, he's embarrassed, you can see,' said Lenny with exaggerated sympathy.

Having transformed the instrument into a shy and withdrawn wallflower, it retained that identity throughout the evening. When he was through, he patted it on the bridge, as if to say he hoped it would be feeling more outgoing tomorrow. This wasn't so much comedy as surreal alchemy, with which he metamorphosed everything around him.

Lenny's accomplice in his raids against hypocrisy was his public. He spoke to them as if they were all members of his own congregation and, like himself, united against the frauds and fakers whose mendacity he was constantly revealing. The tacit assumption behind all his routines was always 'We emancipated, unhypocritical, groovy people understood that', and from there he proceeded to indict or insult the less sensitive, less sophisticated, less scrupulous people who were ranged against 'us'. The tone was similar to that which one finds at Jewish family get-togethers where the vagaries or vulgarities of absent relatives or finagling *goyim* are mercilessly dissected, Lenny's performances were always conducted in the protected parlour of that tight-knit family circle whose shared values unmistakably divided the *chuchim* from the *putzim*. In Lenny's mind – a mind conditioned by the animosities that the Hipster felt for the Square and the Beats felt for the plastic people in button-down shirts and three-piece suits – there was only one *summum bonum* and it was the one the authorities were trying to suppress. Each member of his audience was an ally against that growing horde which had pledged itself to the cold turkey of moral symmetry, the people who knew instinctively that abandonment to the pleasure principle was bad for marriage, bad for the family and bad for General Motors. They were the same detectives, judges, lawyers and finks who instinctively knew that the likes of Lenny had to be combated and ultimately stamped out if decency was to prevail in an America whose icons were painted by Norman Rockwell and whose creeds were promulgated by Cardinal Francis Spellman and Fulton J. Sheen.

But Lenny was a fortuitous warrior in this battle. He had no way of knowing that comedy, freed from moral constraints, becomes hazardous to the survival of the majority; that a Jew who 'talks dirty', who advocates sex against safety, pleasure against propriety and imagination against the tenets of the Bible as reformulated in the provisions of the Criminal Code, is immediately separating himself from the main stream and asking to be victimized. To Lenny it was never a matter of principle nor a moral crusade; it was squeezing laughs out of the absurdity of the world around him – for the sake of the laughter, not for the sake of social reform or changes in consciousness. He was a professional comedian in the same way that Joe Orton was a writer of comedies; the moral and political repercussions were merely spin-offs from what these artists took to be their professional activity. In each case, as they were made conscious of larger implications, they tried to arrogate them into their work and make them part of their personalities, but in both it was after the fact. The Lenny who said, 'I'm not a comedian. And I'm not sick. The world is sick and I'm the doctor. I'm a surgeon with a scalpel for false values. I don't have an act. I just talk. I'm just Lenny Bruce,' had gradually absorbed the implications of his own press clippings. Towards the end, when his unbearable routines were filled with self-conscious poetry about Adolf Eichmann and the injustices of the American judicial system, the old Lenny had been almost totally engulfed both by his champions and his tormentors, and was unrecognizable. And, of course, his personal calamities had siphoned all the comedy out of his *persona*, leaving only the empty wreck that so delighted his four-square, strait-laced enemies. If personal hardship hadn't sunk him irretrievably into heroin, there would have been a few more luminous years, although it seems inconceivable to me that he would have found any real refuge in society. He was too hip to its deceptions ever to play the game for long and, as his more sober critics always said, 'No matter how much you liked Lenny, if you listened to him long enough, there'd come a time when he turned you off.' The image of a smug, balding, buttoned up and respectable Lenny Bruce being given a Lamb's Club roast is simply unthinkable. Lenny was perhaps the first of the comic *maudits* – John Belushi was in the same tradition, so is Sam Kinison – and no doubt there will be others.

The great artists are those who can transcend the forms their genius is constantly inventing and stay in touch with the elusive spirit behind those forms. Like Picasso, like Joyce, like certain matchless jazz musicians, they follow the curve of their improvising natures into uncharted areas which they know it would be fatal to map out. Lenny had the ability to ride the bucking bronco of his comic genius each time he performed, knowing full well he might be tossed in the dirt, but knowing also that the same kind of ride was not possible in a sedate sports car or a sleek limo. To throw oneself constantly against the chaos of streaming circumstance armed only with instinct and *chutzpah* is the mark of the great comic, what separates a Bruce from a Bob Hope or a Mort Sahl. Lenny failed almost as often as he succeeded and I frequently saw him sprawl and die on the stamp-size Establishment stage, but, when he scored, he was the biggest Lotto winner on record. His win, and ours, was dizzying and incalculable. He penetrated certain areas of consciousness (simultaneously blowing the vaults of unconsciousness) in a way that raised stand-up comedy on to plateaus where only the names of Rabelais and Swift, Molière and Fielding could begin to describe the magnitude of his achievement. Having the ability to dredge up the imagery and create the mimicry to 'really tell it the way it is' is no mean feat – and he demonstrated that it can be 'told' as legitimately in stand-up comedy as in literature or the theatre.

It has often been said that it was Lenny who opened the gates for America's contemporary crop of comics. What a dubious distinction! To have paved the way for Shecky Green, Buddy Hackett, Jackie Mason, Johnny Carson and Joan Rivers! No, the fact is Lenny's tradition died with him. There were no descendants at all. What was bequeathed was only the licence for which Lenny paid those heavy dues, a licence which is now blithely exercised by foul-mouthed club comics and vulgar Las Vegas headliners. Despite his own insistence that he was merely a child of show business, Lenny can only be appreciated when compared to the advances of literature that took place in the Sixties. He was the comedic counterpart of Kerouac, Burroughs, Ginsberg and Corso, and to appreciate fully both his style and his content, reference has to be made to the best that was being written and published between 1956 and 1970.

After his death, Harold Hobson, in one of those puerile Sunday pieces for which this critic was especially noted (Hobson on the *Sunday Times* was the pious counterpart of Tynan on the *Observer*; one went from Tynan to Hobson as one might from a gang bang to a prayer meeting), maligned Lenny for being a malicious informer. Although I knew in those last, grim days he had informed on several of his pushers, I couldn't abide the idea that someone as po-faced and piddly as Hobson was doing a little jig on Lenny's grave, and so I wrote a letter defending Bruce and saying that I loved the man. What I meant by 'love' was a passionate affirmation of Bruce's ethos and his way of looking at the world. A few months later, I was told that one of England's leading gourmet and food critics, was interested in seeing me, as he had always wanted to meet 'Lenny Bruce's last lover'. On several other occasions in subsequent years I would be approached by gays who wanted to know what Lenny was like as a lover. In order not to squelch anyone's pleasure, I always lifted a thumb, winked an eye and said, 'Far out.' I knew Lenny would have appreciated the joke.

4   *An acting diversion*

In 1959, after three years of living in London at the behest of the GI Bill, the Government teat was cruelly withdrawn and I found myself holding a passport which ominously warned that I was not permitted to undertake remunerative employment while in the UK. The object of the Home Office stricture was to get its student aliens back to their native countries and off the British welfare rolls.

I wrote a variety of long and eloquent letters asking to be allowed to stay. In them I concocted a long-standing love affair with British culture and fulsomely pledged allegiance to the Queen. They were preposterous letters and, no doubt, read as such. Each time I sent one I included my passport and respectfully requested an extension of my stay. It usually took about six months for the Home Office to reply. The answer was always: request not granted, please leave. No sooner did it arrive than I wrote another fulsome and obsequious letter, again enclosing the passport. Another six months elapsed, and I was again directed to quit the country. This went on for about four years. By the end of that time the authorities got the idea that this was one Yank who had no intention of returning to the colonies.

During those intervening years, being barred from official employment, I had to scratch around for a living. As I described earlier, I did a bit of reviewing, started a Method workshop at the Unity Theatre, directed a few plays without remuneration and more or less starved. My economic salvation came in the form of a US Air Force programme called On Target, which was administered by Jack Briley, an American stationed at the South Ruislip Air Force base.

On Target was the cutesy name of an information and education programme conducted by the Air Force to disseminate basic information to American airmen stationed abroad. Little playlets written and directed by Briley were toured to NATO bases throughout Britain. The object of these playlets varied from month to month. One concerned the dangers of sucking alien objects into jet engines; another dealt with base security and how, in an era of Cold War politics, one could never be sure with whom one might be discussing troop movements or aircraft design; a third extolled the virtues of the chain of command and demonstrated how each airman could contribute to base efficiency. Not exactly great drama.

I always thought of Briley as Jack Armstrong, the All American Boy – he had the kind of face you'd find beaming out at you from a box of Wheaties. He was thirtyish, good looking, a well-scrubbed mid-Westerner who had learned the great American art of playing both ends against the middle. While running On Target, he was writing films for MGM, which then had a sizeable operation in England. He was baby-makingly Roman Catholic, 'gung ho' for America, straight as a dye, a combination of patriot and wheeler-dealer, and given to interminable anecdotage. One learned early with Jack that the last thing one asked him to do was to recount an incident from the past as this unleashed a three-hour monologue which thoroughly immobilized his captive audience. But he was basically easy going and liked me, I think, because I brought an element of 'class' to his act: not everyone at the Ruislip Air Force base could quote Shakespeare and allude to the icons of American literature. The fact that our joint project was intellectually contemptible made it all the more important that we shared an appreciation for culture, even though it never had an opportunity to insinuate itself into the work.

Each month Briley was able to hire one British actor, who would rehearse with the airmen and presumably inject a note of professionalism into their amateur frolics. The salary, by British standards, was considerable and, since we had become friends, Jack offered to hire me as the authorized British actor for these tours.

At the start of each performance I was duly presented to a great bustling battalion of us airmen forcibly gathered for their monthly dose of I&E and, with the kind of exaggerated Blimp-like British accent that one associates with the grossest parodies, offered a few introductory words: 'So heppy to be with you, chaps. Do hope you enjoy the performance, what? Looking forward to meeting you all after the show. Pip, pip.'

After the show, of course, sitting in the PX cafeteria polishing off burgers and milkshakes, my guard was down and so my dentalized lower East side, New York accent would automatically resurface. Airmen, having just seen me give a stirling imitation of David Niven or Ronald Colman, listened suspiciously as a crude, guttural New Yorkese came streaming out of my mouth. 'Bilingual actually,' I would have to explain suddenly reverting to Brit. 'I do so fancy the crude *argot* of East coast American speech, don't you?'

My fellow players were, with one exception, assigned their jobs by the duty roster. The exception was David Healy, a roly-poly Texan actor who, like myself, was resident in London and for whom this job was a convenient sinecure while trying to hammer his way into the British theatre. The others were simple, brash, American mid-Westerners or Southerners who knew nothing about acting and cared less. For them appearing in On Target skits was the equivalent of KP and nothing that Briley or anyone else said could possibly engender any conscientiousness. They were peeved at being assigned namby pamby chores like 'acting' and so invented a number of ways to take their revenge.

The 'performances' of On Target were unlike anything I (or anyone else) have ever experienced on a stage. Usually actors are anxious to impress so as to enhance their chances for future employment or simply because they are committed to the craft of acting, but for these airmen-actors this was a loathsome chore and the only way to tolerate it was to treat it as a farce. They converted each performance into a daemonic test of will. Realizing a play was predicated on suspension of disbelief, they tried, by every means possible, to destroy that belief. To sustain character or situation would have been to accept the impositions of military discipline and become something they were not, viz actors, but in revealing its pretence, shattering its illusion and subverting its purpose, they got the better of it.

One of their favourite tricks was the Frustrated Entrance. Having heard my cue and being just about to step on stage, one of them would clutch me forcibly by the testicles, while another clung to the seat of my pants. Thus immobilized, many desperate moments elapsed while other 'actors' improvised aimlessly and

I struggled to free myself. Once on stage, they would manoeuvre themselves into down-stage positions facing up stage (so as to face away from the audience) and proceed to mug, cross their eyes or convert their faces into Javanese masks, the object being to see if they could flummox me into corpsing.

Another favourite ploy was the Unexpected Prop. During one scene I had to open a packet containing a test tube and brandish it for all to see. In place of the tube an unrolled condom had been deftly substituted. It was always treacherous to leave one's seat, because, when one returned, one would find wrenches, hammers or razor-blades waiting to collide with one's posterior. In one sketch a particularly enterprising mummer had engineered a pillow soaked in the kind of white, sticky tar that is used to immobilize mice. When I sat in it, it was virtually impossible to rise again – and one of the most ingenious comedy moments since Lloyd or Keaton was wasted on a perplexed audience seated in an overhauled Quonset hut in Bentwaters Air Force base.

Scenes which involved eating or drinking were particularly hazardous. I can recall being passed a piece of toast buttered with mucilage and beginning to drink a cup of tea that had been flavoured with ink. Sometimes the ingenuity applied to these pranks was awe inspiring. In one scene, having to sit down in a swivel-chair perched behind a desk, someone had arranged the castors in such a way that the weight of the seated person immediately launched it into a backward spiral directly off the stage.

Eventually one's own ingenuity was dramatically brought into play. After all, this was my chosen profession and, if I applied myself, I should be able to outdo the amateur competition. I became more adept than they at cracking them up, substituting props and obstructing needful moves and, having the ability to stay in character in the midst of all these calamities, managed to imply that all deviations from routine were their doing.

When Briley was on hand, the maniacal improvisations were considerably reduced. But, as soon as he left, the rampaging spirit of devilry which his skits inspired returned with a vengeance. I could never determine whether the audience realized what was going on. They never responded to the lunacies which enveloped the cast. Occasionally they laughed at perfectly normal lines, but

I can never remember them laughing at some of the manic horse-play which so aggravated my bladder that I sometimes had to leave the stage to relieve myself, an unscheduled exit which never seemed to distress either the audience or my fellow actors.

For more months than I can vividly recall Dave Healy and I woke at some ungodly hour in the morning, jammed into his minuscule Austin Sprite (his flatulent collie Pepper wedged between us) and set off for some far-flung outpost in the North or the Midlands, where we donned our costumes, mounted a makeshift stage and proceeded to negotiate some of the greatest hazards ever devised by the twisted mind of man.

When he was ready to move on to bigger and better things, Briley, knowing of my literary and directional inclinations, asked whether I would be interested in taking over the programme. The money was irresistible and, since I was still officially prevented from accepting British employment, I agreed. The stint only lasted about six months as the ludicrousness of what I was doing gradually overcame all financial rewards, even the extra perk of having access to an endless supply of American malted milks in the PX cafeteria.

Six months after I resigned the job at Ruislip, I was asked by Briley whether I was politically active in the Communist Party. I blinked at the question, said that I wasn't and wondered what prompted the query. It turned out the OSI (Office of Security Information) had initiated an investigation against me prompted by the suspicion that I was a fiery radical living with a Communist spy who was regularly beaming broadcasts to behind the Iron Curtain. Since at that time I was consorting with a blonde Windmill dancer named Michelle who would have found it difficult to tune in a radio let alone transmit broadcasts to the Commies, it all remained an insoluble mystery. I was a little chuffed to think there was big fat dossier on me sitting around HQ elaborating some extravagant, Bond-like imbroglio and, after the passage of the US Freedom of Information Act, often thought of requesting access to whatever files might exist. I never got around to it and by the time I was actively involved in the theatre my curiosity had abated.

Jack Briley, who wrote quite a number of film scripts for

American production abroad, went on to fame and fortune as the author of the Oscar-winning Richard Attenborough film *Gandhi*. He also wrote *Cry Freedom* and remains an active and much sought after screenwriter. No doubt there is some small alcove in his study where the On Target scripts await enshrinement in the Academy of Motion Picture Arts and Science.

David Healy became a successful American actor in England, playing with the National Theatre and in London's West End. As for my fellow actors, I have no doubt they went on to become highly wanted criminals throughout America converting their diabolical ingenuity into more grandiose acts of desecration and rapine.

Although I cringe to admit it, those two or three larky years touring with On Target afforded some of the most enjoyable moments of my life. It was an entirely unreal situation and therefore conjured up transports of surrealism which, in retrospect, are fondly recalled as holidays from sense. We were all wicked children behaving irresponsibly and cocking a snook at order and reason in a way that reaffirmed our impishness – the quality that later life seemed resolutely determined to squelch. I've come to believe that what we call 'fun' can only truly come about by subverting some rigid man-made order; the more effectively we subvert it, the more fun we have.

5   *Happening in Edinburgh*

According to official mythology, the first Happening in Britain took place at the Edinburgh Drama Conference organized by the publisher John Calder at the MacEwan Hall in 1962. Although I was part of it and helped construct it with Ken Dewey and Mark Boyle, I'd be very surprised if some nutty students in Liverpool or Kirbymoorside didn't beat us to the punch long before Allan Kaprow ever coined the word 'happening'. In those days the theatre was nothing if not shared impulses, shared between people in different continents who never learned of each other's existence until many years after their respective impulses had been expressed. But the one in Edinburgh, probably because it was televised and therefore disseminated throughout the country, succeeded in bringing the whole concept of happenings to public consciousness. Originally, the conference was intended by Calder and its chairman, Kenneth Tynan, to be a serious, in-depth discussion on a variety of topics, a kind of *quo vadis* on the contemporary theatre. All the international heavyweights (Esslin, Pinter, Olivier, Ionesco, Albee, Frisch, Wesker, etc) were there, but unfortunately so were the television cameras and gradually the awareness that one's opinions, as well as the thrust of one's kleig-lighted personality, were being beamed to millions of viewers produced subtle personality changes in those who came forward to speak.

It was generally acknowledged that the first day was a write-off with each delegate stepping up to deliver a three-minute party piece on the topic 'Who makes today's theatre: the writer, the actor or the director?' – an inane question which everyone later agreed had no answer and only encouraged pointless partisanship. The second day an inquiry into 'commitment' – one of the unshakeable shibboleths of the sixties – was enlivened by an ego-*krieg* between Wolf Mankowitz and critic Bernard Levin made memorable mainly by Mankowitz calling Levin 'a Fascist Jew'. The most striking contribution was made by a hydra-haired, hoarse-throated John Arden who, proclaiming his Dionysian concept of the theatre, said among other things, 'I don't believe you can convert people in a theatre. What you can do is confirm them in something they have just begun to think.' The third day was given over to nationalism in the theatre and again was listlessly predictable. The session on censorship and subsidy, like the first day's discussion, was self defeating as almost everyone was for subsidy and against censorship, although the stream of anecdotes illustrating the Lord Chamberlain's fatuousness was consistently amusing, and by then the conference had reached that pass where levity had become a desirable anodyne against pomposity.

By the fifth day many of us had become disturbed by a sense of aimless drift. Each day produced two or three fruitful ideas, but they were never explored, nor did they condition subsequent discussions which touched upon the same issues. The platform gradually came to resemble an official dumping ground where innumerable views, some sensible, some lunatic, were all piled on top of each other. My own depression became very acute and, I thought, exceptional, but conversations with other delegates soon revealed that the torpor was widespread. A genuine intellectual chaos seemed to have been created. People were trying to sort out their own ideas in relation to the loosely expressed, half baked opinions of others. Whatever frame of reference had begun to emerge gradually collapsed as each televised day led to the next. Preposterous ideas went unchallenged. Esslin, for example, said at one point (I am paraphrasing here), 'Despite the fact that this play is entirely lucid and comprehensible, it still remains an important play.' Language difficulties complicated every session. Through multilingual earphones, cautious translators tried desperately to be true to the meanings of terms the connotations of which they did not always understand.

On the sixth day the subject was to be the theatre of the future and on that day representatives of the *avant garde* such as Ken Dewey, Allan Kaprow, Mark Boyle and myself, had been invited to present a sample of a curious art form called a Happening which had been burgeoning in America.

The night before, Dewey, Boyle, Kaprow, Charles Lewsen and I had met to work out the final details of the event's strategy. We were unanimously pissed off with the pretentiousness of the preceding days and wanted the Happening in some way to express our disgust with the empty showmanship into which the conference had dwindled. Since so many speakers had been putting puerile resolutions, I suggested I put one regarding Beckett's *Waiting For Godot*, that it be interrupted by a planted member of the audience (Charles Lewsen) and that Dewey's scored events proceed from that peg. Very quickly we had managed to muster the people, articles and elements needed to create the Happening: giant masks poised on the galleries above, a bagpiper, a nude model, and a tape of the previous days' debates which included some of the more fatuous excerpts of scholars and critics and a long, cruel excerpt of Ken Tynan stuttering. Dewey was its prime mover – Lewsen, Boyle and myself adding features along the way.

The sixth day, devoted to theatre of the future, began with Joan Littlewood describing her 'fun palace', a giant amusement park she was planning on Thameside. (It never happened.) Omens appeared almost immediately. Littlewood had barely begun her talk when a tanked up Irish director interrupted her and tried incoherently to express an antagonism which appeared to be motivated entirely by the amount of porter he had previously consumed. After a lot of convoluted chat from other speakers, speeches ponderous with overstatement and giddy with oversimplification, the Happening began.

I came forward to put my resolution before the conference. I explained that, because certain plays inspired a multiplicity of interpretations making it difficult to fix their 'true meaning', I was proposing an 'official' interpretation of one of these, viz. *Waiting For Godot*, which, when passed by the conference, would become 'standard' and appear in the appendix of each printed edition thereby removing any confusion about the author's intentions. I suggested that the play, Christian and existential interpretations notwithstanding, was, in fact, about the racial situation in the southern United States; that Lucky represented the Civil War plantation slave; Pozzo, Jefferson Davis; and Estragon and Vladimir, the Generals Grant and Lee, albeit cleverly disguised. When the resolution became unbearably preposterous (and I must say I was listened to with respectful attention much longer than I would have thought possible), I was interrupted by a heckler planted in the audience (Charles Lewsen). A bitter feud ensued or would have had I taken heed of his objections, but in fact I just droned on as if nothing untoward was happening. Gradually one became aware of the low, throbbing sound of an organ and an electronic tape feeding back carefully edited excerpts from the week's discussions. Then a stationary nude on a trolley was drawn across the balcony above the speakers' platform. Carroll Baker, the American actress, who had been seated on the platform took this as her cue and began clambering over the seats at the back of the hall as if hypnotized by Allan Kaprow, who, Valentino-like, was spooking her from the front of the hall. By this time a group of strangers had appeared at the windows overhead hollering, 'Me, can you see me?' and a mother ushered a baby across the stage pointing out the celebrities in the crowd. The final beat was when the curtains behind the speakers' platform suddenly tumbled down to reveal rows of shelves containing over 100 sculpted heads illuminated by footlights. The object of these actions had been to disperse attention and create a number of different areas of interest. The television cameras, under the direction of David Jones of BBC's *Monitor* programme, was completely flummoxed because here was a 'show' with over a dozen different focal points and only one or two cameras to catch them. As often happens in Happenings, the visual 'centre of gravity' was totally removed and a certain kind of alarming drift set in.

A Happening is seen from as many standpoints as there are participants and witnesses; that is, in large part, its allure and what sets it apart from a play, in which there is common consent about centres of interest and, usually, meaning as well. Unlike a theatrical production, it is dynamically conditioned by the perceptions of those involved, who tend to respond to stimuli and incidents not specifically intended by the happeners – although often brought into being by their prepared events. In subsequent reports of the Edinburgh Happening I have always been struck by the great disparity between the different accounts. To try to describe the full impact of what *seemed* to be taking place, I include here two independent reports. One by Ken Dewey, its major planner, and the other by Mark Boyle, a collaborator who, like everyone else, had his own perspective.

A list of the elements, in the order in which they were intended to appear, was as follows:

A platform speaker (Charles Marowitz) making a pseudo-serious proposal that the conference formally accept, as the definitive interpretation, his explanation of *Waiting For Godot*.

An audience member (Charles Lewsen) attacking the speaker for being unclear and not heroic enough.

From the outside, a tape of cable-pullers at work.

Low and barely audible organ sounds.

The silhouette of a large head at the top of the dome of the hall.

A second tape made from fragments of speeches at the conference.

A man walking the tiny ledge high up at the base of the dome.

Figures appearing at other windows high above the hall and occasionally staring down at the people.

An actress on the platform (Carroll Baker) beginning to stare at someone at the back of the hall (Allan Kaprow), eventually taking off a large fur coat and moving towards him across the tops of the audience seats.

A nude model (Anne Kesselaar) being whisked across the organ loft on a spotlight stand.

The men at the high windows (Rik Kendell and Patric De Salvo) shouting, 'Me! Can you hear me? Me!'

Carroll Baker reaching Allan Kaprow and both running out of the hall together.

Tape, organ and debate continue.

A bagpiper (Hamish MacLeod) crossing the top balcony.

A sheep skeleton hung on the giant flat with Cocteau's symbol of the conference.

The piper reaching the other end of the hall as all other sounds stopped, and a blue curtain behind

the platform dropped to reveal shelves containing
about fifty white plaster deathmasks (or, to be
more precise, phrenological head studies).

A woman with a baby, and a boy with a radio
entering the hall, mounting the platform, looking at
everything as if in a museum, and leaving.

The piper tapering off in the distance.

(Running time of the piece was calculated as
seven minutes.)

The piece was intended as a surprise to be
introduced without prior comment. However,
through some mistake, it was announced. Feeling
angry enough to call the whole thing off, I gave
a premature cue, which sent the nude and several
other elements on their way very near the
beginning. As it worked out, this was the perfect
accident to offset whatever expectations the
announcement might have generated in the
audience. Where a slow build would have been the
right tempo for a situation in which nothing was
expected, a quick surprise was better suited for an
audience that was waiting to be 'shown'. It is not
unusual for change, accident or unusual
circumstances to supply such a piece with its most
appropriate rhythm.

Ken Dewey

Quite suddenly we are performing the piece.
Charles Marowitz is called to the microphone
on the platform and starts to give an absurd lecture
and the audience listens politely. It is no more
absurd than most of the talk that has gone on
during the conference, but it has the
distinguishing quality that it is meant to be absurd.
He is brilliant. He has captured very precisely
the air of arrogance and conceit that has
characterized so many of the contributions . . .
Somewhere you can just hear someone
interrupting. It is Charles Lewsen affecting a

high, squeaky voice, looking very diminutive in the vast sea of the audience. Marowitz ignores him and goes on with his nonsense speech. But Lewsen continues interrupting with his shrill voice, and every now and then Marowitz makes little gestures to the audience as though to say, 'You see what I have to put up with.' But Lewsen is now standing on his chair and people round about him are shouting for Marowitz to give him a chance. But Marowitz goes on, saying he only has a few more points to make and then the audience are invited to speak. Lewsen starts to climb forward through the audience, over the seats, stepping from seat-back to seat-back, supported by hands and shoulders, and all the time getting nearer to the platform and letting forth outbursts of shrill heckling, until the audience more or less lifts him bodily on to the platform.

Even now Marowitz, in the most overbearing way, refuses to let him speak. The audience are baying for Lewsen to be given a chance. Finally, with a deep sigh of bored resignation, Marowitz surrenders the microphone and, as Lewsen begins to speak, the microphone goes dead and the whole hall erupts in noise and action. A shattering, cacophonic tape-collage of all the speeches made during the conference, superimposed and jumbled together, blares out from all the loudspeakers with the constant refrain, 'I love the theatre! I love the theatre!' as spoken by one of the ageing heroines of the English stage on the opening day of the conference. But now it is repeated and repeated, fading away and returning, again and again throughout the rest of the performance. Carroll Baker and Allan Kaprow are clambering about, doing what looks like a kind of *avant-garde* ballet on the shoulders of the audience ... Shadowy figures of men appear at the roof-light windows of the hall, windows that are impossible to reach, and they knock and scratch to be let in, which no one can possibly do.

A motorcycle and a horse are being raced round the perimeter of the audience. Across the balcony at the back of the platform, a nude mounted on a trolley . . . makes her triumphant progress across the stage, and men bring trolleyloads of animal skeletons and dump them on the stage.

The people are now standing on their seats and everybody is shouting. I reach the pile of skeletons and diseased, wax human parts from the basement, and start to nail them all over the ten foot high Cocteau drawing (the festival's logo) . . . [then] I make my way to the back of the platform . . . the audience seems to be baying and roaring and all the important theatre people turn towards me with bewildered expressions on their faces. Some are delighted, some angry. Ionesco winks at me. Then I open the curtains and reveal the row upon row of plaster heads. As I turn to the audience, I realize that they are shouting at one another. About half seem to be for us and the other half against us. Then Joan [Hills] appears, heavily pregnant and serene, with Sebastian in her arms and Cameron at her side. She is pointing out to the children the statues, Ken Tynan, the audience, a couple of critics, the TV people, and so on, as though they were all items in some museum of the future.

As suddenly as it started the performance is over.

Mark Boyle

The event became the subject of the remaining afternoon's session. For the first time since it had begun that staid old conference dominated by dour Philistines and frumpy littérateurs was bristling with feeling. The majority, led by a harried Ken Tynan, apoplectic with rage, deplored the disturbance, although the Happening had been announced on the first day and duly scheduled as part of the last day's agenda. Celebrated directors from Yugoslavia, India, Ireland and Germany called it 'nonsense' and 'child's play'. Joan Littlewood immediately sprang to its defence, dismissing questions such as 'What did it mean?', 'Was it theatre?', 'Did it succeed?'. Alexander Trocchi spat the word 'Dada' in Tynan's face and exclaimed that critics could not merely explain away new forces in art by bundling them into ready-made classifications. Martin Esslin, consciously steamrollering his own antipathy, pointed out that the Happening had forced the conference to distinguish between what was real and what was contrived, and therefore had exerted a healthy influence. Jack Gelber looked pained. Edward Albee was noncommittal. Alan Schneider tried to change the subject.

Ken Dewey was hauled up before the conference like a kid who had thrown an inkpot into the electric fan and asked to explain. Dewey, who was later to become something of a legend in the field of performance events and who the night before had been luminously articulate about aims and attitudes, mumbled and stuttered. Finally, to try to resolve the welter of contradictions simmering in his head, he pointed out that in any contemporary theatre, three broad elements always co-existed: the past, the present and the future, and that no one could afford to be involved in all three. He was interested in the future and, to a certain extent, the present. As he found his voice, he delivered the most beautiful and honest talk to come out of the conference: a direct, unvarnished expression of his most deeply felt beliefs triggered by the pressure of having to justify not only his event but his entire approach to art.

In the papers the following day, the nude, predictably, had become isolated from the Happening and most people simply gained the impression that a prank had been played. A statement issued by the Lord Provost of Edinburgh bravely attempted to face down the barbarians: 'It is a very great pity indeed, in a way it is quite a tragedy, that three weeks of glorious festival should have been smeared by a piece of pointless vulgarity. I am advised that the incident can be technically described as a Happening. As a mishap it might have been explained away; as a planned Happening there can be no explanation or excuse.' And then, to show that it would take more than a pair of bare bodkins and a gaggle of beatniks to destroy the Scottish sense of virtue, the Lord Provost concluded: 'In spite of [this], I have faith in the drama today and I have faith in the drama of the future. I do not contemplate surrendering to the irresponsible actions of a few people sick in mind and heart.'

As Adrian Henri, the art historian, said: 'Ever since then, the Great British Public has associated happenings with naked ladies.' For her fifteen to thirty second appearance twenty feet above the speakers' platform, the nude model, Anna Kesselaar, was formally charged in an Edinburgh court with shameless and indecent conduct, and John Calder, organizer of the conference, with allowing the incident to take place and not exercising proper authority. At the trial several months later Kesselaar was acquitted and charges against Calder were dismissed.

In fact, despite the lack of coherence on the part of both those outraged by the event and by its perpetrators, the Happening unmistakably delivered its message. The *animus* that the happeners felt towards the delegates of the conference and the travesty it had become were powerfully communicated. As each delegate in turn came up to deliver a broadside against the 'child's play', the 'offensiveness', the 'lunacy' of what they had seen, they were unconsciously responding to the fierceness of the criticism which the event had lodged in their bellies – just as in the months and years to come Philistines and squares of every stamp would rail against the 'corruptiveness' and 'decadence' of future 'events' and see in them, quite rightly, a challenge to their settled way of life and that *Weltanuschaung* which the hairier members of the Sixties were progressively and gleefully eroding.

The facts are that the week of the conference had been filled with intellectual belching and critical one-upmanship. The television cameras had encouraged showmanship and unfelt passion. (On the second day, Harold Pinter had prophesied this when he spoke about the 'vanity' which brought people to such a platform – perhaps in the deluded desire 'to become movie stars'.) Serious and talented people were put into positions of self-deceit in order to save face or explain themselves in aimless discussions where each delegate had his own definition of words such as 'reality', 'style', 'commitment', 'aesthetics', etc. Ionesco, the long awaited star attraction, arrived on the final afternoon, spoke about fifty words and then fell into a sullen silence. After twenty minutes of emanating waves of inconsolable *ennui*, he left the platform for a smoke and never returned.

Dewey had taken all these strands in the conference and woven them into a quasi-spontaneous combustion. The taped excerpts exposed some of the muggier thinking and contradictory proclamations made by the delegates. The nude, in some inexplicit way, acted as a voluptuous surrogate for Carroll Baker, the glamorous delegate from Hollywood who spoke sensibly, but was essentially a sexual apparition on a platform dominated by male writers and intellectuals. The huffing bagpiper metaphorically musicalized the hot air that so many of the delegates vented into the atmosphere. The mother and child and the screaming intruders at the windows made a comment about the vaunting egotism of so many of the speakers, and the rows of gaping faces revealed at the end of the Happening were the graphic counterpart of that part of the audience which ogled vapidly, listened indiscriminately and waited docilely to be given *the word*. Ken Dewey, the nude, the audio-retrospective and the attendant panic had forced people to examine their behaviour during the week. In doing so, it was only natural they should be outraged.

Happenings galloped apace after that. In the basement of Better Books on London's Charing Cross Road (then owned by Tony Godwin of Penguin Books) and at UFO on Tottenham Court Road, aesthetic *provocateurs* such as Jeff Nuttall, Mark Long, Bruce Lacey and innumerable others began brandishing paint, flashing lights, tossing textures, orchestrating sounds and juxtaposing texts for the greater glory of counter culture. Anything served as a pretext for a Happening: traffic accidents, disturbances at public lectures, the involuntary posturings of certifiable psychotics, musicians playing endless repeats of compositions by Erik Satie, long-haired gits getting a public haircut while video cameras recorded 'the act' for posterity and, of course, young men and women spontaneously stripping, streaking or flashing in any kind of public situation where such exposure would outrage, offend or merely incite giggles.

I became very interested in the form itself. It seemed to be a welcome alternative to texts and conventional *mise en scène*. The fact that it environmentally liberated the theatre, enabling it to 'happen' in any venue it chose, either indoors or out, was genuinely exciting. At the Open Space, Dewey and I did one other event entitled *Exit Music*. This involved a number of people arriving at a theatre only to be ushered into buses and transported all over London whilst a number of specific calculated events took place at designated points *en route*. Of course spectators saw much more than we laid on for them – or at least thought they did. It was all a kind of lesson in seeing. Once the audience members in their bus seats realized that the nature of the event was to spot actions and activities through the bus windows, they began to see things which had always been there but had been rendered invisible by their own routine lack of perception. After the event, when spectators reported fist fights, the sighting of strange animals and glimpses of famous celebrities who couldn't possibly have been there, it became clear to me that 'seeing' was only the threshold of 'imagining' and, if properly orchestrated, one could easily (sometimes fatally) lead to the other.

Happenings matured into events and theatre pieces and, ultimately, performance art, which, by distilling and refining the outdoor hurly-burly of the early events, formalized a trend that had begun as a rough, spontaneous, truly unpredictable mix of random factors. But, as we all know, everything in the Sixties got packaged, merchandised and taken over by the advertising moguls, so it is no surprise that you can now buy subscriptions to performance art series and that its exponents, heavily subsidized by leading cultural foundations, have retreated to the safety of posh museums and galleries. '*Avant garde*' itself has become merely another form of chic and, whereas once upon a time it took generations, sometimes centuries, for *avant garde* art to be discovered and appreciated, it now flourishes like any other item in the overstocked cultural supermarket.

But, for a little while there, it was, as we used to say in our juvenilia, 'a gas', and some of my fondest and most indelible memories of danger, excitement and suspense are of being bombarded with sights, sounds and silliness by a wide variety of aesthetes and zanies who didn't always understand what they were doing, but were as committed to it as the orthodox are to the coming of the Messiah.

6   *Milligan Madness*

I arrived in England too late for the Goons, but their myth was everywhere. People imitated Peter Sellers' Eccles voice and acted out classic bits from the more memorable programmes and of course, before long, *Monty Python's Flying Circus* was spawned out of the surrealism which Spike Milligan, Michael Bentine and Eric Sykes had wrought a decade before.

What I was just in time for was Milligan's emergence as a national wonder both on stage and in television. In 1964, reviewing for *Encore*, I was present on the historic occasion when Milligan transformed Goncharov's *Oblomov* into one of the wildest and most anarchic improvizations of the British stage. On the first night of that woefully misguided entertainment the cast was still under the impression that Ricardo Aragno's footling dramatization of the Goncharov novel, leadenly directed by Frank Dunlop, still had some dramatic validity. The first night reaction proved conclusively that everyone concerned had been suffering from a collective delusion. The second night Milligan, who is nothing if not a survivor, let out all the stops, and left them out for the rest of the run.

Milligan, financially strapped and realizing the show was going to take a nosedive, began to thread the play like a scarlet ribbon, weaving a crazy pattern around drab burlap. It was the sort of performance that recalled those wacky Hollywood comedies where the lead comic somehow finds himself inveigled into a stage play and tries vainly to impersonate the actor he isn't. It's Harpo Marx in the *Il Travatore* scenes from *A Night at the Opera* and Danny Kaye in that picture where he stumbles into a classical ballet company and tries desperately to remain inconspicuous. On one level it was nothing more than Milligan larking about, but on another it was the introduction of a demonic element into a work so square and staid that its being sabotaged became the only remarkable thing about it.

There was something devastatingly Brechtian about Milligan's performance. He torpedoed the fourth wall. One was constantly aware of the stage, the actors in costumes, and that Milligan, through some incalculable misadventure, somehow had landed himself in a nineteenth-century Russian manor as a landowner in debt, in bed and in love. But the mind never really absorbed Oblomov as a character, it was too busy following the permutations of Milligan the clown, watching him repeat fluffed lines ('Just a minute, folks, I'll say that again!') or prefacing a love scene with, 'Watch it, this is the big serious acting bit coming up.' Brecht creates his illusion and then throws cold water in our faces to snap us out of it; Milligan scaled the periphery of illusion squirting us with a water-pistol at regular intervals.

Milligan's art of comedy lay in acknowledging the obvious. He goes down on bended knee to profess love to his beloved. Embarrassed, she turns away. He suddenly focuses on himself. He is on the floor. He looks at his beloved. She is turned away. He looks to where she is looking to see what she is looking at. She quickly looks back at him. He regards himself quizzically. The scene continues. These simple 'takes' produce laughter that grows out of Milligan's questioning of himself and his circumstance. He questions it even though he himself initiated it, even though he of all people should know what it's about, and in that questioning he objectifies his own words and actions, thereby drawing attention to their conventional formality. Did I say that? What did I mean by that? Is this me? Is everyone out there watching me? Is this a play? Am I a character in a play? Who is this beside me? Are those lights out there? What's going on here?

Oblomov opened to disastrous notices at the New Lyric theatre in Hammersmith in October 1964. In December, almost wholly improvised, rerouted by Milligan and ironically retitled *Son of Oblomov*, it reopened at the Comedy Theatre and was a resounding success. It is the only instance I know of in the theatre, British or otherwise, where a comedian's maniacal will to survive thoroughly alchemized lead into gold.

When I was fielding an improvisational programme to BBC-2, I suggested that we bring together Milligan, Barry Humphries, Barry Stanton, Jacqueline MacKenzie (and another actress whose name I no longer recall) into a troupe, and spend three or four weeks just improvising. At the end of that time, an interconnecting tissue having formed between the performers, we would then launch a wholly improvised comedy programme before a live audience. The BBC chieftains, at that time mainly refugees from Fleet Street, were sceptical, but agreed to give it a try.

Each day the troupe met in a rehearsal room at Shepherd's Bush and I contrived a variety of improvisational pretexts for them. One, as I recall, was a scene in which Milligan and Humphries answered a classified ad which read 'Wanted: A highly cultivated, well-spoken gentleman to act as valet and butler for a member of the Royal Family.' The actors had to come up with the unlikeliest applicants they could conjure up. Humphries, as I recall, entered as a one-eyed hunchback with a slobbering speech defect; Milligan, as an incessantly scratching eczema victim dragging a club foot. At other times I set up makeshift musical instruments, rattles, spoons and pans, penny-whistles, half-filled milk bottles, etc., and led the troupe in a series of changing rhythms and acoustic sonatas. Each day, for several hours a day, Milligan, Humphries *et al.* improvised according to some of the most challenging pretexts I could devise. The rehearsal room was beserk with outbreaks of uncontrollable energy and rocked by incredible acts of comic invention.

Barry Humphries, at this time, had not yet thrown himself irretrievably into Dame Edna Everage. He was an eye-twinkling, surly scamp of a comic with a strong surrealist bent. (He once described to me a revue he wanted to assemble, the main feature of which would be a grossly overweight naked lady just perched on the side of the stage as a kind of human anchor. No mention would ever be made of her and at no time in the evening would she participate in the action.) He and Milligan shared a similar world view and their scenes together had the kind of unity you would expect if two trolls stumbled upon each other in a Norwegian grotto. His improvisational flair was prodigious and, unlike Spike, he had a literary facility which enabled him to invent a prolix comic language which perfectly captured his most off the wall and wayward thoughts, a quality he has since perfected in his Dame Edna exchanges with live audiences. There was something almost Dickensian about Barry. He was a character fashioned in the old style, full of quibbles and quiddities, in whom life seemed to trigger larger-than-life impersonations, not, as in Spike's case, to elude reality, but to transform it into something more grotesque and amusing than it actually was.

Needless to say, the idea of a scriptless programme sent the BBC heads into a flap. As in all improvisational programmes, if you are lucky, fifty to sixty per cent of the product is astounding and usable and the rest almost entirely expendable. I had asked for us to record twice as much as we needed so we would have something to cull from, but the Beeb couldn't see the point of recording 120 minutes when all you needed was thirty. The pilot had highs and lows, but was, on the whole, disappointing. It never reached the manic heights of the rehearsal room work. The producers then suggested that we codify some of the better improvised scenes and play them as rehearsed items. I argued that this was contrary to the whole spirit of improvised comedy, but couldn't persuade the three-piece suits. The Beeb wanted something tangible that they could put in the can and seemed not to notice that what we had, in embryo, was a first-class, crack squad of improvising comics which in time would develop both muscle and consistency. Like many of those efforts which were temperamentally opposed to the buttoned up character of the Corporation, the programme, after some pathetic attempts at first aid, was abandoned. But, for me, the exposure to Milligan and Humphries was more than sufficient compensation.

Milligan, as he often said himself, was driven mad by the BBC. Over the years they treated him shamefully, curbing his finest instincts and negotiating him into corners which made him feel like a barely tolerated hireling. Of all the British comedians, he was the only one who was ever truly possessed. You could actually feel his possession. In the middle of a routine he would begin to talk in some indecipherable tongue, jabbering away like an epileptic, transported into realms of comedy which were just short of certifiable lunacy. In my view, this was Spike's safety valve. Behind the inspired zaniness was a ferocious hatred of the bigoted, bureaucratic and Blimpish British character, and, rather than take up a knife and hack away at that, Spike would 'pass over' into that zone of demonic gibberish which could still be construed as comedy, but was palpably the ego's defence against going spare.

Spike was a 'medium' for comedy which came from some

incorrigible spirit world above and beyond the personality of the man himself. Comic energies invaded his being. When the spirit was with him, he spoke in tongues. His comic *personae*, that bevy of weird characterizations that shuttled in and out of his personality, were aspects of a schizophrenic delirium which occasionally took him over. In Spike's case, it was either comedy or madness, the two copulated regularly, sometimes one was on top, sometimes the other.

In social conversations, at dinner or in a pub, Spike would be matey, breezy, clever, playful (he loved talking about jazz and was an accomplished musician), but it always seemed an enormous effort for him to adjust to social intercourse, as if it involved descent from a much more abstract plane on which social conversations were thoroughly alien. In his company I tried (usually in vain) to establish contact with the extra-terrestrial Spike – the one who prepared and rehearsed the terrestrial comedian with whom I was in only earthly contact. I wanted to climb into his head, loll around on his inner landscape, see the outrageous spectacles about which he brought back such tantalizing, albeit fragmentary, reports.

I have always had a strong predilection for comedy and comedians, which for many seemed an interest incompatible with *avant-garde* inclinations. (Irving Wardle, I recall, once complained of my 'tin ear', since so many comic offerings at the Open Space fell flat.) For a short period in my adolescence I wanted to be a comedian and even went so far as to enrol in a gagwriters' institute. There were also a couple of *gauche* comedy acts during the high school years, in one of which I was garishly saronged as Tarzan and another in which I did a soft shoe shuffle with a partner who instinctively danced left everytime I danced right, and *vice versa*. I grew up in New York with a profound admiration for the early explosive comics – men like Milton Berle, Irwin Corey, Jack Carter, Jack E. Leonard, Red Buttons and Larry Storch. I am sure much of that early enthusiasm ripples beneath the plays I write, most of which are comedies. And in England, when I had the opportunity to mount the première of Ionesco's *Makbett*, I brought together Harry H. Corbett, Terry Scott and Victor Spinetti, and resolved to turn that metaphysical parody into a vaudeville turn. It opened in Coventry and then played successfully at Sam Wanamaker's Globe Playhouse in Southwark. Scott and Corbett had both been big television names, and there was an unspoken sense of rivalry between them, or at least there was from Scott's standpoint. Corbett, riding high on the success of *Steptoe and Son*, automatically assumed he was the star of the show and behaved accordingly. At the end of certain performances when audience reaction was particularly warm, Corbett would step forward from the curtain call and, blithely assuming leadership of the ensemble, make a little speech on behalf of the cast. Scott, frozen in the line behind him, would seethe quietly and go purple in the face. I don't think his contempt ever manifested itself, and throughout the run Corbett would smile his goofy, ineffectual smile and assume everyone loved and adored him as much as he did himself. But, compared to these comedians, Spike was in another world. They were all commercialized *farceurs* of one sort or another dependent on scripts and gagwriters. Spike was a palpitating, self-contained comic emanation. Although bred in vaudeville and cabaret, like Lenny Bruce, he, like Bruce, had transcended the confines of conventional show business to inhabit some other realm. You could see his roots clearly: they were in simplistic British comedy and music hall. But his topmost branches were out of sight.

In 1963, while working with Peter Brook on the Theatre of Cruelty season, I acquired Spike's translation of Jarry's *Ubu Roi*. It was a riff on the original work, more Milligan than Jarry, but perfectly caught the airborne quality of that surrealist extravaganza. Peter was quite right to say we needed Goons in order to bring it off and that in the hands of RSC actors it would never leave the ground, but for years after the RSC stint I stroked the script lovingly. In the late 1970s, in collaboration with the Central School of Art and Design at the Jeanetta Cochrane Theatre, I managed to interest the comedian Charlie Drake in playing Ubu and we actually assembled a production. But Drake, although cut from the same cloth as Milligan, a variety, radio and television comic, could not carry the show alone. The rest of the cast were 'just actors', whereas it became clear that it needed the same kind of comic ensemble that had been gathered together for the

Milligan and John Antrobus comedy *The Bedsitting Room*. It needed, in fact, the kind of shared anarchy that had characterized the Goons themselves.

In *Confessions of a Counterfeit Critic*, a collection of reviews from the Sixties and Seventies, I wrote: 'If some cruel genie suddenly appeared to say that every performance I had seen in the past twelve years was to be mentally banished – save one – it is the memory of *Oblomov* which I would choose to retain.' In some ways I still feel that seventeen years after it was first written. Milligan gave me a sense of comic transcendence, what Jonson would have called 'transports of joy'. With some performers, you feel they represent high-grade professional accomplishment. You speak of their talent, their skill and their presence. But with Milligan it is like recalling an encounter with an unreal, other-worldly being and I think back to him as one might an apparition, a poltergeist or a verifiable UFO.

7   *Sinning in Glasgow*

In December 1965, at the Glasgow Citizens Theatre, I had one of the most memorable openings of my life. Or rather, didn't have, since my production of Marlowe's *Doctor Faustus* was cancelled on opening night with a full audience in anxious attendance. Although I'd never actually had a show shot out from me moments before the curtain was due to rise, in a curious way the experience itself was reminiscent of many other scrapes I'd had with authority ever since high school and so, being part of a psychic pattern, was not as exceptional as it might have been.

I had put together a new adaptation of the play loosely identifying Faustus with J. Robert Oppenheimer, one of the chief architects of the atom bomb, and drawing a parallel between the necromancer who experimented with forbidden knowledge and the nuclear scientist who, in the minds of many, had transgressed the permissible bounds of science. Faustus, dressed in the modern togs of a university research scholar, sat at a desk inscribed with the equation $e = mc^2$. His Mephistopheles had the air of a governmental defence chief, the kind of man who appropriates brilliant scientists for the greater glory of militarism. In this rendering, Faustus exchanged his considerable intellectual gifts in return for the bounties of experimentation and research. The diabolical part of the pact was that Faustus knew he was morally trespassing into areas which were hazardous both to himself and society as a whole.

Since medievalism was not a factor in this version, the Seven Deadly Sins had to be rethought and reinterpreted. I hit upon the idea of fashioning a caricatured mask for each sin identifying them with different heads of state: de Gaulle was Pride, President Johnson Gluttony, Mao-Tse-Tung Envy, etc. In this version, it was Mephistopheles himself (Peter Halliday) that played each of the Seven Deadly Sins in quick succession while all the members of the cast huddled around Faustus like a makeshift audience conjured up especially for the diabolical entertainment. For Sloth,

I chose a mask of Queen Elizabeth II. She wore the familiar Elizabethan tiara and spoke in that thin, dehydrated voice that one associated with the Queen's Christmas messages. Everyone seemed to be delighted with the invention and the cast treated the scene as a hoot.

At a final preview, Michael Goldberg, chairman of the management committee at the Close Theatre, in which the production was to open, saw the scene for the first time and went white. He called me to one side and wondered whether this was in the best taste. 'No,' I said, 'you might well consider it bad taste – if you happened to be the head of state being pilloried, but it's perfectly in keeping with the style of the show.' Goldberg was not persuaded. Although not too concerned with the other world leaders, he pointed out that the characterization of the Queen might be offensive to members of a Scottish audience. And besides, the Queen was not slothful, she worked very hard on state occasions, diplomatic visits and at local and regional events. 'This is not personal to the Queen,' I pointed out. 'She herself is symbolic of a certain class in British society and for many this class is perceived as slothful – living on unearned income, lolling around baronial mansions, hunting and shooting, etc. It is only her symbolic significance we are dealing with.'

Goldberg remained unconvinced and during the next twenty-four hours a variety of people connected with the theatre tried to dissuade me from the impersonation. I found the whole thing amusing – this neurotic concern for protecting the delicacy of the Queen from a two-minute review turn in a production of *Doctor Faustus* being staged in the Gorbals, then the most tawdry and impoverished district in Glasgow.

The following day, the day of the première, Goldberg, now bolstered by other members of the board, rounded on me.

'Will you delete the impersonation of the Queen?'

'Do you mean have *Six* Deadly Sins instead of Seven?'

They paused for a moment, aware of the incongruity of such a move, but then boldly replied, 'Yes!'

'I'm sorry,' I replied, 'Marlowe would come back from the grave to haunt me if I did anything so sinful.'

Obviously my levity was misplaced as the rising ire of Mr Goldberg and his cohorts made it very clear that in their minds they were defending, not only the tenets of Good Taste, but the honour of Her Majesty the Queen, and they had no intention of allowing a bearded, New York upstart to administer such an insult. I still felt they were carrying on like jackasses, but my stage manager reported that they would cancel the show if the offending impersonation was not expunged. Such a course of action seemed so incredible to me that I couldn't give it any credence.

On the night of the première there were a lot of backstage rumblings going on, clusters of tuxedo'd officials like schools of penguins kept waddling from the front of the lobby to the back of the stalls. I became the object of pointed looks and poisonous whispers. The press and the subscribers were in their seats; 'beginners' had been called; the first light cue was about seven minutes away; and then Mr Goldberg, in a natty dress suit, rose to address the house. The performance, it appeared, was to be cancelled 'due to differences between the director and the committee of management'. The director had introduced an impersonation of the Queen, personifying Sloth, which in the opinion of the committee was 'needless and gratuitously offensive' and, since Mr Marowitz had refused to modify the scene, they had no alternative but to cancel the presentation.

The audience moaned, hissed, laughed and broke out into dozens of cross conversations. Since I was now the object of many people's attention, I rose and protested this 'outrageous act of censorship' against my production. Marlowe's own intention with the Seven Deadly Sins had been satirical and I didn't see why I should be disallowed a licence which had been issued to the playwright over 300 years ago.

Duncan Macrae, a leading Scots actor and one of the board members at Glasgow, entered the fray, saying the director's allegation that he was being 'censored' was 'nonsensical'.

'He's not satisfied with Marlowe's text,' brayed Macrae, having been told several of the comedy scenes had been rewritten, 'He's got to have his own text!'

'You're talking baloney!' I replied deductively.

'You should have some sense of responsibility,' cried one of the senior board members, 'towards this committee who are actually carrying this theatre. It's losing money and is dependent on public support.'

'If you cancel this show,' I pointed out, 'it will only lose more money. Furthermore, this is a club theatre, which has been especially created to avoid the censorship of the Lord Chamberlain and here am I being censored by four gentlemen in dress suits.'

'Don't use that word!' said Goldberg, getting so hot under the collar I feared an apoplectic episode. 'We have no right to offend people gratuitously.' Then, turning to the audience and playing shamefully to the house, 'I pleaded with him to make a minor adjustment to remove references to the Queen which may be offensive to many people.'

When Macrae, not having entirely shot his bolt, rose again to say that he refused to sacrifice what little authority he had, there were strident shouts of '*Sieg Heil!*' from the back rows. 'Why should an American director come here,' he asked venomously, 'and insult the Queen?'

'I agree,' replied an indignant Scottish wag, 'he should deliver the insult directly to Buckingham Palace where it belongs!'

As people began repeating themselves, I threw my pigskin jacket over my shoulders and strode out crying, 'I quit' – which was an entirely pointless gesture since the work had already been done and my job was over in any case, but in the heat of the moment there were many of us spouting lunacies. By this time the audience, realizing there was to be no performance, began shuffling out, many of them assuring each other that in many ways this was one of the most stimulating evenings they'd had at the Citizens for some time.

The next day the cancellation was headlined in newspapers throughout Scotland and England. In most cases the stories perfectly captured the surreal pandamonium of the evening. 'Slur On Queen Halts Play' screeched the front page of the *Scotsman*. 'Producer Offensive To The Queen' chided the *Glasgow Herald*. 'Play Banned For Insulting The Queen' declared the *Daily Mail* in its most offended royalist tone.

There then followed a variety of storm conferences between the theatre's directors, the members of the board and, ultimately, Goldberg and myself. All the talk was about compromise. No, I would not remove the scene. No, I would not 'put it on tape'. No, I would not substitute King Farouk for the Queen. Would I remove the tiara? Could it be replaced by something else? Britannia's helmet, I suggested helpfully. Yes, Britannia's helmet! After all, Elizabeth doesn't wear a helmet, but she does wear a tiara. Fine, I said, aware that the cast were now frightened they might lose their jobs if the run were cancelled, we'll substitute Britannia's helmet for the Queen's tiara. Concession granted.

That night, with actor Peter Halliday wearing a helmet instead of a tiara, the play finally opened. But of course, since the characterization depended not on the hat but on that thin, regal voice, there was no question in anyone's mind that the Queen was intended. Even if there had been, the publicity from the night before removed all doubts.

Next day in the *Glasgow Herald* Jack Webster wrote:

> I wait for the scene that I have been told has been changed so that Her Majesty the Queen will *not* be represented as Sloth and, when it arrives, what do I find? The same mask that was intended for the original performance! Still unmistakably the Queen . . . Is [Mr Goldberg] satisfied that the offensive parts have been removed? 'The mask was doctored with a Britannia helmet being added and the voice changed so that it would not represent the Queen,' he said. 'I feel our point was made . . .' 'Was it intended to be the Queen?' I asked Marowitz. 'Did it sound like the Queen to you?' he asks. I say it did. And he gestures as if to say, 'Of course.' So, having clarified that the only concession was to dress up our Queen in a Britannia helmet, I call over Mr Goldberg and bring the two men face to face. I repeat what Mr Marowitz has just told me, whereupon Mr Marowitz points out that I have misrepresented him. This was NOT meant to be our Queen. It was simply a regal figure. As for the voice well . . . who knows what kind of voice Britannia had?

The most salutary effect of the controversy was that it keyed up the cast so intensely that they were bursting to play and, as a result, gave a walloping good performance. The reviews were on the whole favourable, although each critic felt the need to state their political positions on the Queen, censorship and the quarrel that had developed between managerial control and freedom of expression. Had Mr Goldberg wanted to obtain maximum publicity for the show, he couldn't have acted in a more effective manner on the opening night, but I am sure he was sincerely motivated by considerations of propriety. The publicity ensured a sell-out run and, I am sure, helped fill the coffers of a theatre that was then badly in need of box-office takings.

Once the controversy had died down, I had to acknowledge a strong dissatisfaction with my own adaptation. The Faust–Oppenheimer parallel, once established, was never permitted to develop because of the nature of Marlowe's play. At a certain point the morality play, which is at the base of *Doctor Faustus*, took over and the nuclear implications got lost in the Christian *dénouement*. It was one of those bright ideas that needed more radical revision to the original if it were truly to implant itself. In a later production, at Gothenburg, I went further with the treatment, but never really brought it off.

The only other opening that can compete with Glasgow happened a few years later in Wiesbaden, when I directed Webster's *The White Devil* in a German production designed by John Napier.

Wanting to avoid the lame duels which were a regular feature of classical productions throughout Europe, I asked Napier to create a device which would enable blood to spurt from victims as the deadly steel entered their flesh. (The climax of *The White Devil* is awash with perforated noble men and women.) Being both conscientious and ingenious, John came up with an invention which I christened the 'spurting scum bag'. Those characters who had to receive the deadly steel were fitted with a blown up condom into which stage blood had been carefully impacted. When the blade pierced the unseen condom, the blood would spurt as if an artery had been hit, splattering the assassin and ghoulishly soiling the victim.

Because of a shortage of rehearsal time, we could not be sure the effect would work on opening night, but it did, better than anyone could have predicted. In the last moments of the play Vittoria Corombona, Zanche and Flamineo are fatally stabbed, and, as the blades entered, three geysers spurted on to the stage creating a wave of audible nausea which swept from the stalls to the balconies. The audience, which had already shown their disdain for the show's black comic effects (Lodovico took a full three minutes to strangle Brachiano, only to have him suddenly resuscitate after he appeared to be stone cold dead) began booing, catcalling and launching their programmes on to the stage as if it were an aerial display. The cast assembled for their curtain calls in the midst of this abominating furore and were pelted with orange rinds and chocolate boxes. John and I, who, according to the German tradition, were supposed to go out and take our bows along with the rest of the company, beat a hasty retreat giggling demonically. The Wiesbaden audience had expected lofty tragedy, were unprepared for sick comedy and, in the best German tradition, let the artists feel the full measure of their scorn.

There is something heady and intoxicating about 2,000 spectators venting their loathing on an unprotected group of actors involuntarily lined up to receive their plaudits. Although, over the years, certain of my productions have received standing ovations and spirited huzzas, I recall the Wiesbaden roasting with a certain affection. It was in that same theatre that an unrepentant German director whose production was violently loathed (and who, in turn, loathed the *bürgerlich* Wiesbaden audience) stepped on the stage at the end of his première, pulled down his dress trousers and mooned his first night audience. There is something about a tumultuous emotional reaction which, whether positive or negative, confirms the liveliness of the dramatic event and makes one glad to be in a theatre.

8   A *Theatre of Cruelty*

Throughout my life in England I was haunted by Peter Brook. The haunting occurred even during those periods when we actually worked together. For me, he was never simply an English director, but a constant psychic preoccupation; an exemplar of what was best in the British theatre, an unattainable ideal, a friend, a mentor, a model, a nemesis, a mixture of childlike innocence and Nietzschean complexity, a pioneer, a pretender, a genius, a dupe.

One of the first shows I saw on arriving in London (indeed, it may have actually been *the* first) was Peter's 1957 Stratford production of *Titus Andronicus*. Inebriated with its theatricality, I wrote a heady notice for the *Village Voice*, which began: 'A short, scalene-shaped man named Peter Brook, aged 33, is the greatest director in England', and ended by intoning, 'The production is great theatre because it's *all* theatre. It indulges itself in theatricalism and cuts the umbilical cord that theoretically links life to art ... Every so often an art form triumphs solely within its own boundaries, without deference to the reality it is supposed to be reflecting. When such theatre fails, it is hopeless and agonizing; when it succeeds, it is *Titus Andronicus*.'

My maturer sensibility wriggles at the effusiveness with which my adolescent self expressed itself, but I respect the passion in many of those early, let-it-all-hang-out *Voice* reviews, and here I was clearly responding – without knowing it – to certain Artaudian imperatives which, because I had not yet read *The Theatre and its Double*, had not even begun to formulate themselves. Something in *Titus* was speaking to me as directly as if the director had leapt down from the stage, taken me by the collar and begun to bellow into my face.

One of the attractions of *Encore* magazine, the theatrical bi-monthly, was its vague connection with Peter Brook, who had contributed articles to its early numbers. It was quietly tantalizing to know that, as I was reading his pieces, he was reading mine and that, although no dialogue had yet taken place, we were studiously eavesdropping on one another. At some point I wrote to him, an outpouring that was something of a *cri de coeur* disguised as a fan letter. I know it went into my profound dissatisfactions with the English theatre, but I don't remember much more than that. At the time I was directing the In-Stage experimental group at the British Drama League and Peter attended my production of *A Little Something for the Maid* by Ray Abell, a short, discontinuous play which involved a fragmentary encounter between a man, a woman and a telephone. After that, we met in London and then again in Paris, where we first discussed the possibility of collaborating on an experimental scheme Peter was hatching for the Royal Shakespeare Company. Much of our conversation had to do with whether to attempt it in London or in Paris, which I could not fathom. It seemed incredible to me not to create such a theatre in London and I couldn't for the life of me understand why Peter was seriously considering France. I didn't realize then (lessons which had already been notched in Peter's gut) that there was in England a shallowness of soil which threatened the growth of any serious artistic enterprise. I was still a virgin and my love affair with English culture was only at the hand-holding stage.

Before the formation of what came to be the Royal Shakespeare Company Experimental Group, Peter was scheduled to mount *King Lear* anew at Stratford-upon-Avon with Paul Scofield. Somehow I wangled myself into the position of Assistant Director on that show and in the late summer of 1962 found myself at the first read through, sitting in a draughty rehearsal room in Stratford, being eyed suspiciously by actors who were always on the look out for unannounced replacements. Peter had received a note from Gordon Craig, which he read to the assembled actors; the gist of it was that *Lear*, like the Oriental husband who had lost his wife, knew that she was somewhere and so had to look for her everywhere. Lear, likewise, was somewhere, although no production had ever successfully realized him, and so we too had to look everywhere.

The reading, from the company's standpoint, was the typical, under-energized trot through which signals actors' uncertainty in the face of a daunting masterpiece. Not sure where they are heading nor what route was to be taken, they tended to sidle alongside the text clearly implying that nothing they said should be taken very seriously. Scofield, on the other hand, threw himself into the reading as if it were an audition before employers sceptical of his talent. He growled his way into the thickets of the text, constantly testing and re-testing scansion and stress, like a hound chasing an elusive hare through densely wooded terrain. Gradually the company transformed into something of an audience for Scofield's 'performance'. The actors were both awed and frightened by the muscularity of his attack, the unmistakable sense that something difficult and perhaps unachievable was at stake. In that first reading Scofield set the whole tone of the rehearsal period. 'This is a precariously steep mountain face with a sheer drop below,' he seemed to be saying, 'so we'd all better get out our sharpest picks and our sturdiest boots.'

My role on *Lear* was primarily reflective. Like an insidious *kibitzer*, I haunted the rehearsals, taking copious notes on how actors were or were not fleshing out their characters, conveying the implications of their relationships, assimilating *mise en scène*, muddying or clarifying prearranged intentions. A lot of this *kibitz*ing was done with Peter at his home in Kensington or strolling around Kensington Gardens, tussling, for instance, with the intricacies in the Edgar–Edmund relationship, trying to discover what certain passages meant – or *could* mean – in the context which was gradually unfolding. Although, after the event, Brook's *Lear* was attributed in large part to Jan Kott's essay 'King Lear or Endgame' in *Shakespeare, Our Contemporary*, I can't remember any direct allusions to it in our discussions. Peter was obsessed with the *leitmotif* of 'nothingness' which wound its way through the scenes of the play; also how certain characters like Lear with all their faculties intact could not 'see' – while others, like Gloucester, after having been blinded, could 'see' for the first time. How seeing, seeming, sight and blindness seemed to weave themselves into a lanyard.

Beckett's pessimism was a natural foil for Brook's. He didn't need Beckett's bleakness of perception in order to express the nullity at the heart of Shakespeare's vision. He had plenty of that himself. The fusion between Brook and Beckett took place, I think, quite accidentally. Perhaps because Brook's setting was as spare as Beckett's in *Godot* or *Endgame*, or simply because at that time Beckett's nihilism saturated the work of many playwrights, anything that even superficially resembled the Beckettian world view was automatically taken to be a Beckettian offshoot. The real existential dread of *King Lear* belongs more to Shakespeare than it does to either Beckett or Brook, but in Brook it found a compassionate interpreter. In the mid-Sixties God was already dead and the 'Word' was rapidly dying. An apocalyptic view of the universe was not only widespread, but fashionable. (Ionesco was flogging it to death, as were other French writers such as Genet, Arrabal and Schéhadé.) In many ways the excesses of the Sixties were nothing more than desperate sublimations of that cosmic melancholy.

As a director, I wasn't given much to do on *Lear*, nor did I expect very much. This was clearly Brook's vision and my job, as I saw it, was to refine and clarify that vision by applying whatever objective perspective I could to the work. To justify my title Brook gave me certain scenes to direct with some of the lesser actors, but there was no real point. When a director of Brook's magnitude is shaping a production, it becomes irrelevant for an assistant to try to sculpt moments or add interpretation. Although certain members of the company seemed to think I should have shouldered more direct responsibility for the production, the joy and reward were piecing together Brook's thoughts in conjunction with Brook himself, questioning and analysing the minutiae of choices that constituted his vision of the work. I was an oarsman on that ship and quite content to follow the course set by the navigator.

When we started work on the RSC Experimental Group, I felt myself suddenly come forward into more familiar territory. With Shakespeare I had been a tyro and eager to learn. When we started the RSC Theatre of Cruelty season at LAMDA, which was to be an application of Artaud's ideas on stagecraft and writing, I had already been experimenting for some seven years with my own company (In-Stage) and before that in New York. Although fascinated by sounds, games, movements and improvisations, this was an area that Peter entered tentatively. Most of his experience had been in opera or on the West End stage with solid, four-square but largely commercial actors such as Olivier, Gielgud, Edith Evans, Anthony Quayle, Rex Harrison, etc. Now, inspired by the promise of astonishing breakthroughs implied in the rhetoric of Artaud's prose and Peter's own dissatisfaction with mainstream work, he was setting sail for uncharted territory. As David Williams has pointed out in his *Theatrical Casebook* on Brook: 'Brook's production of *King Lear* ... marks a major crossroads in his career ... a new beginning; the genesis of ensemble concerns, work on the actor as supreme creator, the primary source in an empty space; starkness and provocation, clarity and visibility at every level; the uneasy fusion of Artaud, Beckett and Brecht in search of a prismatic density of expression and form, a truer reflection of the spirit of our age. *The theatre as disturbance* . . .'

The seeds of all that were planted in the Theatre of Cruelty work in which there was a dynamic shift of emphasis. The 'word' was no longer the starting point; it was now the collective imagination of the actors harnessed in such a way as to discover what an ensemble itself might 'author'.

It was my task during those first alchemizing three months to invent a series of provocations by which actors' untapped creativity could be flushed out of their systems. This was in many ways a more arduous task than either writing or directing a play. It involved accessing areas which lay beneath behavioural psychology and the camouflaging techniques on which professional actors prided themselves. It meant finding and touching the *personal* metaphysic which lay deeply embedded beneath an actor's talents for verisimilitude and his simulation of emotional states.

Many of the exercises I invented during that period I still use twenty-five years after the event. They are some of the most durable tools I know for opening up an actor and blowing away the cobwebs. Because they transcended psychology and were deliberately pitched against the easy virtues of Method training, they enabled me to dredge up those states of being which lie far beneath expressions such as love, fear, ambition and joy. I had always believed that behind the sub-text (Stanislavsky's most crucial discovery) was something resembling an *ur-text* – a complex of needs, drives, symbols and unformulated emotions which eluded the analyst, the sociologist and the priest, and existed in that stratum which Artaud described as 'that fragile, fluctuating centre which forms never reach'. The exercises, when successful, managed to penetrate that centre. They coaxed the actor into sounds, moves, spatial metaphors and non-verbal improvisation which, once glimpsed, were immediately understood to come from the labyrinth out of which human communication springs. In themselves these impulses are useless – like isolated atoms – but combined with pertinent dramatic material they nourish action and language in ways that charge the performance.

When the Theatre of Cruelty season came to an end, many of its members were integrated into the company and, to all intents and purposes, experiment *per se* ended at the RSC. Something else ended as well – a period in which Peter himself had absorbed a manner of work about which he had had an enormous curiosity, but not very much experience. It may appear both doltish and presumptuous to suggest that I taught Peter things he had not known before, but I know I did. The whole range of non-naturalistic improvisation and a *modus operandi* by which Artaud's metaphysic could be grafted on to psychologically realistic material was a very tangible off-shoot of the RSC's LAMDA work; and I believe a large part of it was due to the exercises and games I created for those dozen actors. The aesthetic overview, the larger objective of both the training and the season itself, was certainly Peter's, but without that basic training he couldn't have created the machinery by which that company perfected the style which would eventually be applied to *The Marat/Sade*.

It has often been said that Brook is eclectic. When you break down the meaning of that word in concrete theatrical terms, it means a director appropriates what he needs from one source or another and integrates it into his own way of working. After our LAMDA season, Brook went on to graft much of Grotowsky's teachings on to his work – as he did with Joe Chaikin, whom he invited into later collaborations such as *US*. It was that period in his life when he was consciously trying to transcend the habits which some twenty years of commercial work in mainstream British theatre had made second nature, and what better way to do that than to pick the brains of people immersed in alternative disciplines? It was all part of the process of becoming, as it were,

Peter Brook Mark II, the one who started the International Centre for Theatrical Research in Paris and would go on to evolve the *Conference of the Birds* and *The Mahabharata*, the man who realized that beyond conventional success in the commercial theatre lie mines of untold riches, if only equipment could be fashioned to extract them.

When the Theatre of Cruelty was being formed, it was my job initially to screen the candidates. We were seeking not so much talented performers but performers open enough to accommodate highly unorthodox techniques without triggering the rejection symptoms so common among British actors, particularly in the early and mid-Sixties. Instead of seeing actors on a one-to-one basis, I worked out a system of collective auditions whereby groups of eight and ten would interact with one another on improvisations, nonsense texts and various theatre games engineered to test both their imaginations and their critical temper. Some of the candidates when they heard what was going on in the audition room fled the theatre. Many more had their agents ring and cancel. It had been bruited about that what was happening at this particular branch of the RSC was decidedly unBritish and even exotic. The bourgeois members of the acting profession, who make up the majority, caught wind of things very early and either stayed away or began to cast opprobrium on the project. One of the actresses who came and stayed was Glenda Jackson.

I have always felt possessive about Glenda Jackson – as if I had personally delivered her from bondage or rescued her from some fate which, though not worse than death, was almost as obscuring. Of course I did nothing of the kind, and the feeling has no rational basis whatever, but in 1964, when we were making the final selection for the Theatre of Cruelty season and Glenda was nose to nose with an odds-on favourite for the final place, I found myself mounting a frantic campaign for her to be chosen.

My fervour was so uncharacteristic that Brook wondered if I had sexual designs on the woman. I assured him that was not the case and, when asked to state my reasons, found myself explaining lamely that she was beautifully screwed up and that after a four-hour work-out I had developed the impression that she was, in some inexplicable way, 'mined'. I remember the very first interview I had with her in some woebegone shack appropriated by Cub Scouts and whist drives (in those days the obligatory setting for London rehearsals): watching her stark, nutty eyes shifting slowly in her head like arc-lights; feeling that behind her studied stillness was a cobra ready to spring or an hysteric ready to break down; choosing my words carefully and getting back short, orderly answers that betrayed the very minimum both of feeling and information; being perpetually conscious of a smouldering intelligence rating both my questions and her own answers as she shifted her focus from within or without, mimicking the mechanism of a hypersensitive tape-recorder that could fast-forward or rewind with the flick of an invisible switch. I had no way of knowing at the time that banked up behind that interview were two years of anguished unemployment and the soul-destroying poverty that imposes. I was aware only of a disconcerting presence, something inaudibly but palpably ticking, something capable of 'going off'.

The flap in regard to Glenda's selection had to do with the fact that Peter was being pressured to consider another contender (i.e. Eileen Atkins, not exactly a slouch herself). After alluding to this hassle in various articles and interviews, I received a letter from Peter prior to the publication of my book *Prospero's Staff* in which he enjoined me once and for all to desist from disseminating the fiction that he was opposed to Glenda's selection:

> In the name of pure honesty I must ask you to revise the story you've already written elsewhere about how Glenda was engaged. I happen to remember it all very exactly. When she auditioned, we were both quite electrified by the sudden plunges she took and by her intensity. At the same time, we were both very impressed (rightly) by Eileen Atkins. We both weighed one against the other from all points of view and were both sharing a real question and a genuine indecision. There was no moment when you fought against me for Glenda. What my very

exact memory has recorded is how the question was ultimately clinched. You said: 'I've an idea that Glenda's marriage has just broken up – she's all screwed up and I think that's a better starting point for the sort of work we're going to do than Eileen, who seems to be comfortably settled down.' It was in fact not true, but it did not matter, because I completely agreed with the finesse of the theory and it was just this that tipped the scales! As so often, truth is better than fiction!

Well, memory is the one tribunal to which everyone has equal recourse and which always adjudicates in one's own favour. For myself, I cannot remember even putting Atkins through her paces, let alone being in a quandary as to which way to go. My only memory is arguing hard for Glenda's inclusion – not because there was any opposition on Peter's part, for there certainly wasn't – but simply because a strong campaign had been mounted in favour of the other actress. In any case, Glenda was eventually chosen to join the company of twelve and her dry, acerbic, languid demeanour (which was certainly not everyone's cup of tea) implanted itself firmly on the character of the group.

Each day Peter and I would put the actors through a series of acting tests and exercises. Unlike conventional rehearsals in which, from the start, actors are gravitating towards roles for which they have been chosen, these involved interminable improvisations and games in which the actor's personal imagination was constantly being nudged, wooed or flagellated into action. In circumstances such as these one sees the centrifugal talent of each person in clear, unmistakable terms. Glenda's choices were staggering; consistently unexpected, often tinged with sarcasm or perversity, occasionally droll, with a hard, urban kind of humour which was three quarters irony and one quarter absurdity; a complex sensibility spiralling up out of Stygian depths.

'God, she's so negative, so destructive,' I can remember one of the less talented actors in the group complaining after a particularly arduous session. Without realizing it, he was really protesting against Glenda's loathing for lame and easy effects. Glenda, wearing a permanent scowl, radiated disgust in those days, but its object was the sloppy, ill-defined, unthought-out mugging which passed for acting in the British theatre and, particularly, the appearance of those characteristics in herself. Whenever she worked, one could hear her built-in bullshit detector, that most delicate of all precision instruments, ticking in the background, and the actors who resented her most were those whose execrable effusions were being scrutinized and judged in the glare of those cold, sleepy, cruel eyes. I have vivid memories of her lounging around the rehearsal room looking like a scrubwoman, her face not only unmade-up but scrubbed raw as if to obliterate her features, emitting great waves of languor tinged with *ennui*, a softly pulsating indictment of everything crude, crummy and unworthy in our work.

The first fruits of the company's effort was a kind of surrealist vaudeville made up of brief pieces by a wide variety of authors including Alain Robbe-Grillet, Paul Ableman, John Arden and Shakespeare. Peter had written a short collage piece ingeniously combining the personae of Christine Keeler and Jackie Kennedy, which involved Glenda being stripped down and bathed in a small tin tub. Before it actually came to the final stripping rehearsals, I remember that Peter and I wondered whether the actress would refuse. These were the heady, pre-*Hair* days when the Lord Chamberlain was still exercising censorship on the British stage and the Age of Permissiveness was only just beginning to flash itself. When it came to the delicate, last-day rehearsals and the stripping had to be rehearsed, I remember Glenda's dry, undramatic resignation accepting, not the embarrassment of appearing nude, but the necessity of the act if the play were to fulfil its intentions. Whatever convoluted thought process and emotional wrenching may have paved the way, the decision itself, like everything else in her life, was brisk, clear and decisive. It was the role, not her directors, which had persuaded her and that was the only authority she ever obeyed implicitly.

Brook and Jackson had a winning chemistry. In a piece I did on her for the *New York Times* Magazine Section, she said:

> What I can never understand, talking about
> Brook, is when people cite him as an example

of an autocratic dictator of productions when, in fact, the reverse is the case, for he just sits and says nothing for weeks and months, and you have to find it yourself. Then he will suddenly come in and orchestrate it. What is interesting working with Brook is that he is looking, as much as you, to see if there is anything to be *found*, whereas with other directors you know they start out from the premise that there is *their* production to be discovered. Brook starts out thinking: *Is* there a production to be discovered?

In many ways that was always Peter's great strength – having both the interest and the patience to see what actors, instinctively interacting, could come up with. But the hidden corollary to this open-ended approach is having the discipline and determination to expunge and delete that which was not nourishing the work. In the later phases, when he was already ensconced in Paris, he learned that, if you laid the right foundations and immersed actors in the relevant research, the chances of their making the 'right' choices were greatly enhanced and the work acquired an organic forward motion which almost made it seem to be creating itself. But unlike a tangible structure, a play cannot be built to blueprint, and so no matter how valid the foundations seem to be, as the structure develops, one storey is askew, another undersized, a third insupportable, a fourth the wrong way round. In the final analysis, even the most fiercely collaborative work is *directed* even if 'direction' consists only in rejecting or discouraging what is irrelevant or counterproductive so as to allow more pertinent choices to assert themselves. Amorphous as it may seem in the early stages, there is always a vision which is being fleshed out and this has been true in all of Peter's work.

After the RSC, Glenda, like the shooting star she was, shot into higher and higher reaches of the stratosphere, often scoring outstanding successes in off-the-wall and extraordinary films, many of them directed by Ken Russell. In 1965, Roy Hodges, her ex-husband, perceptively observed: 'She moves through life like natural royalty – never carries any money. She thrives on work. If she'd gone into politics, she'd have become Prime

Minister. If she'd gone into crime, she would have been Jack the Ripper.' Although a life of crime seems quite unlikely at this juncture, it is conceivable she might wind up in Parliament. In 1989, she was asked to stand for selection for Hampstead and Highgate, and, when I last saw her, she spent a lot of time trying to deracinate Margaret Thatcher and plumping for the Labour Party.

The secret of Glenda's success as an exotic actress is her suburbanity. Most of her professional London life has been lived in Blackheath; her closest friends are drawn from the working class. Her husband Hodges married his (then) assistant stage manager in Crewe in 1958. After the break-up of that marriage, Glenda's longest liaison was with a talented, proletarian lighting designer from the Royal Court. Throughout her career she has clung to that earthy common sense and undiluted directness bred in her native Cheshire. Because the temperament is so rootedly suburban, she also has the suburbanite's fascination with both the *haut* and *demi monde*. It is the flat-pancake ordinariness of her background which enables her to fantasize characters such as Charlotte Corday, Gudrun and Elizabeth I, and it is that same dry-as-dust background that inclines her toward performance choices which are exotic and hierarchical. She is the most fully rounded schizoid character that I know, her true social self bearing no relation whatsoever to the roles she essays – other than, of course, an imaginative one.

After the RSC collaboration, Glenda and I met on several occasions, and even worked together in the West End on a black comedy called *Fanghorn*, which, because it involved a central character who cracked a great black whip and wore long Gothic Charles Adams gowns, appealed enormously to Glenda's sense of the decadent. Many years later we tried on several occasions to join up on one project or another – a nebulous *Duchess of Malfi*, an updated version of *The Shrew*, an American play about the Empress of China – but they all fizzled out. During our sundry meetings, posh dinners in New York supper clubs or talk-fests in her splendidly upholstered hotel suites, I could feel the gap that had settled between us. Glenda had become a star – indeed, a superstar – and the decisions by which roles would be accepted and projects undertaken were no longer simple enthusiasms for the material, but appropriate career choices, often determined by film tycoons or high-powered agents who buzzed around in the background protecting their 'investment'. I don't mean to imply that Glenda went grand. Her bedrock commonsense would never have permitted that and any public signs of swelled headedness would have been firmly rooted out. It was simply that the adventurous, innovative, experimental phase of her life as an actress was behind her, and she was now in a larger arena where a different set of priorities prevailed. I, on the other hand, was still knocking around with *avant garde* projects and off-beat ways of realizing them, and it soon became clear that, despite a mutual warmth, we were in different worlds and, though they would occasionally intersect, they could never really combine.

The opening of Peter's production of *US* in 1966 coincided with the first issue of *International Times* and I was asked to review it. I found the play politically pretentious with a lot of expressionist devices being used to project clichés about the hopelessness of the American involvement in Vietnam. Somehow the combination of high aesthetic devices and leaden political thinking created an effect of obscenity which rubbed many of us up the wrong way. After a roster of heartfelt negatives, I ended the piece by saying:

> I had come to the theatre – as so many people
> will come – out of a hunger to do something,
> see something, say something which cuts a path
> out of the chaos. One doesn't need a theatrical
> performance to explain that we are at an *impasse*.
> The role of the theatre in times like these is to
> elucidate and give a positive lead. A conventional
> play may end up in a state of fascinating ambiguity,
> but a social document dealing with red-hot
> contemporary crises cannot take refuge in artistic
> ambiguities, or else it becomes only another cinder
> in the eye. A century ago the theatre's task,
> according to Chekhov, was to ask questions. This
> has been superseded by a world situation in which,

if the theatre is to pull its weight, it must – at such times and on such themes – begin to supply answers.

The review triggered the following exchange:

Dear Charles,
In your review of *US* you say that the theatre must stop asking questions and must start giving answers. If this is so, it must surely mean that negative criticism is also at an end. In other words, if you, as both critic and a very active director, discuss a show concerning Vietnam, you too are challenged by your own words. What can you suggest as a positive solution of the Vietnam horror? Note your own proviso – this must not be a formula already covered by news, broadcasts, films, TV or the press.

Peter Brook

Dear Peter,
No one is wacky enough to suggest that a handful of writers and actors working off the Strand is going to arrive at a solution to a problem, which has defied the best political minds in government today. One didn't expect a formula from the Royal Shakespeare Company, but a viewpoint. The press, TV and film coverage tends to be objective reportage; it doesn't presume to have a viewpoint. But a theatrical performance dealing with the same material must confer an attitude, if it is to avoid being merely a rehash. What the theatre can (and, in my opinion, should) do is put the issues in such a way as to make certain solutions visible to an audience. The first job is elucidating those issues, and this is urgently the case with Vietnam, where everything is a welter of fact and pseudo-fact, half truths and outright lies.
    In effect your letter is asking me to supply you

with a viewpoint and my innate sense of tact must refuse to do that. If, however, you are asking me my own viewpoint and what line might have been laid down in such a production, I can suggest that. Three legitimate lines that could have been taken are these. [I then enumerated three premises on which the work could have been predicated.]

As to your first suggestion: I roundly disagree that negative criticism should come to an end. What is needed at the moment is a much more discerning and perceptive form of negative criticism than London reviewers offer . . . Many reviewers, in my opinion, have been subtly intimidated by the urgency of this subject and the unfamiliarity of the treatment, which both you and I know is nothing more than living newspaper techniques brought up to date. This has angered me, and many like me, who would like criticism to stare down the po-faced intensities of productions like *US* which, with the best intentions in the world, produce superficial flurries on incendiary subjects that can be justified neither on artistic nor ideological grounds.

Charles Marowitz

This cooled relations between us. When we met in a London theatre, Peter pointed out that this review, reprinted in the *Tulane Drama Review*, was the only word that many American readers had of the production and that therefore it was unjust. There were other objections, but the gist of it all was: Peter, who was always prone to betrayals, real or imaginary, felt I had betrayed him by writing bitingly about his work. Relations remained strained for some time afterward – not helped by a critical notice of *A Midsummer Night's Dream* which I had written for the *New York Times*, especially when this production was, in most other quarters, being generally regarded as a masterpiece.

A few years later, having been approached to write a profile for the *New York Times* Magazine Section, I contacted Peter to ask whether he would be interested. He felt it would be a good opportunity to remove some of the frost that had settled over our relationship and was eager to meet. The piece, like all *Times* profiles, was generally laudatory, more puffy than pithy, and, I think, went a long way towards restoring normal relations – but throughout the years Peter has always maintained a certain wariness in regard to me. I think he feels that someone who has been so close to the 'palace' should resist all offers from the press to divulge confidences – although reviewing a work in which one was not involved seemed to me to confer the requisite objectivity for a fair critique. I understand his sensitivity, but have never believed that sharp criticisms need be construed as gestures of disloyalty. On the other hand, I must admit to the niggling doubt that, since I know so much about Peter's metapsychology, perhaps I can no longer be truly objective about his work. My admiration for the man and his work remains unshakeable and sincere, but I persist in my belief that it is the most ambitious and the most challenging pieces of theatre that require the most stringent assessments, and Peter, because he has achieved international cult status, is too often let off the hook.

Like many creative artists, he has always been highly vulnerable to criticism. One way to transcend criticism is to create an artifact so unique that conventional criteria cannot be applied to it. A play must answer a play's critics, but a performance piece, a happening, a surrealist vaudeville, an eight-hour evocation of ancient rites and unfamiliar mythology eludes the critical tentacles of those who would clutch, squeeze and ultimately label what artists do. If you astonish sufficiently, there are no convenient words with which critics can put you in your place. By creating outside the established convention, you rob convention of its power to circumscribe you. 'The theatre', Brook has said, 'has one precise social function – to disturb the spectator.' A 'disturbance' is a breach of order which nullifies customary expectations, thereby rendering them immune from ordinary assessment. But is one creating a 'disturbance' in order to disrupt the order of a spectacle or the rules of procedure by which it is ordinarily assessed?

I don't say that creating a form that eludes criticism was the sole or even the most significant motive behind the works of

Peter Brook from 1971 to the present, but I do say it is one of them, and that part of Brook's fecund creativity and overweening ambition derives from his attempt to escape censure by over-whelming ordinary expectations – by creating work which causes conventional yardsticks to crack.

The Royal Shakespeare Company 'bridge', the first bricks of which were laid with Peter in the mid-1960s, was effectively 'burnt' in the mid-1970s, when I was asked by Trevor Nunn to direct Philip Magdalaney's *Section Nine* at The Place. It was one of three offerings in the smaller venue and the only one invited to transfer on to the Aldwych stage.

The play was a well-constructed farce about Watergate and the CIA. Directorially, it required little more than editing and suppressing the sillier inventions and more ludicrous choices of actors so steeped in classical work that they approached this modern comedy in a frolicsome and even hysterical frame of mind. I quickly lost friends and de-influenced people when, for the good of the play, I proceeded to repress their irrepressible high spirits and put bounds on their boundless energy. In any case, the trick worked and the early performances were a success.

The play never really had an end and so, to provide one, I came up with the idea of a series of cartoon slides showing various heads of state embracing one another. It was a simple, even obvious device, but it succeeded in putting a punctuation mark to the evening where before there had been none. One of these cartoon slides was a drawing of Queen Elizabeth embracing Idi Amin of Uganda, which, from the start, incensed the play-wright's sense of propriety. (Shades of Glasgow!) After all, here he was an American being produced by the leading classical company in Britain and so, he felt, it behoved him not to be seen to be giving offence. The slide, however, brought the house down and, being a sucker for explosive audience reactions, I fought to retain it. The bigger the laughs it got, the more Magdalaney seemed perturbed by its implications. ('This is the *Royal* Shakespeare Company, after all,' Magdalaney kept repeat-ing.) Finally, fearful that he might be the subject of some Royal summons, he brought Trevor Nunn into the dispute. Trevor didn't want to be placed in the position of dictating a political cut to an outside director, but, on the other hand, he didn't want to distress his visiting playwright and so merely straddled the fence. After a good deal of backroom finagling and insidious infighting, the shameful slide was dropped from the Aldwych preview without my being informed. I flipped my lid to Trevor, lambasted Magdalaney and fulminated against this craven piece of censorship. Relations with Trevor cooled since guest directors, by tradition, were expected to leak gratitude for just being allowed into the royal enclaves of the RSC and here was I trumpeting my indignation. Magdalaney's horror of Royal sacrilege was assuaged and the show, poorly drilled and with newly substituted stage management, opened and did far less well than it had in its first incarnation. But the main upshot was that I had revealed myself 'difficult' and 'unbending' to a management which, though it professed Left-wing sentiments, was essentially conservative in its demeanour and terrified of giving offence.

This was a burnt bridge I rued torching because I had a variety of grandiose and beloved classical projects in my ditty-bag and none of these could now be pursued. Several years later and eight years after I had returned to America, as a kind of ironic footnote to this disaffiliation, Terry Hands, who succeeded Trevor as Artistic Director, asked me to direct Jean Genet's *The Blacks* at the Barbican, a play for which I had a deep fondness and some pretty startling production ideas. When the 'translation' by Wole Soyinka arrived, it was clear that it was not a translation at all, but a free adaptation with wadges of new material wholly unrelated to Genet's original. When I pointed this out to Terry (who had not yet read the version), he immediately concurred that one could not take liberties with an author only ten years dead and we all started looking around for a viable translation. None could immediately be found, but, meanwhile, I had cast the entire play and was itching to start.

The date of the first reading came and went. Still no translation. One week passed. Attempts to secure Robert David Macdonald's version or to have one quickly worked up by David Rudkin failed. Another week went by. Actors provisionally booked started to fall away. After three and a half weeks Terry announced that there was no way to proceed with *The Blacks* as originally intended and that a postponement had to be made. Of course, 'postponement' in the theatre almost always means cancellation, as it did in this instance.

After eight years of American resettlement, I had been cooling my heels in hated London, living in a foul and disreputable hotel in Holborn with all my loathing for England gradually being reinforced. Terry then asked if I was prepared to sweat out a few more weeks so rescheduling could be effected. I begged off, citing fictitious commitments in Los Angeles and left London after having killed a month with a sheaf of ambitious ideas for *The Blacks* rapidly dwindling in my mind. This 'cancellation' was followed almost immediately by Terry Hands's disastrous production of *Carrie* on Broadway, which created an RSC backlash. Some months later Terry resigned. When I now look back to that burnt bridge, I can almost smell the fetid smoke still streaming in my nostrils.

9   *Just a thing called* Joe

In 1966, when I was a director with the London Traverse at the Jeannetta Cochrane Theatre, Michael White, then a fledgling producer with *avant garde* inclinations, approached me about staging Joe Orton's play *Loot*. He and Oscar Lewenstein held the rights jointly and were in no way put out by a regional try-out which, according to the grapevine, had been disastrous. I had not seen the production, but knew it had had a strong cast including Kenneth Williams, Duncan Macrae and Geraldine McEwan. The word of mouth on the project had been that, believing the play was 'in trouble', the cast had magnanimously come to its aid with a wide assortment of ribald one-liners and comic interpolations. When I heard this, I was in no way surprised by the result. Nothing kills a comedy faster than the delusion of a group of actors who believe the only salvation of a problematic script is the protein injection of their collective invention.

I asked Michael if I could see the original, pristine version – the one that existed before the comedians got their pickers into it. When I read it, I was astonished, for here was a subtle black comedy studded with sophisticated literary constructions and infused with an air of perversity more reminiscent of Ronald Firbank than the Crazy Gang – the exact opposite of what I had been led to expect. I agreed immediately to mount it in our first season and promptly set about persuading my fellow directors that it was worth a shot.

When I first met the author, I was struck by his impish good looks and his fiercely protective attitude to the script. His 'baby', thought to be a mawkish and mentally retarded offspring, had been mauled by a lot of tasteless West End types and he was determined to reintroduce it to the world as the healthy and precocious infant he believed it to be. He exuded an air of conspiracy, as if both he and I working in concert knew the true merits of the piece and could easily rehabilitate it despite its unfortunate start in life. He was snidely confident and didn't come on at all like a writer who had just had a widely publicized disaster in the provinces.

Because it had been a comic fiasco, Joe was obsessive about 'playing it straight'. When he talked about the play, he often alluded to Chekhov and, when he spoke about its situations, he might have been describing a Strindbergian drama. Even before his exhortations, it was clear to me that the secret of the play lay in making its social and moral excesses utterly plausible, finding *its* truth – which, at that time, no one would have dreamed of describing as Ortonesque. But he was so insistent about resisting its comic pull, he practically blanched when I referred to its comedic texture or extravagant characters. To say that he was overcompensating for the provincial disaster would be a massive understatement. Inside, Joe was hysterical that a second cock-up – this one in London – would nip his career in the bud.

Having been an actor at RADA, Joe was very knowledgeable about casting. He came up with some apposite ideas and, with the help of Michael White's wily instincts, most of the company was quickly assembled. Oscar Lewenstein had put in a strong bid for Ann Lynn, the daughter of Ralph Lynn, to play the role of Fay. Although I didn't know her, Oscar's enthusiasm was so overpowering I assumed she must be a great find. We didn't actually meet until the first reading. When we had finished the read through, I took her aside and apologetically explained that a serious mistake had been made and that she was simply all wrong for the role. Fay needed a certain brisk authority, a slightly camp manner; she was a lady who easily took charge and whose darker side was hidden behind a blunt, confident façade. This actress, though clearly talented, possessed a certain urban sarcasm that would have given the game away as soon as she walked on stage. I mustered as much *politesse* as I was capable of, explaining the problems and we agreed to part amicably.

The next day I learned that Lewenstein was incensed by the dismissal. Apparently there had been a personal bond between Lewenstein and Miss Lynn or her family, and the role had been intended in the manner of a gift to an old friend. Since there was no question of reconsidering Miss Lynn – Sheila Ballantine already having been cast – all Oscar could do was sulk and splutter. Although our relations always remained kiddingly cordial, I think his indignation against what he took to be directorial high-handedness never entirely dissolved. Simon Ward and Kenneth Cranham were chosen as Hal and Dennis respectively. For Inspector Truscott we had all agreed on Michael Bates, a gifted comic actor in the old mould whose speciality was imminent explosiveness (a kind of reversal of the Edgar Kennedy slow burn) and who had recently completed a comedy series on television.

During rehearsals I could feel Joe rankling every time I introduced a bit of comic business or orchestrated a laugh. In his mind every attempted comic moment was a throwback to the provincial trauma. He kept talking to me about Chekhov and finally, one day in Regent's Park, I turned on him and said, 'Look, Joe, this isn't *The Cherry Orchard*. It's a black comedy and unless the comedy gets slotted in, it's going to fall flat on its face.' In defence, Joe reiterated that Truscott was based on a true case of Scotland Yard corruption and that Hal and Dennis were extrapolations of people he had known and *been*. That's why the comedy will work, I countered, because it's rooted in something real and plausible, but, if it is played as the unvarnished truth, it goes against its own grain. To overcome the fear of another comic disaster, there was something in Joe that was guiding him away from comedy altogether. If we don't try for laughs, something seemed to tell him, we won't get clobbered.

The direction of comedy is always something of a tightrope – but when the style is arcane, parodic or oblique, it becomes a veritable nightmare. If one throws all comic pointing to the winds and neglects stress where it is needed to point up a paradox even *The Importance of Being Earnest* can come across like a frost. *Over*stressing or throwing a spotlight on what is already a perfectly visible fairylight is just as disastrous and can bring ruin just as quickly. Balance is all – but without an *assumption* of comedy, comic moments do not evolve. In the old saw about all good comedy being based on truthful behaviour, the key phrase is, of course, 'based on'. When an actor bases a performance on something outside of himself, he is incorporating all the artifice and falsifications that make art different from life. The moment an actor begins to embellish, underscore, inflect or transform the 'truth' for the purpose of revealing it artistically, strictly speaking, the departure from truth has already begun.

Of course, I said nothing of this to Joe and, had I attempted to do so, he would have hauled up his mental drawbridges and barricaded himself away. He was impervious to theory and, perhaps because of his RADA background, saw acting strictly in terms of pragmatic choices which needed neither explanation nor justification – so long as they worked. This, in a nutshell, *is* the British Acting Method: just do it, darling, and try not to fall over the furniture! It was institutionalized in the Twenties and Thirties, and, despite lip service to Stanislavsky and Brecht, was as deeply embedded in the mid-Sixties as it is today.

When we got into the final stages of rehearsal, Joe's buddy Ken Halliwell began to make appearances. His handshake was like the slot of a dead-bolt and he brought with him an air of proprietorship that made you believe he was the show's primary investor. Joe had regaled us with tales of his quaint *ménage* and thus had already introduced Ken as a central character in his life. When questions of the play were discussed, he would nod affirmatively behind Joe as if to say, 'That's right, that's just the way "we" intended it to be, just the way "we" wrote it.' Later in the run Joe gave us a peek at his birthday gift to Halliwell – a full, flowing wig. It was difficult afterwards to take in his full head of hair without wondering precisely where the joins were.

Generally there was a larkiness about Joe that pervaded the entire rehearsal period. He often told me about the new play he was writing which he would refer to only as 'the one with Winnie's cock in the sweet tin' – shortly destined to become *What the Butler Saw*. He was always conscious of being outrageous and worked at it assiduously. It was as if he was getting back at people for certain crimes they had committed against him, and his strongest weapon of revenge was pointed offence. He once told me his greatest pleasure would have been to blow fart rings through the air-conditioning system at Scotland Yard. This, in some inexplicable way, would have atoned for his brief imprisonment for desecrating library books. Once, he rolled down his trousers to show me some horrible scabs which he assured me were all over his body, mementoes of a Moroccan holiday. He displayed them with glee – as if they were medals he'd won in battle. He not only looked impish, but consistently played the imp. There was a certain undergraduate crassness to him which he might well have outgrown, but which was boorishly alive in 1966, one year before he died.

On the opening night of *Loot* at the Jeannetta Cochrane Theatre, Joe was a swirling bundle of nerves. Suddenly the old provincial terror had returned with a vengeance. His compulsive levity had been a shield against his fear that the play, once trounced, might well be battered again. The first act was sluggish, and the laughs came one beat late in almost every case. You could almost hear the audience, unfamiliar with Orton's tongue-in-cheek style, consciously adjusting their expectations. After a boozy interval, the second act swept along at a good pace and the laughs fell into place. It was as if Act One had been a crash course on Orton's style of comedy and in Act Two the audience passed with flying colours. When I saw him in the foyer, Joe looked incandescent. The play *could* work on its own terms – which meant this morally dubious, artistically fanciful Ortonesque talent was viable; that the provincial disaster had been, as he had always contended, a mistake foisted upon him by faint-hearted, short-sighted professionals. Confirmation of that fact lifted Joe to a plane on which he could now confront his own uniqueness and revel in it. Halliwell was also beaming – or, to be more accurate, training his torchlight grin on to Joe's resplendent luminosity to snag from it what wattage he could. From that night on a certain new garishness began to appear in Joe's attire: broad, brightly coloured ties, flashy jackets, Paisley shirts. He had gained celebrity and was now determined to costume himself for his new role. The reviews were positive, some of them deliriously so. It transferred to the West End in January 1967 and won the *Evening Standard* Award for Best Play of the Year.

Despite the transfer and the glowing notices, *Loot* was never everyone's cup of tea. Whenever I was there noting the performance from the back of the stalls, there would always be a certain number of disgruntled patrons scurrying up the aisles and out of the theatre obstreperously demonstrating their chagrin. On some nights the draught they generated was enough to induce flu. This was the period of the so-called dirty plays controversy when Prince Littler, a portly incarnation of Jeremy Collier, came stoutly to the defence of traditional British morality by trouncing those plays and theatres which were dispensing immoral debris under the misleading title of 'new drama'. Orton was one of Littler's chief targets and the writer responsible for his major apoplexies. Nudity and promiscuity were bad enough, but homosexuality without guilt was an abomination to the thinking Englishman. Littler's crusade was spontaneously supported by a large number of fuming prigs, of which England has never had a shortage, and it was these same moral vigilantes who, two years later from the gallery of the Queen's Theatre, were to barrack Sir Ralph Richardson on the opening night of *What The Butler Saw*, a fracas which triggered off a volley of mixed to poor notices from critics who seemed unable to distinguish deliberately contrived demonstrations from genuine audience reaction. In the enlightened and permissive Sixties it was easy to forget that, along with the hippies and the beautiful people, the stodgy, uptight, morally straitjacketed British Puritan flaunting his 'sense of decency' and brandishing his banner of Good Taste made up a sizeable majority of the theatre-going public.

While *Loot* was playing at the Criterion, unbeknownst to myself or most of the cast, Oscar Lewenstein was negotiating the film sale. To maintain the heat of his deal it was necessary to keep the play running – despite the fact that houses were thin. Early in the run, I had been asked to waive my royalty – an almost ritual tactic when plays do not immediately flourish – in the hope that business would pick up, but really because the producers needed the visible West End production to clinch their deal. The *Evening Standard* Award gave the show a certain boost, but by the summer it was flagging badly.

When I returned to it after an absence of about eight weeks, I was appalled to see Michael Bates playing as if he were in *Charley's Aunt*. The performance, which had been honed to a cutting edge, was now about as sharp as a brass knocker. Every subtlety had vanished and Bates was wringing every dram of comedy he could from moments which were intended to be expository or merely transitional. He had succumbed entirely to the whoredom which beckons to every lead actor in a West End comedy. For the sake of audience reaction, he had sold the style down the river and reverted to obvious ploys which I had painfully eliminated during rehearsals. Back stage, when I confronted him about this, his virulent excuse was, 'I'm getting all the laughs and more, aren't I?' – totally unaware that that was the problem; that in scrounging laughs where they were not pertinent, he was undercutting his own best effects and giving the entire evening a sense of baggy-trouser-red-nose-end-of-the-pier music-hall frivolity. Walking out of the theatre, I experienced that kind of wholesale renunciation that a priest must feel when a converted sinner, lapsed for the thousandth time, clearly indicates that he is too enamoured of his excesses ever to reform.

About ten months into the run with the houses falling off and summer closeness encouraging flight from the city rather than treks to the West End, Ken Halliwell hammered Joe Orton to death in his sleep and then took an overdose of sleeping pills. The papers headlined the gory details of the murder-suicide and business at the Criterion suddenly leapt forward. On the night following Orton's death there wasn't a seat to be had in the house. All of London suddenly wanted to see the play written by the playwright who had been beaten to death by his lover. Not only did the size of the audience increase, the laughs came faster and more furiously than ever before. Sitting at the back of the stalls, listening to those uncontrollable cachinnations when only days before spectators had fled down the aisles in disgust, I thought to myself: 'It's Joe – having the last laugh!'

After his death innumerable researchers came to me wanting to know of Joe and, slowly and painfully, I was obliged to construct some viable memory of him. This is always something of an artificial exercise. Talking to posterity rather than friends over a cup of coffee invariably stimulates the pontification glands, so what I say now should be read in the perspective that it was framed long after Joe's demise.

There was something contradictory in Joe's nature. He was very charming, very boyish and jolly, but never without his convict's mentality. Having been 'inside', his attitude towards the outside world was always that of the inmate to the screws. There was a built in antagonism between him and people in authority which extended even to directors and producers who loved and admired him. Whenever we had a difference of opinion, it was always as if something more was at stake. As if the 'screws' were out to get him. It was a Them and Us mentality. It required strenuous effort for a young man with this sense of 'outsiderness' to come to terms with the adulation of the British intelligentsia. It meant not only suppressing his contempt but also converting it into something socially acceptable. In the last months of his life I was conscious of him trying to make this adaptation. It required great willpower on Joe's part – not only to come to terms with an 'outside world' but to distance himself from Halliwell – friend, lover, mentor, fellow jailbird, his oldest ally and the person who probably originated the concept of 'Us' against 'Them' in Joe's mind.

Joe had the most highly developed bullshit detector of anyone I have ever known. Knowing intimately the seamier side of life, prison society, the world of the London bedsit and the ravenous gay underground, there was no angle he could not see, no hype he was not immediately on to. When his agent Peggy Ramsay or his producer Oscar Lewenstein conspicuously associated themselves with his success, he allowed it – knowing full well they were as Philistine and 'square' as any of the characters he satirized. When he started to become a celebrity, he knew he was trumping up a persona that was far removed from the suburban mongrel he really was. 'I can play that game as well as the best of them,' said Joe and proceeded to wear the right clothes, manufacture the right chat and accept invitations to move in the right circles. Although it was Halliwell who had initiated him into the *haut monde*, it was several echelons below the real thing. The *real thing*, as Joe came to know, was not the Angus Steak House, but The Ivy or San Lorenzo's. That bugged Halliwell, that 'real' society, into which he had never penetrated, was now teaching Joe new tricks. He was also bugged by Joe's ability to sleep – a bitter aggravation to a chronic insomniac. I always believed that's what caused him to take the hammer to Joe that unfathomable night of August 9, 1967. Joe's ability to sleep was, in a way, his most unforgivable offence. After he'd spilled his blood, Ken took a massive dose of Nembutal and finally got some rest himself.

Twenty years after Orton's death, John Lahr, the American critic, dug up Joe's bones and proceeded to sell them piecemeal to every medium he could find. After writing the biography *Prick Up Your Ears*, a title coined by Orton, the book was turned into a film and Lahr went on to edit and publish *The Orton Diaries*, introduce *Collected Plays*, produce a one-man show drawn from the diaries and loose a bevy of articles largely cobbled together from the aforementioned material. For all I know, he may also have been distributing Orton T-shirts and perfecting a line of Orton body-building equipment based on the design of Joe's bar-bells. In my view, never before has one man gone so far in packaging a dead artist.

My complaint is not with Lahr's hyperdeveloped entrepreneurial sense – more power to he who in the capitalist rat-race can build the better mousetrap – but his obsession with the scandal and his critical obtuseness in regard to the *oeuvre*. Reading *Prick Up Your Ears*, it is hard to avoid the impression that the author's middle-class sensibility is secretly regaled by tales of sodomy in men's urinals and gay lovers hammering each other to death. Throughout the book, Orton's relationship with Ken Halliwell is seen as the pivot of Orton's life and Halliwell's frustrated ambitions and his envy of the rising acolyte who was outstripping his mentor, are the main strands in the Orton saga. This, for me, is voyeurism posing as academic criticism – a writer having a wank while expostulating on the vices and virtues of the *poète maudit*. If it provided new insights or deft connections between the life and the work, it might possibly justify itself, but it doesn't and so we are left with the Orton Manufacturing Company posing as literary criticism.

However, one of the results of Lahr's merchandising frenzy was a renewed interest in Orton's work. In Los Angeles *Entertaining Mr Sloane* and *Loot* were revived at the Mark Taper after similar productions in New York, and, when Bill Bushnell at the Los Angeles Theater Center asked me to suggest a play to fill a gap which had suddenly occurred, I threw him a copy of *What The Butler Saw* and within two weeks was in rehearsal for the professional West Coast première. Although when I recommended the script, I didn't actually have myself in mind as a director, I realized, when Bushnell automatically assumed I would mount it, there was something providential about coming to *Butler* almost twenty years to the day after *Loot* was first performed in London.

In 1969, when I saw the barracked and subverted production

of *Butler* at the Queen's Theatre, I had written: 'There is no question in my mind that *Butler* is Orton's masterpiece'. Twenty years later, getting into bed with it and discovering every wart and wrinkle in the text, I was riddled with reservations. In many ways it remains an unfinished play. The bowdlerized New York version merely cut what it could not contend with and did the play a great disservice. I worked from the authorized printed version which, overwritten and poorly structured, still contains the Ortonesque essence. Clumsily plotted and constantly halting for gratuitous gags which drain its plausibility and impede its flow, gallumphing to a clumsy Act One finish which arbitrarily posits the missing Winston Churchill penis joke, mixing one-liners (which get laughs) with literary conceits and whimsies (which do not), the play is an inspired mish-mash which, in the final analysis, works because of its driving, anarchic spirit. Despite its bumps and potholes, its detours and roundabouts, it delivers a heartfelt kick in the pants to a bureaucratic normality which would rob us of our untrammelled animal spirits. Although its brain is addled, its ear is impeccable and its heart resoundingly in the right place. No one in Los Angeles could have known that its inspiration was the near-lunatic theories of R. D. Laing, for whom schizophrenia was merely a passage through which the psychotic must blithely pass, nor that Joe believed that *chic* psychiatrist to have had his head wedged irretrievably up his ass. None of the sub-textual allusions to the Sixties and its fanciful idiosyncrasies could have conveyed itself to those audiences in Los Angeles. But what they did hear was the sound of stained glass being shattered and the thud of dead cats being lobbed through the windows, and that was enough for them.

The passage of time has also encouraged me to consider the real, as opposed to the time-warped, relationship we actually had. The fact is, although our basic attitudes to one another never surfaced, I never much liked Joe, nor he me. Having grown up in New York's Greenwich Village and then been transplanted to London for twenty years, I had become weary of that snide, shallow homosexual humour that believes itself to be most outrageous when it is in fact being most banal. It is a campness which equates broad, scurrilous insolence with bold volleys of withering sarcasm and persuades itself that bitchy put-downs and anatomical ribaldry are somehow on a par with Swiftian satire or the wit of the Algonquin Round Table. I have always found it reminiscent of the dreariest Thirties film comedies with people such as Patsy Kelly, Charles Butterworth or Hugh Herbert gormlessly trying to squeeze laughs out of inert, hackneyed *shtick*. Its antithesis, it seems to me, is the genuine wit of an Oscar Wilde or a Ronald Firbank. In his private life, Joe was much given to the former – just as in his creative work he emulated and often reincarnated the spirit of the latter. He knew that personally I didn't find him amusing as I never made any attempt to conceal the fact and, for him, that was an indication of intellectual solemnity. It wasn't at all. It was just that I preferred my clowning genuinely anarchic or cerebrally sharp and found sub-standard Danny la Rue imitations tedious. What I most had in common with Joe was his abhorrence of authority (I'd had my own run-ins with Truscotts in the US Army) and it was that which charged my work on *Loot*. What I least had in common with him was the gay badinage about cocks and bums which, on a conversational level, seemed to regale him as much as actual promiscuity delighted him in his private life. It was often the case in gay English circles that, if you didn't carry on as if camp comedy was the acme of scintillation, you were thought of as a party-pooper. The fact is that mincing, limp-wristed, mindless levity tended to poop a lot of *my* parties.

At the moment Orton is still basking in the wake of his revival, but whether any of the plays retain currency after the media hype totally subsides remains to be seen. *Sloane* will always be a little marred by its Pinteresque origins – its clammy Theatre of the Absurd redolence. The mechanism that underpins *Loot* is as solid as the Feydeauesque clockwork which inspired it. *Butler* will always retain a certain period flair and jejune frivolity, and Orton himself will always have the artist's advantage of having died young, noisily and in sensational circumstances.

10   An Open Space

When I first saw Thelma Holt she was wearing a brocade corset, black net stockings, high heels and a bowler hat. She held a whip in one hand and her countenance was one of the most wicked I have ever seen in a woman. The play in which she was appearing was Andreyev's *He Who Gets Slapped*, a rather inert production at the Hampstead Theatre Club. Alexis Kanner, an actor friend who had delivered a striking Hamlet in my collage version of the play (first in the Royal Shakespeare Company's Theatre of Cruelty Season at LAMDA and then, even more memorably, at the Akademie der Künste in Berlin) had suggested I meet Thelma, as she might be interested in backing the experimental theatre I'd told him I was intending to open in London.

As it turned out, Thelma *was* interested in the theatre – but only if she could have some active managerial role in it. Since the entire staff at that point consisted of myself, I told her there was no shortage of staff positions. I began to describe the kind of theatre I wanted to create: a permanent home for a small nucleus company; a place to mount esoteric and unorthodox works – some of them plays from America and the Continent, some not plays at all but projects or collaborations which would be collectively devised by the ensemble. This had become such an ingrained creed I could recite it in my sleep, but it was never said perfunctorily, I believed in it implicitly.

Thelma, by her own description, was 'one of Binkie Beaumont's girls', by which she meant she had played in some Shaftesbury Avenue productions under the aegis of H. M. Tennent Ltd, which at that time was managed by Hugh 'Binkie' Beaumont, a man whose unimpeachable commercial taste then dominated the West End theatre. She spoke in that languid, upper-middle-class accent frequently affected by RADA-trained actresses whose class origins were often far removed from the social manner they uniformly adopted. After I'd explained about my theatre, I didn't believe for a moment I would ever see her again. I could think of nothing more antithetical than an aesthetically driven experimental theatre with a radical bias and the temperament of this slithery, almond-eyed ingenue bred on Noël Coward and Terence Rattigan. Evasively, we told each other we would meet again and, exposing the residue of the half-baked Andreyev to the merciful vapours of the night air, I trundled off.

In my search for premises I had come across a disused basement in Tottenham Court Road and, if I could raise a deposit of £5,000 or £6,000, I stood a chance of acquiring it. I had been everywhere and tried everyone, but, instead of providing balance sheets neatly outlining potential profit and loss, I had spent many febrile hours describing the aesthetic of the theatre, the need to develop new techniques and attempt groundbreaking methods of production. Needless to say, I came away empty handed and it wasn't until years afterward that I realized how painfully tolerant all those would-be backers must have been listening to a bearded, New York git eulogizing the Théâtre du Vieux Colombier and the Group Theatre while they were trying to conceptualize running costs and a bottom line. On one occasion, after being courteously fobbed off by Christopher Burton at London Weekend Television for what must have felt like the thousandth time, I can remember sitting down in a hallway in Soho and finding tears pouring down my cheeks. That lasted about thirty seconds. I then bustled myself together, swore off the enterprise and strode through Golden Square gratefully relieved that the obsession was finally exorcised.

The next day, as if none of that had ever happened, I was once again on the telephone trying to collar some well-heeled patrons into parting with seed money and busily hammering out manifestos. Paradoxically, Burton and London Weekend Television became one of the first backers of the enterprise. Roddy Maude Roxby agreed to invest £2,000 and about £1,500 eventually came from Bernard Delfont. I threw in all the money I had, which, as I recall, was all of about £500.

To my astonishment, Thelma rang again a few weeks later. The spidery threads of our discussion were drawn together and before long it became clear that she was in earnest. She actually wanted to help found and run a basement theatre in Tottenham Court Road. I was elated by the discovery. I knew in my gut that the only way such a theatre could ever get off the ground was through a determined public relations effort. That meant meeting people, charming them, involving them and establishing the kind of social rapport on which an artistic framework could be built. I knew I could never do this. Quite apart from lacking the necessary social graces, I had no real desire to mingle or fraternize with Arts Council bureaucrats, financiers and captains of industry, the very people on whom such a theatre depended. I had sensed from the outset that the vital factor was missing in me – both as a talent or a proclivity – just as I sensed that Thelma had it in spades. She not only charmed people, she enjoyed charming them. She had that rare ability to convey a deep rooted, inviolable intimacy after spending only a few moments with a stranger. One left her thinking one had made a friend for life and that impression remained until one saw that same deeply grounded intimacy being blithely bestowed on yet another stranger. The cocktail party was her element and she thrived in it. To be the nominal producer of a new theatre and to meet a wide assortment of affluent, culturally ambitious, middle-class people in a *milieu* tintinnabulating with wine glasses and the sound of quiches being politely crunched conferred a *frisson* which no West End play could equal.

I had all the initial contacts. I knew Bernard Delfont from a production of *The Bellow Plays*, which I had directed at the Fortune with Miriam Karlin and Harry Towb in the leads; had a nodding acquaintance with other producers such as Michael Codron, Michael White and Donald Albery, as well as critics such as Irving Wardle and Ken Tynan, and so could gingerly open the appropriate doors allowing Thelma to swan through and move in for the kill. In many ways it was a perfect union. I could preoccupy myself with 'art' while she saturated herself with business and promotion. Further, she could do what I could never have done for myself – dramatize the persona of the artistic director, a vital factor in the creation of any theatre.

It was the first of Thelma's many attachments to a father figure, an overpowering male chieftain to whom she was happy to subordinate herself and in whose name she could worship the greater good of art. Twelve years later, at the Round House, she concocted the same relationship with Robert Maxwell and the male-dominated board of directors, just as in the mid-1980s at the National Theatre she was to transform herself into the adopted daughter and loyal amanuensis of Peter Hall. One hesitates to slither into the upholstered chair of drawing-room psychologist, but in Thelma's private life there was always a mother and virtually never a father. (Significantly, during the course of our collaboration at the Space, I was actually nicknamed Father while she dubbed herself Mother.) Throughout the ten years or so during which we worked together, I can never remember a single reference to her own father. For Thelma, Father always had to be recreated and invariably it was the dominant male leader of the organization to which she pledged her filial allegiance – just as the members of our quasi-permanent group of actors became 'the children', which is precisely the term she used in referring to them. Gradually I came to realize that running a theatre was not so much an extension or diversion of her activities as an actress but a compensation for a life which, though filled with friends, lovers and itinerant husbands, was painfully devoid of a family. I was probably the first of her surrogate fathers, but no sooner did she feel betrayed than she would select another. Not just anyone could qualify. The man in question had to be powerful, creative, somewhat ruthless and, most important of all, prepared to reciprocate unwavering attention in return for blind idolatry. Like everything in Thelma's life, it had to be a trade off.

It was generally assumed around London that Thelma and I were sleeping together, that being the logical extension of our professional liaison. This was never true. Had it been, our relationship would have been much less complex. During the decade or so during which we virtually lived in each other's pockets. (If the phone rang at some ungodly hour in the middle of the night, it would be Thelma trying to head off a crisis or wanting to review a parenthetical observation casually tossed off during yesterday's three-hour lunch discussion.) We were privy to each other's flings and affairs with an intimacy not unlike that between the Marquise de Merteuil and Valmont in *Les Liaisons Dangereuses*. However, sharing the same struggles, being pole-axed by the same crises and screwed to the sticking point by the same objectives, a deeper, more symbiotic relationship developed between us not unlike that which evolves between soldiers in combat whose affection is bred during those in-between moments when the din of warfare is temporarily stilled. For something like ten years we were always there for each other, providing the kind of psychological and tangible support that one associates with tribal allegiance. During interminable lunches at Bertorelli's and various Indian restaurants strewn around Goodge Street and Fitzroy Square, analysing, fraternizing, fantasizing and lunatizing, we hammered out the pylons and pillars which became the Open Space. In the course of those marathon discussions, we also elaborated a philosophy of life, a theory of love and relationships, and an ethic which made it possible to live and work in a society dead set against the creation of art. I became intimately aware of the lineaments of Thelma's Byzantine personality and she got to know me better than any woman with whom I'd forged a romantic relationhip.

Given the flimsiness of our finances and the fact that the fringe theatre was not yet established in London, it was essential that our first production put us on the map in such a way that all future cartographers would take note of our existence. The grotty basement on Tottenham Court Road had been designed for a number of moving rostra, which could be used either for seating or as acting areas. Each production would have a different permutation so that essentially we were working in a space rather than an irreversibly designed auditorium. Although I wanted to open with a Shakespeare adaptation, I was aware that since we had no ensemble, we had not yet created the collective expertise which would make our classics any different from anyone else's, and so I chose John Herbert's *Fortune and Men's Eyes*, a drama set in a Canadian reformatory which is a mixture of hard, social observation and mawkish sentimentality. I was fully aware of the play's unevenness, but felt I could turn it into something – a common motivation among directors unable to find irresistible new work and one that many people do not credit as legitimate.

I decided to create the play within an environmental setting, starting it the moment customers arrived at the theatre, even before they took their seats. The original Open Space, which sat about 200, had a long fire exit stairway that led from the street down into the basement where the theatre was located. In order to give the audience the sense of incarceration on which the play was predicated (i.e. to try to reproduce the convict's sense of being caught in a totally programmed existence), as the customers arrived, they were ushered down a long, iron staircase, past a cell (originally a coal shute) in which three forlorn prisoners sat staring out myopically, and under a catwalk on which a uniformed guard with a machine-gun peered down ominously. Once they got to the bottom of the stairway, they turned a corner and found themselves in an official chamber, where two prison guards took their fingerprints. This done, they were allowed to turn the next corner which found them inside a cell with the door bolted. (The cell was, in fact, the set of the play.) From within this cell they could see the auditorium into which they would soon be released, but for the moment all they could do was peer out into the confines of the theatre where their seats vainly beckoned. Throughout the perambulation into the theatre, the audience was assaulted by distant sirens, the sound of alarm bells and droning voices making prison announcements about meal times, church services and other details of prison routine. It was an ear-piercing din which made conversation virtually impossible. Those that asked questions of the uniformed guards were studiously ignored. It soon became clear that it was considered an effrontery to question the discipline which had been imposed upon them or to seek explanation from guards phlegmatically following instructions. Eventually a long alarm bell sounded and the cell door swung open, releasing eight or ten members of the audience and allowing them to take their seats. No sooner did they leave the cell than six or eight other audience members, duly fingerprinted and harassed, took their place in the cell to become exposed to exactly the same routine.

By and large the British audience unflinchingly accepted the insolence of this opening. Occasionally, a woman averse to confined spaces became hysterical, started screaming and demanded to be 'released'. Invariably this was taken to be part of a staged incident and so, as she scampered for the exit doors, she received virtually no sympathy or support. One came to realize how easily totalitarian regimes are created and accepted. People cannot resist a positively organized, efficiently conducted behaviour structure. They are too busy fulfilling its pattern to question its purpose. I kept waiting for someone to say 'Screw all this fingerprinting shit. I came here to see a show!' No one ever did.

Afterwards, once people were in their seats, the effects of the regimentation lingered on. People would ask permission from uniformed guards to use the rest rooms, whether it was all right for them to smoke or walk across the auditorium to visit friends. The guards were instructed to be totally impassive and to resist all attempts at fraternization. No sooner did the normal signs of social courtesy disappear than people became sullen, silent and aggrieved. When the play started, more than half the work was already accomplished. Everyone in that theatre knew what it felt like to be an incarcerated prisoner.

The play benefited from the environmental entry and drew positive notices and large audiences. In a matter of weeks we were on the map. Those that saw through the *mise en scène* to the play beneath had to castigate the thin, melodramatic material, but something had been laid over the production which paid an extra dividend. For good or ill, the Open Space had been launched. Within a few months the play transferred to the West End (the Comedy Theatre) and we were into our second production, a slightly *risqué* play by Paul Ableman called *Blue Comedy*, which ended in a romp of terpsichorean nudity, a finale which gave it rather more fillip than it had elsewhere. My two most salient memories of that show are that one of the actresses who had been rehearsed right up to the previews suddenly contracted a mysterious psychological disease and checked herself into the Middlesex Hospital. Since we could not possibly replace her in time, Thelma and I journeyed down to the hospital, persuaded her it was all in her mind and got her checked out in time for the opening. She seemed to survive both the hospitalization and the experience of being sprung as nothing more was ever heard of her complaint.

On the first night Lesley Frances Ward, a delectable and zany actress friend, pointed out that I had bought no flowers for Thelma, who was appearing in the play, and that she might take this amiss. Since the performance was already in progress and there was no way to obtain flowers from conventional outlets, Lesley and I went around the corner to Middlesex Hospital and I appropriated a ten-foot potted plant. With Lesley as my cover,

I spirited the leafy object out of the hospital through a side entrance and manoeuvred it into the theatre just in time for the curtain calls. As the actors were bowing to the audience, I hulked it on to the stage and, in lieu of a bouquet, deposited it in front of Thelma, who tried hard to keep her cool but, as I recall, did not succeed. The audience, accepting it as a stand-in for flowers and seemingly aware that this was a special occasion, gave the plant a tumultuous ovation.

Lunatic events and wayward behaviour seemed to emanate quite naturally out of the ambience of the Open Space. I can recall another occasion when, angry with Thelma over a frustrated contract negotiation, I found myself pulling the fire alarm on Tottenham Court Road. Within minutes, three enormous fire engines and a couple of dozen firemen descended in full regalia. Thelma and I stood in front of the theatre hotly castigating the 'wicked fools' who could have raised such a false alarm and, after the fire engines left, being unable to explain our preposterous behaviour, took refuge in psychopathic laughter.

The first years of the Open Space were beset with financial woes, an inability to attract quality actors or soften intransigent agents, and rows with writers, directors, stage managers and the Arts Council – and yet, through it all, we managed to mount one production after another, eke out a living and build a reputation. Apart from about half a dozen Shakespearian adaptations, there were a whole sheaf of British premières (Barnes, Barker, Griffiths, Brenton, Hopkins, Mowat) as well as work by Brecht, Sternheim, Büchner, Handke, Dürrenmatt and Beckett. There were special presentations such as our adaptation of *The Chicago Conspiracy*, derived from court transcripts of the hearings of the Chicago mavericks that pulverized the 1968 Democratic Convention in Washington, in which I cast mainly McCarthyite victims such as Carl Foreman, Clancy Sigal and Larry Adler. A dry as dirt William S. Burroughs, constantly masticating non-existent cud, played Judge Hoffman. As members of the audience entered 'the court-room', they were frisked at the entry stairs. It was a time when environmental openings and coercive audience participation were *de rigueur*.

Over a period of some twelve years, including lunch-time shows, late-night attractions and tours from abroad, we mounted well over a hundred productions. Most of them have merged like the vegetation of a landscape viewed from the window of a passing plane, but a few stand out like bodies of water in that same landscape. In collaboration with Sir Roland Penrose, Picasso's official biographer, we mounted the world première of the artist's *The Four Little Girls*, a costly and elaborate effort which involved turning the entire theatre into a fantasy terrain with the audience lolling on pink grass surrounded by tubular trees trellised round with knitting-wool foliage, and invaded by four adolescent girls painted in different colours performing (literally) in their laps. In one of the trickiest pieces ever attempted, I invented a dramatic sub-text for Oscar Wilde's *The Critic as Artist* by means of which Wilde's brilliantly loquacious essay became the pretext for an elaborate seduction between an experienced older man (Wilde) and his young and inquisitive prey (Alfred Douglas). To strike that delicate balance between Wildean conceits on art, literature, politics, religion and the burgeoning desire one man begins to feel for another was as much a miracle of innuendo and inference as it was memorization. Timothy West never played with more wit, nuance or intellectual gusto. Language was never so much charged with ulterior motive and sublimated desire.

There were, for me, memorable mutilations of the plays of William Shakespeare – a black power *Othello* with Rudy Walker and Judy Geeson which harshly commingled black American street argot and traditional '*Othello* music', a lightning-quick collage *Hamlet* (played by Nikolas Simmonds) with specks and shards of the play flashing by like racing cars on a speedway; a necromantic *Macbeth* with three synchronized actors triplicating the title role and Thelma creating a nude sleepwalking scene which was subsequently cadged by Polanski for his movie version; an admixture of *Merchant of Venice* and Marlowe's *Jew of Malta* with Vladek Sheybal's hooded eyes and swarthy mid-European demeanour conjuring up a Zionist Shylock who, for the first time in the history of that decimating trial scene, with armed Jewish insurrectionists ringed around the courtroom, emerged victoriously.

But this is no place for an Open Space retrospective. Suffice it to say, during those years one felt a power in one's artistic loins and a freedom in one's overall musculature which was tantamount to that experienced by an Olympic athlete at the top of his form. The ideas came in a heady profusion; there was never time enough (nor money) to realize the unreachable goals, to test out the more tantalizing theories, to bend the pliable art form into a thousand different shapes – to break it, even – then re-cast it anew; to explore problems which unearthed discoveries more revealing than depth analysis, more mind-boggling than space travel.

The real significance of those early years was that we were what we were because the Sixties had unleashed a new sociological force and our dotty, off-the-wall capers were the inevitable artistic spin-offs of the new era. Some clearly discernible chain linked our experiments with what Tom O'Horgan was doing at La Mama and Joe Chaikin at the Open Theatre, with Grotowsky in Poland and Lavelli in Paris, with the Living Theatre's travelling circus in Europe and the Cage–Cunningham–Rauschenberg forays in the American dance world. The plays we chose, the Happenings, the Shakespearian cut-ups – were all grist for the mill in the 1960s and 1970s, and no matter what form they took, they tried to close down old mineshafts and dig for gold in fields where no one had ever dreamt of prospecting before. The excitement was more in the times than in the artifacts, the art more in the demeanour of the public than the accomplishment of individual artists. That was what made it such fun and, in retrospect, caused us to judge it so harshly. But no matter what its artistic limitations, there was something precious and indelible in the joy they unleashed, and I wouldn't have traded it for the most finished masterpieces.

I I   *The case of the Vanishing Playwright*

At the Open Space it sometimes befell that a play, duly announced and verbally contracted, was gazzumped by a larger, wealthier theatre. This was the case in 1974 when we were about to begin rehearsals for the première of a new British work which we had every reason to believe was ours for the staging. In the event, we found ourselves with a blank slot and about three weeks in which to fill it or suffer the displeasure of our subscribers and, more to the point, sustain some hefty financial losses at the box-office. To avoid such a fate, I was exhorted by Thelma to pull something out of the bag. 'Can't you write something,' she hectored, 'you've got two weeks?' The unimpeachable logic of her remark penetrated the interstices of my skull. No matter that most playwrights worked two, three or four years on their *magnum opus*, confronted with a hiatus of fourteen days there was no good reason in the world why an industrious chap couldn't come up with a play.

As it happened, I'd had this idea for a play some seven or eight years before but, like most writers, found good reason to postpone its creation. I had always wanted to put together a work in which Dr Watson, the bumbly, slow-witted, long-suffering stooge of the great detective, gets his own back. Inspired more by the memorable performances of Nigel Bruce in those late 1930s and 1940s American films than the stories of A. Conan Doyle (which I hadn't even read), it had always struck me that the Holmes–Watson relationship cried out for moral redress. Rathbone's supercilious sleuth always seemed to be lording it over his less mentally agile companion, making him feel backward and incapable. I fantasized a murderous envy on the part of the good doctor which eventually resulted in the perfect crime: the dissolution of the great Sherlock by the last man in the world who would ever be suspected of the crime. Now, confronted with the yawning void of our blank slot, I was impelled to see if the bugger could indeed be written. God knows, it had been gestating long enough!

To make a long, tedious story into a short, tedious one, I wrote the first version of *Sherlock's Last Case* in the appointed fourteen days. It was a long one-acter running about ninety minutes and it finished where the first act of the later version now ends. It was a very different play from the one it turned into ten years later, inexorably black and culminating in the Grand Guignol murders of both Mrs Hudson and Liza Moriarty (the diabolical Professor's unexpectedly unearthed daughter), each of whom was discovered hanging upside-down in a broom cupboard.

We quickly garnered a first-class cast, which included Julian Glover as Sherlock, Peter Bayliss as Dr Watson and Kate O'Mara as the pulchritudinous Liza Moriarty. Being both the artistic director of the theatre as well as the director of this hastily assembled entertainment, I felt it was pushing nepotism to insufferable limits also to be announced as the author, and so concocted an imaginary playwright called Matthew Lang. Mr Lang, I told the company and anyone else in earshot, was an old GI buddy of mine who was essentially a painter. He lived at some *poste restante* address near Marrakech and was constantly on the move, although, whenever the need arose, I could (miraculously) get him on the telephone. Glover and O'Mara listened in wonderment to this tale, although, judging by the quiver of Peter Bayliss's nostrils, I suspected he was beginning to smell something fishy.

We began rehearsals; I trying conscientiously to fulfil the author's demands as I understood them. On several occasions when disputes arose and I insisted that I knew precisely what the author meant in a particular phrase or speech, the actors demanded to know how I could be so certain. I could only reply that we had been very close buddies in the army and I felt I had the measure of Matthew's mind instinctively. When I cavalierly threw out two pages of text and replaced them with a single line, one of the actors playing a smaller role took me aside and urged me to examine seriously whether what I was doing was really conscionable. Bayliss's nose was twitching like mad.

As interpretational disputes began to arise with some regularity, I staunchly insisting I knew exactly what the author intended, a cloud of suspicion gradually settled over the rehearsals and more and more probing questions were asked about our absent playwright. I parried all thrusts with an aplomb developed over several years of outwitting narky actors committed to one-up-manship and the play finally got on. It garnered some very upbeat notices and one or two critics prophesied that, no doubt, we would be hearing more from Matthew Lang.

Then a development occurred that I had not foreseen. Alexander H. Cohen, the Broadway impresario, became interested in the script and began negotiations for the New York rights. As Lang's appointed representative and using Thelma as the mouthpiece, I conducted these negotiations as deftly as I could.

'Do you mean he's not going to be here for revisions and rewrites even if the play's going to be done on Broadway?' asked an incredulous Cohen.

'Yes, I'm afraid that's the case,' I had to reply fixedly stone-faced. 'Lang is a peculiar chap who considers himself primarily a painter and has very little interest in theatrical matters. Nothing can dissuade him from his art-researches in [I believe by this time it was] the Negev, however I, as his appointed representative, am empowered to act on his behalf in any matter that may arise.'

These strained and somewhat incongruous discussions continued for something like fourteen months – with regular requests for Lang to make an appearance and Lang tenaciously refusing to do so. You see, by this time, 'the author' had acquired a genuine persona and I was quite enamoured with the eccentricities of his wilful nature. In any case, after protracted letters and telephone calls with Cohen and the Open Space, the impresario's patience snapped and negotiations were discontinued. Although disappointed, I was also a little relieved as the double life, as any full-time schizophrenic will tell you, is highly taxing.

The play was presented in a variety of repertory theatres – in Liverpool, Peterborough, Salisbury, Pitlochry, etc. – and in each case I carefully prepared a biographical note on the author, situating him geographically and describing his literary and painterly pursuits. At Pitlochry, he was invited to attend the opening but, because he was then on safari in Nairobi, respectfully had to decline. The play made the normal rounds and, over the next five or six years, popped up here and there, although with the passage of time it had begun to recede in my mind.

Almost ten years after the initial production in London, I was skimming the pages of the *Dramatist's Guild Quarterly* magazine and came across a blurb from the producer George W. George of Saga Productions saying that he was interested in thrillers that had a strong core of character about them and, believing my long one-acter to be just such a work, I sent him a copy of the manuscript. To my astonishment, he not only replied but said he was intrigued with the play and would the author be prepared to expand it into a proper, full-length work with the inclusion of a new second act. As I had no desire to exhume the defunct Matthew Lang, I replied, 'Yes, *I*, the author, would be happy to do so.'

At the same time as George offered to option a revised and expanded version of the play for Broadway, Alexander Cohen resurfaced and offered an off-Broadway production of the ninety-minute version. Feeling that the hastily written first version left much to be desired and tempted by the challenge of restructuring a play I had previously closed down for good and all, I opted to go with Saga's offer, wrote Cohen accordingly, and began meeting with George with an eye towards expanding the work into a full-length play.

Extended, revised and dramatically improved, I showed the script to Alan Mandell at the Los Angeles Actors' Theater who immediately became its champion. It was accepted for production in the summer of 1984 and officially included in the Olympic Arts Festival.

Because of a long-standing prejudice against playwrights directing their own works, I was persuaded to entrust the work to another director. I did this very reluctantly as I always contended that, whereas playwrights should never be allowed to direct their own scripts, directors who wrote almost had a solemn obligation to do so. And besides, for over twelve years, at the Space and on the Continent, I had been regularly directing my own adaptations of Shakespeare, Sternheim, Ibsen, Strindberg *et al.* In any case, I was bludgeoned into submission and decided to throw the script into the hands of fate. As it turned out, fate threw it right back into my lap after only two or three weeks of rehearsal.

Our first choice for Sherlock was Clive Revill, a brilliant but dwarfish comic actor who, if anything, should have been playing Dr Watson. To his credit, he realized this after a week's rehearsal and dropped out. The next Sherlock was a good-looking American actor who had studied in England. He was line-shaky and remorselessly humourless, although neither he nor the director seemed to think so. The management, fearing that the production was going badly off the rails, asked me to step in and take over the direction, which I dutifully did, promptly placing the understudy, David Fox Brenton, into the lead. The play eventually received a highly sympathetic press response, won first prize in the Louis B. Mayer Playwrighting Awards and subsequently transferred to the Mayfair Theater in Santa Monica.

As I expected would happen, several spectators and other pernickety types with knowing looks confronted me with the charge that they knew this play well from England and that its true author was one Matthew Lang and what did I think I was trying to pull anyway? Where possible, I explained the convoluted origins of the piece; where not, I simply said that yes, there once had been a writer named Matthew Lang associated with the original work but that I had murdered him in order to take credit for the piece myself. This tended to silence the stroppier critics and cause the others to sidle away wondering whether or not to report the crime.

After a bevy of offers, false offers, options, re-options and lapsed options, the play came into the possession of Frank Langella and his production company, Alfie. Langella, a suave and immensely gifted American actor (the last of the old matinée idols), was also dead set against writers directing their own work and so, once again, I deferred as yet another director hoisted himself into the saddle and took up the reins.

After a tortuous rehearsal period in New York and an even more tortuous try-out period in Washington, I was once again asked to come in and redirect the play, this time before its Broadway opening. Of course, after four weeks of rehearsal and two weeks of out-of-town previews, the amount that a new director can achieve – even if he is the author – is minimal. I changed the tone here and there, tightened the pace of a few scenes and instilled a few character perceptions which, it seemed to me, had been grievously neglected. Eighty-five per cent of the reviews were extremely positive, but the *New York Times* was poisonously negative. It lasted about five months, more or less breaking even during most of the run, but not rounding that magical corner beyond which lay fat takings and voluminous profits. After Broadway, it went on to several triumphs in regional theatres and, at the time of writing, looks likely to resurrect as a television play and possibly even a film.

As for Matthew, I often wonder what part of the globe he is now traversing and if he ever thinks back to the halcyon days of the Open Space and his first, faltering steps on the London stage.

12   *Doppelganger from Shreveport*

I can't remember when in the Sixties I first met Jim Haynes. He seemed to be always there along with the Afghan jackets, brown rice, psychedelic posters and burning incense. I do remember that somewhere around 1964 I had gone up to Edinburgh to direct three one-act plays by Saul Bellow, which eventually became a programme called *The Bellow Plays* and was subsequently mounted at the Fortune Theatre in London with Miriam Karlin and Harry Towb, and during the 1964 Edinburgh Festival I staged Jack Richardson's *Gallows Humour*, while the Traverse was frantically preoccupied with raising the money for a production of Brecht's *Happy End*. I also know that I gradually became a kind of artistic director *in absentia* – constantly on the phone to Jim in Edinburgh suggesting plays, actors, strategies, etc.

Jim had originally been stationed at Kirknewton Air Force Base and when he left the American Air Force, he stayed on in Edinburgh and started the first paperback bookshop in the UK – although, from all accounts, it was more like a club house where, during the day, the browser and the book-worm would be offered coffee and doughnuts and, in the evening, abstruse entertainments such as David Hume's *Dialogues Concerning Natural Religion* and Fiona McCullough's *Trial of the Heretics*.

The original Traverse Theatre at Long Acre in Edinburgh was a medieval turret of a building owned by Tom Mitchell, who, it was rumoured, agreed to one of its floors being converted into a theatre because he was persuaded it would expose him to a variety of rapidly circulating young women. Mitchell, tall, bearded, gimlet-eyed and in his sixties, was unquestionably (and unabashedly) the greatest rake in Scotland. He had the face of an ancient satyr (which in a previous existence he no doubt had been), had acquired considerable wealth from cannery and farming (although he always made a point of keeping all that shrouded in mystery as he believed it added to his allure), and racked up conquests with the same avidity with which American schoolboys accumulate baseball cards. Despite its reputation for encouraging an international repertoire, giving untried actors and actresses their first chance, and fiercely experimenting in the arts of theatre, the primary motivation behind the Traverse was sexual lust.

The original theatre seated fifty-eight with roughly half the seats on one side of the room and half on the other. In the centre a railway or traverse stage no larger than 10′ × 15′ was used to perform some of the most obscure, impenetrable and esoteric plays in the Western repertoire. Mrozek, Pinget, Eveling, Jarry and Duras were some of the more recognizable names. The proximity was such that you were an integral part of an actor's sweat, and one of the occupational hazards was that, in the more forceful moments of a performance, you were likely to be hit in the face by a piece of flying spittle. The trajectory of an actress's bosom was directly at the eye-line of most of the spectators and with a slight tilt of your head, you could effectively nuzzle the more protuberant breasts of *ingénues* heading downstage. It gave the term 'intimate theatre' an entirely new connotation. Apart from some conventional collaborations such as the world première of *The Bellow Plays*, Peter Barnes's first work, *Sclerosis*, and Peter Weiss's *Night with Guests* – all of which I mounted there – there were other, less conventional entertainments. Responding to Jim's exhortation to 'perform' something myself, I remember an evening suggestively titled *Come with Charles Marowitz*, which began with each member of the audience being given a candle with which to light their way up the circular staircase and into the darkened theatre. Once seated, the fifty or so 'keepers of the flame' were exposed to an evening of loosely structured improvisation featuring Harry Towb, Gillian Watt and myself. Afterwards, to buoy up my ego, I would claim that the provocative title of the entertainment was responsible for the large number of females in the audience and the only real disappointment of the evening had been that they didn't actually 'come' with Charles Marowitz. Jim, counting it a tearaway success, rapidly began to sketch out an evening to be titled *Come with Jim*

Haynes, which, had it ever materialized, would have had to spill into George Street to accommodate the overflow.

Jim was considered by many the great catalytic figure of the 1960s – the guy who, by consulting his four-volume telephone book, could almost immediately make things happen. Being able to ring Lord Goodman or Arts Commissioner Jennie Lee or his pals in Fleet Street, he effectively became the bridge between the Underground and the Establishment. In his own undiscriminating world view there was no fundamental difference between a high-powered City industrialist and a junkey who had overdosed on coke and passed out on his living-room floor. Jim had a rakish, Rhett Butler, Southern charm weaned in his native Shreveport, Louisiana, and refined in the Morningside drawing-rooms of Edinburgh, and it consistently worked little miracles on people of all classes – except, perhaps, the intellectual class, because behind that irresistible congeniality, there was very little intellect and, as for originality, only a fierce appreciation of it in other people. (A writer who successfully resisted Jim's charm once described him as 'the man who knows everyone and *is* nobody'.) But the absence of any verifiable talent somehow didn't matter. The warmth of Jim's personality thawed out the congenital coldness that stiffened the joints of most Britons in the 1960s and it was something of a real culture shock to encounter someone brimming over with unfeigned enthusiasm who selflessly wanted to promote cultural happenings with the naïve intention of giving the greatest number of people the maximum amount of fun.

Jim's credo – it was also one of the great credos of the times – was *everybody do their own thing*. Philosophically, it was the essence of what the Permissive Society was all about. In practice, of course, it was a provocative invitation for mediocrities, nonentities and self-deluded bores to flaunt whatever poor, dubious or non-taste they possessed. It was a philosophy which, philosophically speaking, was an *anti*-philosophy because it entirely eliminated the principle of discrimination and eschewed the need for critical standards. Galvanized indiscriminate activity, however, can sometimes produce marvellous things. Once you open the floodgates, apart from effluence and debris, an occasional flounder gushes through, perhaps even a pearl or two. For Jim, the effluence and debris were indistinguishable from the pearls and flounders; the important thing was that the floodgates were open.

After doing a few shows at the Edinburgh Traverse, Jim, along with director Michael Geliot and designer Ralph Koltai, managed to create a London base of operations at the Jeannetta Cochrane Theatre, where Ralph was head of design. Michael Geliot, like myself, had known Jim from Edinburgh, but knew little of me. In the first stages I felt a palpable reluctance on Michael's part to include me in the operation. He and Ralph between them had cooked up the deal to take over the Cochrane Theatre and so, I suppose, there was no good reason for them to include an outsider. Perhaps because of Jim's persuasions or perhaps because I simply assumed I was part of the original Traverse triumvirate, I was grudgingly included in the operation – fortunately for them, as the three most successful productions in those short-lived seasons were Joe Orton's *Loot*, Saul Bellow's *The Bellow Plays* (both of which transferred to the West End) and the C. P. Taylor musical *Who's Pinkus, Where's Chelm*, which was scheduled to move into the Mayfair Theatre until I threw cold water on my own contemptibly compromised production, thus effectively discouraging the investor, a well-heeled, starry-eyed mid-Westerner unearthed, as always, by Jim.

In the mid-Sixties, the Jeannetta Cochrane Theatre held a special place in hippie consciousness. It was where they could see Mark Boyle's experiments with liquid slides and Yoko Ono's destructivist Happenings, listen to poetry recitals, watch late-night experimental productions (my own full-length collage *Hamlet* had its London première there) and generally experience the heady sense of being 'in the swing' of swinging London. A half block down on Southampton Row, Barry Miles (soft-spoken Underground entrepreneur, biographer of Alan Ginsberg and confidant of the Beatles) had opened his Indica bookshop, where for a certain period *International Times* was zealously, sometimes surreptitiously, produced. Rumour had it that the redoubtable Lord Goodman, Harold Wilson's private counsel, had pulled some strings to separate the Cochrane Theatre from the rather bureaucratic Design School, of which it formed a part, an act he subsequently rued when he found that backing the experiments of the counter-culture insurrectionists also meant underwriting the drug-running which invariably accompanied them. Lord Goodman, a socialist liberal in politics, was a puritanical Comstock in the arts. His notion of 'culture' was a private box at Covent Garden and, when he caught wind of the fact that the Jeannetta Cochrane was in some ideological way linked with the general licentiousness of the Underground, he cooled considerably.

Temperamentally, the Jeannetta Cochrane and Jim were also a mismatch. He hated the idea of having to abide by London County Council rules in regard to the operation of the place and he loathed the burnished wood and institutional patina of the architecture. He was particularly rubbed the wrong way by the house manager, who was also the theatre's licensee, a county appointee who dramatically personified the kind of moral rigidity the whole counter-culture was attempting to efface. When the Cochrane all came tumbling down (and possibly even before that), Jim took over an old warehouse in Drury Lane and started his Arts Lab, a kind of cultural doss-house for students and junkies which strikingly evoked scenes out of *The Lower Depths*, except that the Russian peasants were rather better dressed. Here, sprawled on foam rubber mattresses with the pong of sweaty, stockinged feet permeating the air, an endless array of performance artists, actors, writers and musicians floating on a cloud of pot, watched pirated Beatles videos and proselytized the New Bohemia. The motive behind the Arts Lab was to create a meeting-place where artists of every stripe could show their wares, commune with one another and live the good life. It was Jim's most ambitious attempt to 'let everyone do their own thing'. Unfortunately, in the mid-Sixties, most people's 'thing' consisted of turning on and dropping out, and very quickly the Arts Lab became a half-way house for drifters and wastrels far removed from the bohemian ideals that prompted Jim to create it. It also became a kind of sexual seraglio for itinerant students and potheads, which attracted a completely alien strain of voyeur and make-out man, for whom the words 'arts lab' had no artistic connotation, but who perceived it mainly as a convenient place to 'pull birds'. Yet again, one of Jim's Utopias became a grubby stop on the Underground transit system. Although he railed against the excesses, the free-loaders and the pilferers, he was never entirely disappointed by what he had wrought. An upbeat concert or a session animated by 'good vibes' was enough to eradicate a month of empty, aimless, meandering evenings with potheads, skinheads or meatheads. Other Arts Labs sprang up in other parts of England and allegedly flourished, and so, no matter how wretched the original model, Jim could take solace from the fact that he had started a mini cultural phenomenon in Britain.

Although we collaborated on a variety of projects – most notably the original Traverse Theatre Club in Edinburgh, the London Traverse at the Jeannetta Cochrane Theatre and the launch of *International Times*, our deepest bond was the mutual adoration of pussy and, in pursuit of this object, we frequently roamed the town together reconnoitring some of the loveliest, sexiest, most voluptuous and often most impregnable women in London. Occasionally Jim and I would bee-line to the same girl, then, like the gentlemen we were, both courteously back off. On one occasion he almost scored with a blonde Berlin film-maker with whom I had already had a liaison. The melodramatic details of that attempted seduction didn't come down to me until years after the event and, when we spoke about it, he vigorously reassured me he had no inkling of my former attachment. But by then it was all as faded as the rock posters that mouldered on the stone walls behind St Pancras Station, and what struck me was not his passion or my jealousy but the fact that, during those years, the propulsion behind so many of those social and cultural jamborees was merely the quest for pussy – the insatiable (though regularly sated) desire to gobble up as much as one could decently consume and then some.

Permissive was always a misnomer for the society because it implied that everyone 'let' everyone else, and that was never the case then, as it isn't now. Probably even in the last orgiastic days of the Roman Empire there were maidens who staunchly refused potbellied senators and fled the beds of lecherous, tanked-up gladiators. It was not so much that the society was permissive, but that it was passionate – passionate in the finest, lyrical, even operatic sense of the word. We were always bubbling with the lava of uncontrollable desires – wanting to touch, to taste, to savour, to consume that seemingly endless procession of dolly-birds that rustled their Laura Ashleys on the pavements of Kensington High Street or flashed their knickers beneath Mary Quant mini-skirts along King's Road. One of Jim's earliest literary efforts was a book called *Hello, I Love You* – and even before dipping into the volume, one grasped the significance of the title because that was the overriding cry of the 1960s: a swarming, heady infatuation with the Feminine Principle crystallized in a teenager's legs jutting out of what were fancifully referred to as 'pussy pelmets', the swirl of a bra-less bosom cutting a swathe beneath a tight T-shirt, a smile on a pair of lips that pouted smugly beneath a Louise Brooks hairstyle or shone irresistibly out of a face which could just as easily be Jean Shrimpton as not.

When Jim and I met for meals or coffee, our most serious consultations were almost always about pussy, like two practised hunters comparing trophies and giving each other useful tips about the treacheries of the terrain and sightings of magnificent fauna in out-of-the-way places. For those feminists who immediately construe this as the insensitive objectification of women, I should explain that our erotic activities were invariably recalled with awe. We wove rhapsodies around the euphoria transmitted by certain women in certain intimate situations. We reconstructed bedroom scenes like pilgrims recounting Christian miracles. We worshipped the lineaments of those pleasures and, in describing them to one another, tried to reconstruct the poetry which had suffused certain transcendental nights in aromatic trysting places. Sometimes, with Jim, I felt like a kid trading baseball cards – and, as anyone knows who ever indulged in that childish transaction, it engenders an atmosphere charged with reverence of precious and ethereal deities.

Towards the end of the Sixties many of Jim's staunchest Establishment allies – Lord Goodman, Michael Astor, Jennie Lee – were beginning to fall away. What three years before had seemed idealistic and bohemian, now appeared at best naïve, at worst unsavoury. They erroneously associated Jim with the 'druggies' – never realizing that he neither encouraged nor personally indulged, although his open-ended tolerance embraced those people guilty of the worst excesses. When he started *Suck* magazine, which was not only pornographic but with unmitigated adolescent glee exulted in its pornography, he was for many people already beyond the pale. For Jim, it was merely a way of spreading the pleasures of sex, a kind of advertisement for communal euphoria, and it was round about that point that one began to wonder what unconfronted problems might be afflicting someone so desperately committed to the public advertisement of his own sexual appetite.

In the 1980s, I was asked to review his proxy autobiography characteristically titled *Thanks For Coming*. My first instinct was to decline on the basis that I was too close to Jim for objectivity. Then, after reading the book, I thought: why let some Oxbridge smart Alec dispassionately deflate the thing with no real knowledge of the subject. Couching the review in the form of a personal letter to Jim, I wrote in part:

> In many ways you were too good for the 'scene',
> incontrovertibly naïve and life-affirming in spite
> of being surrounded by cynics, savages and
> spongers. You often confused the sex-drive with
> the Life Force and appeared, in my eyes,
> irretrievably *gauche* in many of your enthusiasms.
> Nevertheless, you had them – and having them,
> backed them to the hilt. The Traverse was a
> true cultural harbinger – as was the Arts Lab.
> *International Times* was a genuine tawdry expression
> of the counter-culture at its best. *Suck* always
> struck me as an assinine and sanctimonious spin-off
> of *Screw* and a dispensable part of the Hugh
> Heffner legacy, but it was amusingly sordid and
> celebratory, although I always questioned the
> need for each and every orgasm to be marked
> with a psychedelic jamboree, massed bands and a
> firework display. Why can't people come in
> quiet communion without being proselytized or
> turned into part of Germaine Greer's po-faced
> dialectic? Here, I find myself closer to Mary
> Whitehouse than Wilhelm Reich.

burnt bridges

From the middle of the nineteenth century onward, there have always been jaunty bohemian characters who flit in and out of the pages of major biographies (sort of jumped-up Henry Carrs) adding local colour and accurately embodying the sense of period. In lots of ways you really fall into that category. You're the personification of the Bohemian Spirit which in the last half of the twentieth century was virtually obliged to be libertarian, non-conformist, sexually emancipated and supportive of the latest *avant garde* trends in living as well as art.

As to *Thanks For Coming*, it's an MS found in a bottle, an amalgam of flotsam and jetsam from the decade that formed you and with which you had the happiest interaction of your life. Some inspired PhD student in the twenty-first century wanting to add texture to his treatise on the Swinging Sixties will liberally footnote its seamier passages and all the dons will have a good old chortle and say: 'Well done, Algernon' . . . A lot of the book is simply, in Reich's phrase, phallic narcissism and a lot more, pure and unabashed narcissism. *'Thanks For Coming,'* one is almost tempted to answer, 'and thank you for jerking off!'

Despite trying to balance cavilling and puffery, I half expected Jim to be infuriated – but, in a note scrawled to me after its publication, he thanked me for my review and in subsequent conversation it was clear that he was in no way offended. Of course, I speculated afterward, he must've said to himself: it's just Marowitz doing his satanic little thing, and why not?

I don't think Jim is a writer, a director or an artist. I rarely heard him utter an original idea or make a profound critical observation. His autobiography was essentially 'contributed' into being through recollections and souvenirs by people who knew him at different periods of his life. Endearingly, he would never have dreamt of creating it himself, for autobiography, like everything else, is also an opportunity for 'everybody to do their thing'.

Having, in my view, no outstanding abilities of his own, Jim's attempts at creating theatres, publications and events were essentially artistic sublimations. Because he loved books but couldn't write, he created a bookstore. Because he could neither act nor direct, he created a theatre. Because he wanted to express his feelings about sexuality and the counter-culture, he conjured up *International Times* and *Suck*. Because he was intoxicated by the aroma of a mixed society, he was continually engendering events, parties, festivals and cultural clam-bakes where people could experience the spontaneous combustion of each other's company. Oscar Wilde put his talent into his work and his genius into his life. Jim, having limited talent, and not being a genius, catalysed the talent and genius of others in such a way that both rubbed off on himself, giving him the whiff of both talent and genius.

In the Seventies he found a niche at the University of Versailles conducting what he called a 'rap class' – sessions in which, as far as I could gather, people talked about whatever came into their heads. 'Half the kids in the class', he told me once, 'think I'm terrific, the other half think I'm a fraud – so, you see, I've fooled half of them!' I never quite understood which half he meant.

About fifteen years after the cries of the counter-culture had died down and the Sixties had become a subject of academic curiosity, Jim passed through Malibu, where I was then living with my second (although in the existential sense, first) wife, and we had him over for dinner. He was bigger and paunchier than I remembered him. Less rambunctious – but then that might have just been the company. He still laughed at things which were not inherently funny, underlining with a broad Southern guffaw the absurdity of a paradox or a whimsical turn of events. He had been 'lecturing' in various universities, presumably about the 1960s, and was now a property owner in Paris. His son by an early and long-dissolved marriage was now in his early twenties. He still haunted the book fairs in Frankfurt and London, the festivals in Edinburgh, Amsterdam and Berlin. He was still internationalist in outlook. There were still projects to hustle – care packages to Polish refugees and a one-woman show based on the life of Marlene Dietrich – but mainly he had become a commentator on a period of social history in which he had figured prominently and which had realized his catalytic talents in a way which would never happen again. I could see him fuelling chroniclers of the Sixties well into the year 2,000; telling open-mouthed scholars who revered their Beatles collections and first editions of McLuhan and Marcuse exactly how it was; plying them with refreshments as he did in the late 1950s, when he opened his bookstore in Edinburgh and brought down the usual barriers between proprietor and customer by inviting anonymous browsers and tourists coming in out of the rain to sit down, have a coffee and just shoot the shit.

Maybe it was my imagination, but at certain moments during that ghostly dinner I think we shared an understanding that the sensual highs of the Sixties had now been tabulated and stored away in the archives, and no matter how vigorous or efficacious our present lives seemed to be, like veterans of the Normandy landing, the liberation of Paris or other such watershed events, civilian life would always be a somewhat pale imitation of the incredible moments we had shared around Drury Lane, King's Road or Lawnmarket. But so much of this is subjective, it is wrong to hazard any attributions. Maybe that's only what *I* felt. But I did want to get him alone for a moment and ask, 'James, what the hell was it all about? The parties, the music, the anarchy, the sex? What, in these shapeless Nineties, were the Sixties really all about? Do you know? Can you tell me? If a banquet, in commemoration of what? If an aberration, in relation to what kind of normality? Was it just delayed adolescence for all of us? Nothing more than an elaborate, dialectically camouflaged attempt to stop the clock and elude the grave?' Of course, I never talked to Jim like that and certainly didn't then, but always felt that, if anything like concrete answers to such questions could be found, it would be as a result of an interminable rap session between Jim and myself.

I have often tried to reconcile what I took to be his shallowness and lack of personal talent with the resourceful, warm and charismatic character he has become and I simply cannot do it. There is no verifiable reason why Jim Haynes should be a mover or a shaker, a confidant to artists and quasi-artists from all over the world, an Underground luminary or an icon of the counter-culture. His ordinariness is overpowering. One could just as easily see him on a back porch in Shreveport, tossing feed to the chickens and raising a crumpled straw hat to passing neighbours. I suppose what differentiates him from other people is his unquenchable love of society, of which his love for women in all shapes and sizes is merely a spin-off. Like certain vaude-villians who always played down stage centre to feel the breath of the house, Jim has always needed the impact of a public – not to perform to, but to be one with. Although the word 'humanist' tends to have misleading, altruistic connotations, it is the most appropriate word for Jim. He is one of those rare people who, despite the world's constant abuse and incessant betrayals, actu-ally loves people (unlike myself who regularly recoils from the human race and rails against a divinity that, like Nature's journeymen, 'had made men, and not made them well, they imitated humanity so abominably'). Cynically, I have always looked for traces of duplicity in him, signs that his limitless, take-all-comers tolerance was merely a mask, and that deep down he was fully aware that human nature was fundamentally repugnant and people fatally flawed, but I have never found them. Ultimately I am drawn to a conclusion best expressed by Peter Roberts, the hippie turned entrepreneur who, reflecting on the enduring Sixties types, said, 'Normally a star has to be a star at something: playing the guitar, painting, something that can be bought. The point of the counter-culture stars is that they were stars at living.' In those terms, I guess you could say Jim has always been a headliner.

13   *Raided*

Jimmy Vaughan was a jolly, chortling, big-toothed Indian gentleman who acted as distributor for a variety of Underground films. He had been introduced to Thelma and myself by John Trevelyan, the Secretary of the British Board of Film Censors, because it seemed to John we were both exploring similar territory and ought to know about each other. Trevelyan was an astute, highly liberal, middle-aged gentleman, strangely unshockable and an incongruous choice for Britain's film censor. I always suspected that behind the polished façade and correct Civil Service manner lay an archetypal and rather adorable 'dirty old man'.

When, in our third year at the Space, things got particularly tight (our Arts Council grant at the time was a measly £1,500 – while the kitchens at Covent Garden received £34,000 per annum), Thelma and I decided to arrange a film show to tide us over until money promised from Wiesbaden for our production of *A Macbeth* was forthcoming. We contacted Vaughan, who suggested a new film by Andy Warhol called *Flesh* (actually directed by Paul Morrissey).

The film, very much in the meandering, loosely plotted Warhol tradition, depicted a day in the life of a male hustler (Joe d'Alessandro) who is exhorted by his wife to raise the money needed for her lesbian girlfriend's abortion. Dutifully Joe goes out on to the streets, picks up a few clients, swaps experiences with some drifters and then returns home, where, it then transpires, the wife and her girlfriend have reconsidered the abortion, and all three wind up in bed. Apart from the gruelling ordinariness with which it treats subjects like homosexuality, lesbianism and male prostitution, it contains one deathless soap opera line delivered by an ex-girlfriend reflecting on a 'bad scene' she has just had with a former boyfriend: 'Do you know what it's like', she asks ruefully, 'to dance topless in front of someone who's raped you?' Like many of the Factory's products, it was only a few steps up from home movies, but Warhol was hot and I figured it might do some business at the theatre.

For the first three weeks of its run, playing three or four times a day, it did surprisingly well. A whole new breed of subscriber found his way to the Open Space – clearly related to the raincoat brigades which manned the strip clubs and private cinemas in nearby Soho, a grubby, lascivious, anonymous tribe of respectable businessmen and commercial travellers plus a few cineastes, students, weirdos and perverts.

On 3 February 1970, two or three minutes before one of the showings was about to end, thirty-two police constables and a superintendent from Scotland Yard entered the building, ordered the projectionist to stop the film, turned on all the lights and proceeded to take down the names and addresses of the seventy-five consternated patrons captured in the auditorium. Apparently a complaint had been lodged with the police that the film in question was obscene. Earlier in the week several policemen in mufti had paid the extra half-crown plus two guineas for 'temporary membership' in order to confirm the allegation. 'A report', said the burly officer in charge, 'will be sent to the Director of Public Prosecutions.' The film and projector were confiscated, as were club documents, books and receipts. Thelma, who had been on duty at the time, was flustered and flabbergasted. Her first instinct was to offer all the patrons their money back, although all they really seemed concerned about was hightailing it away from the scene of the crime.

Within moments of being advised of the raid, Trevelyan left his office at Soho Square and taxied to the theatre.

'I cannot understand why it should be raided,' he told reporters. 'This is an intellectual film for a specialized audience. I have seen it and, while it is not my cup of tea, there is nothing at all corrupting about it.'

The next day the raid made headlines in all the papers and, when the full impact of what happened had sunk in, there were protests from every quarter. A tiny, Arts Council-subsidized theatre in the West End with a reputation for non-commercial, experimental fare had been raided by thirty-two policemen because of an allegation of obscenity. Previously the London Arts Gallery, which had arranged an exhibition of prints by John Lennon, had been prosecuted on charges of 'exhibiting indecent material'. Prosecution witnesses at that trial had voluntarily gone into the gallery and then claimed to have been 'disgusted' and 'nauseated' (which reminded one journalist of the old lady who called a policeman because she claimed there was a naked man standing in front of a window in the house opposite. 'I can't see him', said the policeman. 'Of course not,' replied the old lady, 'you have to stand on a chair!'). It was also the time that Ken Tynan and Michael White were finding it difficult to obtain a West End theatre for their forthcoming revue *Oh! Calcutta!*, and Mary Whitehouse was inveighing regularly against the corrupting influence of television. Philistinism and permissiveness were locked in mortal combat and, on the sidelines, bystanders were obstreperously egging on each of the combatants.

Within days the implications of the raid were being discussed in the House of Commons. Labour's Home Secretary James Callaghan, pressed on the issue, declared that he would support the police when they investigated complaints about pornography from the public. The country, he declared, was 'extremely alarmed' about what was going on. Mr Strauss, Labour MP for Vauxhall, asked if the recent seizures were carried out with the authorization of the Home Secretary. Callaghan tried to duck the question by replying, 'These are matters for the police, not for me.' Mr Strauss then fired his broadside.

> MR STRAUSS (Vauxhall, Labour): 'Does not the Home Secretary consider it ridiculous that the Metropolitan Police, who are understaffed and overworked with the increasing crime problem on their hands, should send a force of 32 constables to a small experimental theatre which receives an Arts Council grant to seize a film suggested to them by the British Board of Film Censors and seize the projector and the screen? Can he give an assurance that this was a regrettable isolated incident and does not mean that there is to be a campaign to restrict this sort of thing: a repressive, Mrs Grundy-campaign in London?' (*Cheers*)

MR CALLAGHAN: The police must enforce the law as it now is. Two well-publicized cases can hardly be regarded as a campaign. The House should recognize, as many MPs do from their own correspondence, that there is a great deal of concern in the country about the amount of unsolicited pornography (*interruptions*) being sent through the post.

MR ST JOHN-STEVAS (Conservative, Chelmsford): Would not the police be much better employed checking the disgusting hard-core of pornography and activities such as the Julian Press rather than pouncing upon an experimental art theatre? (*Renewed cheers*)

MR CALLAGHAN: I am not drawing a distinction between the two because it is not my place to comment upon individual cases that are, may be, or have been in front of the Director of Public Prosecutions. This is a social matter. There is a great deal of pornography about that is causing a great deal of concern to many people in this country. It is the general desire of the average person in this country that it should stop. (*Further cheers*)

MR MICHAEL FOOT (Ebbw Vale, Labour): There is a serious question of civil liberties involved here. Some people have had their property taken away by the police and perfectly legitimate activities interfered with by the police. The Home Secretary, instead of answering the question, has referred vaguely to questions of pornography. Does he not think that justifies the demand for an independent inquiry, so that we may see what was the cause of what happened on this occasion? (*More cheers*)

MR CALLAGHAN: I have said on two occasions that this matter is before the courts. (PROTESTS) Therefore I do not intend to comment on them.

MR FOOT: The Home Secretary is under a

misapprehension in saying that this matter is before the courts. The Director of Public Prosecutions has said that no prosecution is to take place.

MR CALLAGHAN: I apologize. Mr Foot is right. This case *was* before the courts. It is not now before them. Therefore it would be possible for me to comment on the individual actions of the police. Broadly speaking, I want the House to know that I will support the police when they act in response to complaints from the public in investigating these matters. It may be that on occasion they will make mistakes of judgement, but the country as a whole is extremely alarmed about what is going on. (*Cheers*)

Mr Gray, the Labour MP for Yarmouth, asked the Attorney General what action had been recommended by the Director of Public Prosecutions on Andy Warhol's film *Flesh*, and in a written reply, Sir Elwyn Jones replied that the DPP had advised the Metropolitan Police that criminal proceedings in respect of this film were not justified, but that the papers had been referred to the Greater London Council to consider whether proceedings should be taken under the cinema licensing provisions of the Cinematograph Act of 1909. Which, in fact, *were* taken. Realizing that there was no case in regard to obscenity or pornography, it was decided that, to save face, the theatre club would be prosecuted for the lesser offence of membership violation.

We promptly applied for a High Court writ against the superintendent who had conducted the raid against the theatre in order to try to get back our equipment, books, etc. Having been advised that the film would not be prosecuted, within a few weeks it was once again showing at the Open Space and playing to full houses for virtually every screening. Thelma was cock-a-hoop. She had never seen so much money being taken at the box-office. No fringe theatre in London had ever had full houses two, three, and four times a day. The gross takings made the Arts Council subsidy look like a mean gratuity.

The furore caused the film to be reviewed by those critics who initially hadn't thought it worth the bother, and re-reviewed by those papers which had given it short shrift the first time around. *The Times* called it 'a nice little film full of bizarre touches of characterization which add up to a curiously believable picture of a way of life. Technically, it is one of the most accomplished American underground films we have seen.' The *Sunday Times* was 'agreeably surprised'. The *Sunday Telegraph* found it 'intermittently amusing, sad and quite moving'. The *Daily Telegraph* observed: 'During the making of *Flesh*, Mr Warhol was shot by a lady who was said to have taken extreme exception to his films . . . it is easy to see what got on her nerves.' And the *Daily Mail*, responding to Warhol's comment that the film was essentially about 'beautiful people', concluded: 'Not even the most beautiful people in the world could gloss over so much badness.'

As a result of the controversy and, as so often happens in cases where the quality of a film is complicated by extraneous issues, Morrissey's manufactured bauble received more sympathetic attention than it would ever have got in the normal course of events. There were those who believed there must be hidden depths in a work which could cause so much havoc and, as a result of such belief, promptly found them.

A few weeks after the raid the film was given a special showing to fourteen peers and peeresses who, allegedly, wanted to find out for themselves what the police had objected to. Shortly after the raid, Lord Snowdon had telephoned Jimmy Vaughan and requested a copy of the film be sent to Kensington Palace as soon as one could be made available. A month after the police seizure, the House of Commons official Order Paper, succumbing to Freudian slipperiness, listed the following question from Dr Hugh Gray, MP for Yarmouth: 'What action had been recommended on A. Warhol's film *Flesh* by the Director of Public Prosecutions?' Cartoons in the *Sun* and *Daily Mail* made much of inspectors trying to uproot their constables from film clubs where they were sitting mesmerized by sex films they were supposed to be confiscating. The *Guardian* ran a cartoon showing a children's sex education film being raided by bullying bobbies.

At the magistrate's hearing, considering the charge that the Open Space allowed members of the general public into a licensed club, the theatre was fined £220, which Andy Warhol, in a wily publicity gesture, paid on behalf of the theatre. Every cinema club in London operated the same form of temporary membership on which the Space was penalized, and of course these practices continued unabated. *The Times* had suggested in a diary piece that the *Flesh* raid against the Open Space had really been a police boner and that the intended victim was supposed to have been Cineclub 24, a few yards down from the Open Space on Tottenham Court Road, which, at the time, was showing *Venus in Furs*. When I mentioned this to the proprietor, he clasped his hands together, turned heavenward and prayed, 'Oh, please, God!'

A few months later Andy Warhol and the prolific Mr Morrissey produced *Trash*, a not so worthy successor to *Flesh*, which had no problem obtaining distribution.

The run of *Flesh* ticked on week after week. The takings were phenomenal, but our more serious members began to wonder what had happened to the original Open Space, the leading experimental theatre in London that prided itself on classical adaptations and the latest off-beat fare from America and the Continent? So did I. Reluctantly, I said to Thelma we had to discontinue the Warhol bonanza and go back to being the struggling little playhouse we were before *Flesh* hit. Thelma had always been in charge of finance, and so a return to erstwhile penury was a difficult adaptation to make. At the end of the year, the Arts Council actually considered reducing our grant since we had profited so royally from the film showing. Being forced by lack of adequate subsidy to fend for ourselves, we had used our initiative to try to improve our condition, but this was a motive the Arts Council would neither acknowledge nor countenance. As they saw it, there were many worthy applicants out there and they were hard pressed to share the wealth, what there was of it. Of course, the major companies, the National, the RSC, Covent Garden, the established reps always came first. A 200-seat experimental stage in a basement on Tottenham Court Road somehow wasn't 'theatre'. It didn't look or feel like theatre. There were no upholstered seats. It had no bar. Its members were dressed like wastrels or gypsies. Its repertoire, if that wasn't too dignified a word for the collages, happenings and freak-outs regularly presented, was not like any they could recognize in Birmingham,

Oxford, Manchester or Liverpool. And in any case, what *was* experimental theatre, anyway? Why couldn't the Open Space, like everyone else, revive a hardy old Coward or Rattigan, a straightforward Shakespeare or some good-hearted domestic comedy which would appeal to the entire family? Although we encountered Arts Council officials at various board meetings and financial sessions, I cannot recall them ever being part of our audience. And, of course, to make matters worse, there were all those vituperative articles I tended to write against the Council itself, criticizing their policies and their priorities, on one occasion exposing the fact that two-thirds of their subsidy recipients were, in fact, members of their own drama panel so that, in a sense, they were merely doling out money to themselves! All of that was, in their eyes, 'a very bad show', and papers like the *Guardian* were irresponsible for playing up such diatribes.

In those days the drama panel of the Arts Council was made up almost exclusively of unimaginative, middle-class clubmen who derived some ghoulish satisfaction from wielding petty power over matters they never fully understood, but the principles of which they pompously espoused. Their values had been formed in the 1930s, usually in Tory strongholds like Harrow and Eton, and, despite lip service to the social transformations taking place around them, they had to be shamefully steered and manipulated in order to behave in anything resembling a modern manner. If the Space hadn't mustered media support by being mentioned two or three times a month in newspaper diary columns and the arts pages, they would have blithely ignored our existence. As it was, they only gave us enough to enable us to hang by our fingertips and none of our requests to subsidize a well-grounded, permanent ensemble were ever granted. I remember one snide bureaucrat pointing out to me that one of the unspoken principles behind its operations was that, from time to time, organizations should disappear in order to make room for others and, in this way, democratize the flow of funds. Of course, establishment monoliths like the National, the RSC or Covent Garden were excluded from this theory; although he didn't say so, he meant small-scale theatre groups and fringe companies desperately scratching for a living.

There was a certain irony in the fact that Andy Warhol saved our bacon in 1970. Warhol's vacuous anti-art attitude spanned so many hyped artifacts that his 'theory' almost seemed to hold water, but it was one that could only be given credence in the mindless 1960s. As Paul Morrissey admitted in regard to the Factory's film products: 'The person who operates the camera, he makes the movie . . . We're not interested in directors, we think directors have ruined the movies. We're interested in actors. And we always use actors. Viva [superstar of *Lonesome Cowboys* and other Warhol *shlockerai*] is a great female. Joe d'Alessandro makes Rudolf Nureyev look like Richard Attenborough – he's really unbelievable looking.' (Only street-jaded hustlers could outpoint d'Alessandro over Nureyev, but then, to Morrissey and Warhol, 'beauty' was always in the jockey shorts of the beholder.) 'We think if we don't interfere,' said Morrissey, 'if we play it by ear and let these great people just act, it'll come out realistic.' But Viva wasn't Garbo – she was just an emaciated dyke – and, when freaky women began to lose their appeal, Warhol switched to transvestites like Holly Woodlawn and Candy Darling. They weren't 'unbelievable looking' either; they were just *outrés* – which, in the 1960s, simply meant banal.

The Warholian aesthetic, so persuasive twenty-five years ago, now looks and sounds like the drivel it actually was even then. 'Everyone is rich,' said Warhol. 'Everyone and everything is interesting. This is my favourite theme in movie-making, just watching something happening for two hours or so.' Thirty years ago, we had a tolerance for an immobilized shot of the Empire State Building or the face of a man receiving a blow-job, or a character sleeping for six hours, which almost convinced us that we were on the brink of a new artistic breakthrough. Today most of these products are revealed to be the vacant products of an aberrated imagination. *Vers libre*, said T. S. Eliot, is all well and good, but a man still has to do a good job. Even anti-art, it seems clear to me three decades after the fad, has to have enough artistic constituents to qualify for the label. *Flesh was Trash* as, in a sense, everything ever made by Warhol was trash – although, back then, we could be persuaded that even debris contained aesthetic intimations. In those days we were ready to be convinced by almost any theory that cocked its snook at the conventional wisdom – even self-indulgent amateurism could be mystified and systematized into New Ideology. Because we had grown sceptical of established patterns, we were prone to believe that any departure from the norm was preferable to the norm and, as a result, we were predisposed to the odd, the quirky, the novel and the perverse. It is one of the curiosities of new, bad art that, so long as it bears no resemblance to old bad art, we are prepared to admit it into our charmed circle. It is only afterwards when we try to rationalize the aesthetic which brought it about that we realize it has gained admittance by false pretences.

The *Flesh* raid did three things. It reaffirmed the maverick, anti-Establishment nature of the Open Space; it spread our 'myth' throughout the country and it confirmed that the permissiveness which seemed to be widespread in the society also had its champions in Parliament, in the legal profession and in the press. The irony was that all these 'virtues' were instigated by a puerile, homo-erotic home-movie that was as far from our true aesthetic as anything could possibly be.

14   *Frolics, fêtes and freak-outs*

Several months before the Open Space Theatre officially opened, I loaned it to John Hopkins as the site for his marriage to Suzy Creamcheese. In the late 1960s, Hoppy had been convicted for pot possession and because of the bust, became something of a cult hero. 'Free Hoppy' buttons proliferated throughout London; wearing one was virtually a badge confirming membership in the Underground. A doyen of the counterculture, Hoppy was involved with *International Times*, UFO, the Notting Hill Free School and, in one way or another, almost every other Underground manifestation of the period. Suzy Creamcheese (née Zieger), his Californian bride, was one of the period's more outlandish ephemera – an embodiment of the ethereality of the 1960s who blossomed like an aspidistra come to life at UFO and other nocturnal clubs around town.

The wedding was a typical (dare one say, archetypical) Underground event wreathed in flowers, backed by rock groups and populated by sprites and dryads costumed by Barnum and Bailey. Like many of the 1960s events, it was noisily serene and commingled elements of holy ritual with bacchanalian excess, pot and incense, as usual, in an olfactory struggle to the death. It felt right and proper to be initiating the theatre with a hippie wedding. It augured well.

But, despite rave-ups and freak-outs in grottos all over London, much of what was most typical of the period was played out in the streets, specifically Carnaby Street, King's Road (from Sloane Square to Fulham), Trafalgar and Grosvenor Squares, and open-air markets in Portobello, Paddington and Islington.

For a time Carnaby Street was the most festive and fun-filled thoroughfare in the whole of England. Quite apart from the variety of its boutiques, there was a constant pulse of rock music issuing from every doorway and an informal parade of 'bright young things' brandishing bra-less net blouses, infinitesimal mini-skirts and personalized ensembles which defied fashion analysis. The procession, for that was virtually what it was, started around noon and began to flag around 5.30. Many of those vaunting their taste, or barbarous lack of it, came from the suburbs, un*chic* outposts such as Streatham, Ealing, Walthamstow and Whitechapel.

The King's Road procession on Saturday afternoons was more unpredictable and, in keeping with its Chelsea habitat, had more of an intellectual patina. It was a pageant, a street festival, an open-air concert, an exhibition by shameless exhibitionists, a place where you could sample the latest in face painting and whorled hairstyles; where Pre-Raphaelites patterned after Burne Jones's paintings and Louise Brooks look-alikes freely commingled; where boys in Elizabethan, Victorian and Edwardian dress consorted with Hell's Angels sporting silver studs, swastikas and ominous lengths of linked chain. Everyone was 'on' and everyone was expected to dig everyone else's performance which, on the whole, they did – evaluating the new gear, passing on bits of arcane gossip, trading information about upcoming rock concerts or trendy new eateries. If this was unorchestrated street theatre, it must also be said that many of these people were playing out roles assigned them by the media. They knew how counter-culture was transforming the face of London society – they'd read about it in the newspapers and seen it on television – and by dressing up and cavorting down King's Road, they became extras in the crowd scenes being gaped at by tourists swarming into 'the swinging city'. For working-class kids from the suburbs and students freed from the academic grind who didn't usually have a chance to perform, it was exhilarating. Streaming flagrantly but anonymously through the crowds of Chelsea on those Saturday afternoons created a sense of communion as palpable as any soldier ever felt marching in strict formation to the beat of a battalion drum.

On Carnaby Street you never quite knew what you were going to encounter. Once the police had to be called to break up a near-riot outside the window of Lady Jane, a fashionable women's boutique which had taken to using live models in their window. Garments were changed in full view of the peep-show public, many of whom had forsaken the Soho strip clubs, where they could see the whole kaboodle, to ogle young ladies in bras and panties. Everyone with a fetish, a bitch against society or a

1 Me and Gillian Watt in 1958

2 1960

3 *Glenda Jackson and Alexis Kanner in an improvised scene from the RSC Theatre of Cruelty season at LAMDA*

4 *With Thelma Holt*

5 *Shortly before the raid on Warhol's* Flesh *at the Open Space*

6 *Applying make-up to Thelma before a dress rehearsal of* A Macbeth

5

10

11

7 *Rudy Walker as Othello and
Judy Geeson as Desdemona in*
An Othello, *Open Space, 1972*

8 *Malcolm Storry as Hoss in
Sam Shepard's* The Tooth of
Crime, *Open Space, 1972*

9 *Thelma as Katherine and
Malcolm Tierney as Petrucchio in my
version of* The Shrew

10 *Peter Bayliss as Dr Watson and
Julian Glover as Holmes in the first
version of my* Sherlock's Last Case

11 *Linda Hayden and Clive Merrison
in my play* Artaud at Rodez,
Open Space, 1975

12

12 *Derek Godfrey and Prunella Scales in a scene from Frank Marcus's translation of Schnitzler's* The Affairs of Anatol

13 *Barry Stanton as Antonio and Vladek Sheybal as Shylock in my* Variations on The Merchant of Venice, *1977*

13

14 Gillian Watt
15 Gypsie Kemp
16 Julia Crosthwaite, spouse number
one, at St Pancras Town Hall,
shortly after the impulsive wedding
17 Jane Windsor, the child-bride,
in an exotic moment

delusional obsession could find a post for himself by the fountain just off Oxford Street and there harangue the passing parade.

The man behind the Carnaby Street renaissance was a dapper Glaswegian named John Stephens. After a fire destroyed all the stock in his Beak Street shop, his fraught landlord deposited him in a small storefront around the corner. That happened to be Carnaby Street. Ten years later, Stephens owned nine of the pivotal boutiques on the street, plus two clothing factories, an estate agency, a fleet of car-hire Jaguars, a vegetarian restaurant and a driving school. Stephens who, when I knew him, had the low-frequency hum of a man who had resolutely made it, allegedly approached the Westminster Council to change the name of Carnaby Street to John Stephens Street, but none of the civic burghers scampered on to the bandwagon for that one.

One of the most theatrical emporiums on the street used to be called Gear. The proprietor once explained the etymology: 'It used to refer to equipment, mainly motor apparel, then it became clothes of any sort, then fashionable clothes, and now it just means anything okay or in.' John Lennon did a lot to popularize the use of the word. Its antithesis became 'grotty' and for many people those were the only two classifications that ever existed. Having categories like 'gear' and 'grotty' made distinctions like 'good' and 'evil' obsolete.

Because Chelsea was an affluent, upper-middle-class district, many of the King's Road boppers, despite the *shlock*iness of their apparel, were extremely well off – the offspring of highly respectable professional families. Cruising suburbanites and masquerading working-class revellers never quite knew who was posh or common, 'gear' or 'grotty', and so you were never quite sure whether you were being chatted up by royalty or navvies. That added a certain spice to all encounters. As in the more fashionable plays of *avant garde* theatre, it was a matter of having to distinguish reality from illusion.

Of the indoor events, only two or three stand out: the launch of *International Times* at the Round House, the original Albert Hall Poetry Reading – memorialized in Peter Whitehead's film *Wholly Communion* – and its disastrous follow up, the New Moon Carnival of Poetry also at the Albert Hall.

The launch of *IT* (which erroneously featured a masthead

photo of Theda Bara when it should have been 'It-Girl' Clara Bow) did as much to establish the Round House as it did the new paper. For years, as Arnold Wesker's haunched white-elephant Centre 42, the building just sat there trying to create a workers' paradise with lip service from Harold Wilson and other Labour Party stalwarts. It somehow knew in its circular, tramshed bones that that was not what it was intended to be. Before long it became a ravers' mecca, the site of mind-blowing rock concerts, occasional evenings of weird theatre (Andy Warhol's *Pork* was performed there, as was Peter Brook's *The Ik*) and discovered its true identity. In the 1970s, brushed up and made respectable, it housed regional theatre companies and became merely an outsize playhouse, but its greatest days were in the mid-1960s, when it was a kind of glorified crash pad for the wild and indigent nomads that swarmed through North London.

International Times was churned out in the basement of Miles's Indica bookshop in Holborn. Right from the start, it was an amalgam of art, cultural radicalism and drug idealization that depended on regular boosts from, or articles about, William Burroughs, Allen Ginsberg *et al.* written in a style that ranged from the semi-literate to the hopelessly inane. In the first issue, I contributed a mordant critique of Peter Brook's *US*; the second gave front-page coverage to a potted version of one of Ezra Pound's pro-Fascist wartime speeches from Italy. It was obvious, juvenile, self-consciously provocative and intellectually con-temptible, but it struck a chord with the young for, whatever it was, it wasn't slick, patronizing, stuck up or predictable like the output of Fleet Street. In its coarseness, amateurism and larky anarchy it perfectly reflected the counter-culture's image of itself. For many it was enough that it *wasn't The Times*, the *Guardian* or the *Telegraph*. It was *alternative* – that was all that really mattered.

The bash at the Round House was a sensational compilation of all the elements that made UFO and other Underground clubs so joyously histrionic. There were three bands playing simul-taneously, a constant splatter of liquid slides by Mark Boyle, a whirligig made up of the beautiful, near beautiful, once beautiful, never beautiful people of London – all drawn together by a sense of the Underground consolidating its power. A newspaper, after all, was an emblem of power. It could now issue proclamations, opine on subjects of national interest, mount campaigns, promote events, evaluate the products of the mainstream as well as its own fringe evocations. All that gave the event a sense of enthronement, of a movement coming of age. If, as many believed, the Underground had arrived, *International Times* was the flag of its disposition.

In 1965, sired by Alexander Trocchi and spearheaded by poets such as Allen Ginsberg, Gregory Corso, Michael Horovitz and Simon Vinkenoog, poetry had made history at the Albert Hall. An overflow crowd of over 7,000, in one fell swoop, demolished the myth of the minuscule poetry audience. At the same time it defined, socially and artistically, much of the character that was to shape hippie Britain in the late 1960s and early 1970s.

As you entered the hall, girls with psychedelically painted faces strewed flowers into your arms. Jeff Nuttall and John Latham had populated the hall with fantastical papier-mâché creatures that added an eerie, surreal segment to the audience. On every side people were turning on and offering pot to their neighbours as if they were Polos. R. D. Laing had brought a number of schizophrenic patients from Kingsley Hall who, in their jibbering insanity, blended perfectly with the hyperactive euphoria of ostensibly normal men and women high on poetry. The Albert Hall commissionaires, many of them World War II veterans accustomed to the restrained gentility of middle-class concertgoers, stood to one side and gaped at the gallimaufry.

A clearly half-crocked Allen Ginsberg gave a poor, crabbed reading. Gregory Corso, trundling through an unsuitable autobiographical work, went on too long. Adrian Mitchell belted out his 'Tell me lies about Vietnam', which momentarily transformed the crowd into clamorous members of a political rally, the last things in the world they actually were. Harry Fainlight started a tirade against drugs which irritated Ginsberg and many of the others who, in their minds, had already made a divine synthesis between pot and poetry. Trocchi, not a born entertainer or a gifted emcee, allowed the evening to plod, lurch and halt. Bad British poets confirmed what most of us already knew, that for every Logue or Mitchell or Paddy Kavanagh, there were a hundred versifying deadbeats squabbling to don the mantle of Dylan Thomas and T. S. Eliot. The most theatrical performance of the evening was Michael Horovitz's orchestration of Kurt Schwitters's 'Sneezing Poem' with half a dozen poets snorting, *schnartzing* and kerchooing in a variety of different rhythms – all of which seemed to validate the prevailing idea of many that, indeed, the Word *was* dead and one could just as meaningfully construct a work of art out of burps, grunts, farts and sneezes as one could out of metaphors, similes and bursts of eloquent lyricism.

Like the *IT* party at the Round House, what the first Albert Hall poetry 'meet' did was to make thousands of people aware that there were thousands of people just like them – from all over Britain. That whatever it was that had transformed their world views and conditioned their idiosyncratic behaviour, there were others likewise transmogrified. They say that certain kinds of crimes inspire copy-cat versions of the same. I'm sure that the visible confirmation of the hippie lifestyle so joyously apparent on that occasion turned many borderline cases conclusively into hippies.

That bash, amply chronicled, has become part of hippie history, so I won't dwell on it. A year later there was a New Moon Carnival of Poetry in the Round at the Albert Hall – which many expected to be the jubilant successor to the jamboree of 1965. Several hundred acolytes were on hand, but the upper tiers and much of the stalls were vacant. In the middle of the great rodeo-like arena stood a kind of flowered dais with an upholstered seat in the centre. It could have been a funeral parlour where Poetry was finally to be put to rest.

The small claque from the upper balconies were invited down into the stalls and there, amidst heckling, hoots and the strident cry of cultivated English voices demanding 'fair play for foreign visitors' we sat swilling boredom for over two hours. Spike Milligan, having an off night, read witty doggerel and clowned about. Clobbered and de-energized, he couldn't be persuaded to return for an encore. Then followed a small parade of poetic contenders – solid Paddy Kavanagh losing a battle with a faulty microphone. Then Robert Graves, Odysseus-like, his white hair flaring like the Greek god he no longer was, plonking his bottom on to the Poetry throne and, after a few more microphonic mishaps, rattling off a few short items from *The Collected Works*.

The poems were small helpings of taut privacy loosed in that Buddha-bellied hall where sound systems crackled and crude *kibitzers* blew raspberries and tried to grab the limelight. Graves, gamely tackling the smouldering disorder, began to speak candidly about the difficulty of communicating to such a horde and about the rivalry and clannishness of modern poetry. Someone called out a question: 'What can we do to get more good poetry published?' Then from another part of the hall, in a voice fanged with venom, the cry: 'Write it!' Nothing in the evening quite equalled that strident moment of truth. More interruptions, assorted cat-calls and wisecracks and eventually Graves, like Milligan before him, declined to parade his genius in such a disconcerting atmosphere. Then followed an assembly line of poets, versifiers and rhymesters, dilly Dylans, maudlin Audens, half-spent Spenders and idiot Eliots. Bland, snotty-nosed Stevie Smith chanting light lyrics in the voice of a Tibetan priestess ready to give up the ghost; Adrian Mitchell, his Vietnam convictions now strained and unconvincing, taking refuge in aggression, reading fiery political verse which flashed like a firework and faded just as quickly; Jean-Jacques Lebel, French doyen of Happenings, rising to perform a sixty-second concrete poem worthy of Antonin Artaud – a horrible, rasping, spiralling rhythm which rang out like a fiery indictment against all the barrenness of the language that preceded it. Then a quasi-Happening: an unscheduled internationalist group calling itself Felen starting to chant nonsense sounds, crescendoing to a wild frenzy of rasping counterpoint. Suddenly, with the evening slipping out of the grasp of its organizers, there is a real sense of danger in the big-bellied hall. But, after a few moments, an irate emcee appears to apologize for the 'nonsense' and promises a return to the gruelling tedium of mediocre poetry amateurishly performed. Vapidity in four different languages, good-hearted bores from Finland and Holland spouting verse greetings to England. A lot of involuntary groaning from the cognoscenti. A Scot demanding that someone recite a piece of McGonagal.

A final Happening moment, a fitting punctuation mark to dead air and squelched expectations: Christopher Logue, Britain's leading showman-poet dressed in Cuban khakis and clinging to Vanessa Redgrave for the greater glory of tomorrow's newspaper headlines, singing a pro-Cuban song in Spanish – as if anyone in that audience needed persuasion about Castro or the revolution, as if the tail end of a poetry reading was the place for a damp editorial squib by what I saw as a dwarfish, superannuated egotist and a horsey, oversize actress. A *gauche* grandstand play that, somehow, was perfectly in keeping with all the other gaffs and miscalculations of the evening. (What, I wonder decades later, does old Logue think of his blue-eyed boy now, as most of Eastern Europe throws off the shackles of Communism and Fidel viciously tries to preserve an old-style Latin American dictatorship?)

Afterwards, the police having discovered a cache of petrol-soaked firebrands on the premises, the torchlight procession to Trafalgar Square was unfortunately cancelled. The entire evening unilluminated, it seemed very appropriate to go torchless into that dark night.

Depending on just how tolerant you were, many of the members of the counter-culture were either adorably or infuriatingly disorganized. Often there was almost a sense of pride in the fact that they couldn't get it together, as if a smoothly synchronized event or a thoroughly coherent project in some way violated the spirit of the times. The same was true of much of their personal behaviour. To be steadfast, reliable, responsible and efficient was somehow a violation of drug culture ethics. To be flakey, forgetful, bungling and spaced out harmonized nicely with the ooze of hashish in the bloodstream and the morning-after pot hangover. For every John Hopkins, Jeff Nuttall, Jim Haynes, Tony Elliot, Peter Roberts and Barry Miles who got their acts together, there were thousands of gormless waifs and intellectual dodos for whom the 1960s were just a great big, gorgeous blur.

15   *Continental diversions*

In 1964 I was visited in London by a towering, blond Swede named Claes Sylwander, whose second distinction (the first being that he had once been married to Ingrid Thulin) was that he was Director of the newly formed Folkteatern in Gothenburg. Sylwander, a roaring, cachinnating Viking of a man with a manner that seemed to imply that everything he was doing was part of some uproarious practical joke, wondered whether I would be interested in directing *Hamlet*.

This was a tantalizing offer, since it was my belief that all the ideas I had incorporated in the ninety-minute collage derived from the original could be ladled back to the play proper with only a minimal amount of tinkering. The desire to validate those ideas within Shakespeare's original work was irresistible and doing it in the Swedish language, which I could neither write, speak nor understand, only increased the appeal. My knowledge of Sweden itself was limited to the prevailing British clichés: sexually emancipated, socially enlightened, neurotically Nordic, etc., and the films of Ingmar Bergman, on which I had virtually been brought up.

Once I got there, I found the Swedes were a hard-drinking, astonishingly childlike people who occasionally fell into broods, but who, most of the time, conveyed a gregarious *sans souci*. This, however, was always coupled with an application to work which was in no way characteristic of the English. They were prone to speech-making and I can recall several occasions when, as a non-Swedish-speaking foreigner, I shifted aimlessly from one foot to the other while a variety of burly and beautiful blond Norsemen waxed eloquent, sometimes for twenty or thirty minutes at a crack, on subjects entirely beyond my ken. These speeches were always punctuated with great bursts of applause directed at me and I found myself having to beam appreciation for approbation the point of which thoroughly eluded me. Then everyone began swigging down drinks as if there were no tomorrow. The start of all these formal occasions was invariably stiff and self-conscious and, just as invariably, ended with women dancing on table-tops or men trying good naturedly to rape their friends' wives.

The *Hamlet*, beautifully played by Iwar Wiklander (an actor who went on to become Director of the company), was highly successful and I found myself not only returning to direct in Sweden but also being asked to stage productions in Denmark, Norway and Germany. The Norwegians had the most primitive personalities, the Danes were the most agreeable and the Swedes the most difficult to calculate either in terms of social behaviour or artistic results. The Germans, however, with whom I worked in theatres at Wiesbaden, Bochum, Stuttgart and Berlin, unquestionably had the finest actors. Their character men, great heaving barrels of inspired sweat, could knock your socks off, and their directors, although quirky and often over-dialectical, usually mustered physical productions which were astonishing in their originality and dazzling in execution.

All in all, I spent some fifteen years shuttling between *Staatsteaters* and *Schauspielhauses* all over Europe, learning first hand the ferocity of Europeans' commitment to the classics and their maniacal admiration for the works of writers such as Peter Handke, Thomas Bernhard and Botho Straus. Most of these stints lasted between ten and twelve weeks each, and while there, I seesawed between periods of engrossing creativity and paralysing melancholy. To be an anglicized American in cosy little ghetto-towns such as Trondheim or Aarhus, Bochum or Wiesbaden can be a heartbreaking experience. As much as the actors take you to their bosoms (and that was not always the case, as I shall soon explain), there remains an unbridgeable gulf between your foreignness and their cast-iron nationality. I remember running into Jonathan Miller in a Frankfurt café and immediately sensing that flailing despondency which is the mark of the British director during his off hours in an alien society. We talked vigorously for an hour or so, both of us lovingly reconstructing memories of England, feeding balm to one another for being spiritually stranded in a country where the money was irresistible and the work, often far superior to anything we ever did in the hemmed-in confines of London. He was with his interpreter, who, in a foreign country, is the tenuous link between the nationals and one's own culture, although, as we both agreed, no matter how proficient the go-betweens may be, they never make up for the sense of isolation. I vividly recall trolling through the streets of Wiesbaden with designer John Napier, trying desperately not to sink into the pit of Teutonic despondency which beckoned at the end of every rehearsal day, sensing the terrible desolation of being culturally cut off from what was natural, normal and usually taken for granted: our sense of belonging. Cruising nightmarish discos and erotic night-clubs in search of a solace which could only really be found across the Channel; artificially engendering 'fun' and conviviality with gormless men and women who related as little to our flip, British levity as we did to their harrumphing Teutonic gravity; reminding ourselves of how many days remained before dress rehearsals, before techs, before the première. It was not only our mind-dulling homesickness that made it so unbearable; it was the awareness that whatever success our work might achieve, we had landed on the other side of the moon and the moon-people that surrounded us, no matter how genial or attractive, simply were not terrestrials.

During rehearsals, strangely enough, there were no language barriers. Either the company understood my English or I their German, Danish, Norwegian and Swedish – not with a grammatical grasp of the language, but by inferring and registering the accents of their speech as they corresponded to the English text spread out before me. One listened not to the words of the foreign language but to the music of its sense (the true international language), painstakingly correlating it to the intentions of Shakespeare and Webster, Ibsen and Strindberg. Though listening studiously to a foreign language, one was constantly thinking in English and, like a vigilant conductor, detecting false notes, which the interpreter would proceed to put right in the actors' native tongue. Curiously enough, in places like Sweden and Germany, reviewers would remark upon the verbal clarity of the performances – always assuming bilingualism on my part. Although I have a fairly good comprehension of German, I haven't even a rudimentary grasp of the other languages in which I worked, and I discovered the more I did it that it was not actually necessary in order to deal with the chore at hand. Since all theatre is the crystallization of sub-text, knowledge of the text is secondary; not irrelevant, just not primary.

In the early Seventies, in an article published in the *Village Voice*, I wrote:

> The German actor has a slave mentality. He wants
> to be told what to do, where to go, what to feel,
> how to speak. The pragmatic approach common
> in England and America is not only alien to
> him, his temperament is positively opposed to it.
> If you use a loud voice and an authoritarian
> manner, you can get a German actor to do
> anything, but once you admit you 'don't know', are
> 'not sure', would like to 'play around a little', you
> are sunk. A German director, as a German
> colleague recently said to me, is a *Führer* and, if
> he isn't, then he cannot function in a German
> theatre. Recently, in Wiesbaden where I was
> directing a production of *Hamlet*, the German
> actors found my laconic New York manner rather
> uninspiring. I gained their respect only when,
> during one particularly pressurized rehearsal, I
> threw a chair at an actor's head. After that I could
> do no wrong.

The incident in question occurred during a technical rehearsal of *Hamlet* at the Wiesbaden Stadtstheater. As always in German theatres, time is meticulously monitored by the stage manager, and, on occasion, I have known them blow a whistle to indicate the end of a rehearsal period. Knowing that I was racing the clock, I was trying desperately to get through some 100 light cues in a very limited time-frame when the actor playing Claudius, a giant, rotund, tank of a man, finding his spot, began to perform the King's prayer scene. I pointed out that there was no time for running scenes as this was strictly a technical, cue-to-cue rehearsal. He shrugged off the admonishment, casually insisting it would not take very long. I reiterated that there could be no rehearsal of individual scenes as we were very hard pressed for time. He continued to drone through Claudius's words, occasionally looking up to see if he was centred in his spot. I again asked him to desist, but he remorselessly pushed on. Without any conscious decision to do so, I found myself lifting the chair on which I was sitting and hurling it towards the praying regent. It landed lamely at his knees; he turned towards me like a bull getting ready to charge and, at the same moment, I tossed aside my table and started towards him. I have no idea what I was planning to do, because he could effortlessly have torn me apart and tossed away the pieces, but some ignorant crusader deep within the shell of the gormless Jew was getting set to commit mayhem. Fortunately, a group of stalwart actors held back Claudius, and a somewhat less hardy band of production assistants did the same for me. Curses flew in German and English. I cannot report accurately on his, but they were pungent, guttural and accompanied by great spurts of froth and sputum. I, to my shame, instinctively reverted to my lower East side upbringing and saturated him in a variety of New York expletives which included such tasty epithets as 'fat, blowsy kraut-cunt' and 'motherfucking son-of-a-bitch'. Within minutes the tumult was over. He was wiping the spit off his mouth and I was calmly readjusting my chair and table. He was profusely apologetic, but not more so than I. We had both lost our heads. It had been a pressured afternoon. We were both sorry. We shook hands and got on with the rehearsal as the moments were still ticking by.

The next day I was deferred to in a way I have never known in any social or professional situation. I was beloved – there is no other word for it – beloved and respected and emulated. I could do no wrong. I could ask for whatever I wished. Had I required Ophelia to climb on the parapet and piss down into the face of Polonius, both actors would have unhesitatingly obliged. I had shown the German company that behind the laconic demeanour of this English-sounding, remote New Yorker, there was a raging lion with murderous claws, and something in them revered what they had seen.

The *Voice* article, edited down and rewritten for maximum effect, was reprinted in *Der Spiegel*, the leading West German magazine, while I was re-rehearsing a production of Edward Bond's *Early Morning* at the Schauspielhaus in Bochum. When, after the successful opening of the show, I returned to Bochum to conduct warm-up rehearsals for the resumption of the run, I was met by my harried interpreter, Frank Gunther, usually a placid young man, who acted as both dramaturg and production assistant.

'All hell has broken loose over that article,' he exclaimed with the kind of trepidation I am sure preceded the pogroms. 'The actors refuse to rehearse. They are demanding a special meeting. You must talk to them.'

It appears the criticism against German actors was taken as a personal insult by the Bochum company, the members of which, ironically, I had not even met when the article was first written. The situation was exacerbated by a second article, a larky interview I'd given to a Communist newspaper in Bochum, in which, among other things, I was quoted as saying I had come to Germany to investigate lampshade factories to see if I could track down my missing grandfather. The interview, given in a manic mood with irrepressible hilarity between myself and the journalist, was reprinted in dead earnest. I had been made out to sound like some kind of macabre, Ortonesque eccentric, taunting my hosts with thinly veiled sarcasm and sick humour.

On the day of the great confrontation, as my interpreter accurately forecast, there was a 'let's lynch the pig' atmosphere on the stage of the Schauspielhaus. Actors with whom I had had a creative and cordial relationship for eight weeks glowered at me from the wings, and even the critical success of the production of the Bond play didn't seem to mitigate their contempt.

Taking the Teutonic bull by its Teutonic horns, I decided attack was the best means of defence. I explained that the views expressed in the *Voice* article represented my true opinions, but pointed out that a great deal of favourable comment about German actors had been excised from the *Spiegel* reprint; that they were reacting to only one third of what I had written and that, if the full context were known, a much more balanced picture would have emerged. As for the sarcastic piece in the local newspaper, my interpreter, who had been present at the interview, could vouch for the fact that it had been a lighthearted meeting full of patent absurdities which had then been recorded with grim seriousness, creating an entirely misleading impression. I understood their chagrin believing, as they did, that I had stabbed them in the back, but if that had truly been the case, I certainly wouldn't have volunteered to return to work on the production. Further, I was fully entitled to express criticisms of the German system – just as they had the perfect right to disagree with them – and that in England this would fall into the category of 'fair comment'. (Silently I envisaged the broad-minded mummers of Birmingham and Nottingham valiantly defending my right to castigate them in the public prints, while a benign Actors' Equity stood by quoting Voltaire's dictum about defending to the death one's right to dissenting opinion.)

The smouldering in the company began to grow vocal. Did I think it was fair, asked one actor, to be invited to a foreign country and insult my hosts? I pointed out that it would be far more insulting to pretend to a *bonhomie* I didn't feel and, besides, a critical attitude was an essential part of work in the theatre. Hadn't actors throughout Germany expressed precisely these sentiments in canteens from Hamburg to Frankfurt, and were there not actors in this very company who, at one time or another, signified that they shared those criticisms? Another asked why I came to Germany at all, feeling as I did about German actors. I explained that elsewhere in the article the question had been fully dealt with and I had said that, if one learned how to tap their energies, German actors were the finest in the world. Also that, for me, being in Germany meant working with large, resourceful companies and doing the kind of large-scale work which was not always possible in England, where I was primarily concerned with small-scale experimental work. Then I added, because I knew it was in everyone's mind, and of course the money is very much better.

After a certain amount of desultory bitching about art and politics, Great Britain and Germany, one actor asked if I was prepared to apologize for what I had written. That made my already simmering blood begin to percolate. I said I had no intention of apologizing to anyone for anything, that I had come from London at great inconvenience and without extra pay to work on a production that I cared about and that I was now going to start work, and anyone who wished to leave would be excused, but, as for the other members of the company, would they please take up their positions for Act One and make it fast. The words were terse; the indignation unfeigned; the spectre of the returned *Führer* clearly hovered over the room. The actors immediately drifted into their positions and, in a matter of seconds, the work was progressing as if it were a perfectly ordinary rehearsal day.

I was half wanting a complete boycott, if only to prove that my original generalization had been up the creek. I wouldn't really have minded a thorough revolt which ended with my being pitched out of the theatre to the accompaniment of *Deutschland über alles*. It would have been a nice, unpredictable emotional dividend to the whole experience. Instead I got a fuliginous atmosphere full of petulance and squelched aggression segueing into an orderly resumption of routine. Significantly, after the lynch mob had dispersed, individual actors were extremely cordial and went out of their way to dissociate themselves with what one called 'the earlier childishness'. My inner self was streaked with guilt, for I recognized that the company had a real grievance and it was only their conditioned reflexes as actors which prevented them from fully expressing it. The *Führer* was silently delighted that a quick flash of the iron fist had immediately restored the proper hierarchical relationship, but the Jew in me lusted for the rebellion that never came.

In retrospect, I still believe that the root problem in the German theatre *is* the German actor and his acceptance of a system of wholesale state subsidy which relieves him of the creative tension without which first-class work cannot be done. In Britain and most places in America, an actor is hired for a job and he knows, if he doesn't make good, he may not work for a long time afterward. The show is his sole preoccupation, the main event of his life. In Germany the show is just another item in the *Spielplan*. If it works out particularly well, he may be able to land a better paid job in a larger theatre, but more than likely he is satisfied with his regular stipend, his house, his car and his security. He is not consciously using his performance as a lever for advancement. The drive of such an actor turns inevitably at a lower rate of RPMs than that of an actor whose livelihood depends on the immediate outcome of transient employment.

Against this one must set the ensemble dividend, being part

of a permanent company. But in most places in Germany this pays a very small dividend. It only counts for a great deal in a handful of companies in centres such as Berlin, Frankfurt and Hamburg. Togetherness is not in itself an artistic asset. (People are frequently together for long periods in the tattiest fortnightly reps without appreciably elevating standards.) The value of permanence is that some kind of artistic cohesion welds together a collective instrument. But, if the actor's attitude is not collective, if it is opportunistic or complacent, the physical togetherness does not automatically produce group quality.

More than anything else the German temperament has to be rejigged so that the onus for creative endeavour is on the actors instead of the régisseur, which means reversing the trend of the past 150 years. In the Sixties and early Seventies, when *Mitbestimung* was all the rage, a communal approach was tried by Peter Palitzch in Stuttgart, at Theater-am-Thurm in Frankfurt and in other ensembles within the repertory system – but not with marked success. Many theatre workers look back on this period as the 'bad old days' and the restoration of centralized authority as a return to an era of good feeling.

Most of my Continental diversions were in Norway and, when I look back on them, they all blend into a phantasmagoria of hideously decorated first-class hotels, 20° below temperatures and an atmosphere of bitter internecine struggle between actors' unions, directors and dramaturgs. This happened to be representative of cities such as Oslo and Bergen in the late 1970s and early 1980s, when there was fierce discontent with Intendants such as Toralv Maurstad, Sven Henning and Svetil Bang-Hansen, who, in alienating the members of their companies, often became victims to a bunker-like mentality and, in consequence, produced fractured and perishable work.

The most satisfying Norwegian experience was unquestionably Bergen in 1976, when I presented a collage version of *Hedda Gabler* at the Ibsen centennial celebrations and subsequently transferred the production to the National Theatre in Oslo. What made this so memorable was the willing transformation of a group of routinized Bergen actors into a crack squad ready and willing to assemble a highly experimental product. The collage took bits and pieces of Ibsen's text and radically restructured them, creating a kind of surrealist version of the events of the play as filtered through the sensibility of the central character. In preparing it, it was necessary to involve the company in games, improvisations and acting exercises, all of which were totally alien to their background and, I suspect, their temperaments. To their everlasting credit, the company jumped in the deep end, giving themselves to the wild heterodoxy of those games and improvisations, and creating a stunning ensemble result. Janne Hoff Brekke, a twenty-eight-year-old actress (exactly the age that Hedda ought to be), produced a haunting, dreamlike performance, and dramaturg Liv Schoyen was invaluable in recementing the pieces of the original (not to mention the more fractured members of the acting company) into a working whole. The Norwegian audiences, particularly in Oslo, immediately responded to the fragments of Ibsen's play in the new dispensation and clearly appreciated the rupture with the Ibsen tradition that the collage represented.

A year or so later I returned to the National Theatre to present a similarly restructured *Enemy of the People*. By this time the reverberations of the *Hedda* experiment had been assimilated by both the public and the press, and I found my tampering with the works of the Nordic master surprisingly acceptable. The Ibsen tradition in Norway, like the Shakespeare tradition in England, is rigorously upheld by academics and theatre professionals – although the average playgoer seems quite willing to chuck it aside. I've no doubt that within the next two decades we will see the kinds of radicalizations of Ibsen that we have now become accustomed to with Shakespeare.

When I think back to my Norwegian visits, it isn't to the plays and the players so much as it is to the sights, sounds and smells of Norway itself. The Norwegians have a standing love affair with Nature (the word is always capitalized when they pronounce it) and their idea of bliss is a thirty-mile hike around fjords or a cross-country ski through forests, preferably when the winds are sharp and the snow frozen on the ground. When, around May or June, the all enveloping darkness of winter disappears, the Norwegians are ebulliently reborn. A gambol down Carl Johan

Street with the sun bouncing off the statues of Henrik Ibsen and Bjornstjerne Bjornson (stationed like ancient tribunes outside the National Theatre, keeping virtue in and licentiousness out) and that endless procession of blue-eyed blondes, each more astonishingly beautiful than the last, is a sight that cannot be surpassed in any city in Europe.

Being a small country, Norway has a visible society that carouses and cavorts within very fixed parameters. A visit to a theatre like the Oslo New to see a traditional comedian like Rolf Juster makes one vividly aware of the cultural commonality that exists between artists and members of the public. There is no clear-cut separation. Art consists of observed foibles and idiosyncrasies that everyone recognizes from their own personal lives, and going to the theatre is as natural as going to the Tivoli after the performance or to the Grand Café for a morning coffee (a journey Ibsen himself used to make with punctilious regularity). The public's appreciation of Ibsen is refreshingly non-academic. He speaks their language and they speak his; indeed, many Ibsenic phrases have worked their way permanently into Norwegian parlance. As with Strindberg in Sweden and less so Shakespeare in England, these are not 'classics', but culturally integrated artifacts as familiar as the implements one finds in one's kitchen.

It is not being patronizing to say that it is in many ways a simpler society than that of London or New York – simple in that there are fewer factors to juggle or assimilate. You see the same faces, you read the same papers, you discuss the same topics, you experience Norwegianness in a way that it cannot be said that New Yorkers or Angelinos experience Americana. The customs and the history of the country are more recent, therefore less taken for granted. Despite the existence of two separate languages (New Norwegian and Rixmoll), the population is unified by their history and their culture, and their characters have been formed by climate, politics and social circumstance. It is a copeable society and does not create that sense of imposing vastness and corresponding alienation that you often get in bustling megatropolises.

It is also somewhat romanticized for me because of the relationships (both amiable and amorous) which have been hatched over a period of some fifteen years. The best way to fall in love with a city is to experience it through a series of love affairs. Norway will always be half a dozen people who have entwined themselves round my soul – a geography of the heart that encompasses all latitudes and longitudes, and ignites vivid memories of women sprawled upon hearth rugs before a roaring fireplace or hurrying over cobblestoned streets drenched in rainstorms.

16   *Wearing two hats*

Wolf Heider was a gaunt, hollow-cheeked, Swiss intellectual with rotten teeth and a vast knowledge of French and German drama. He had a wide forehead and a swish of black hair that started at the brow and then zippered back into a wide v like a crow unexpectedly spreading his wings. It was the kind of a head that cried out to be set on a plinth.

I first met him in New York in the early Fifties, when I was still in high school, recommended by a friend of my sister's who told me he was creating a magazine to be called *International Theater*. He had a vast, cluttered office in a brownstone in the East Fifties and, when I was ushered in, he was having a painful conversation with a woman in London, whom I later learned was his betrothed. (She eventually threw him over for some flashy West End director and even from her picture, which was prominent on the mantelpiece, I could see she wasn't the sort of woman to appreciate the intellectual refinements of her sensitive Swiss beau.)

I explained that I was really a director (although at fifteen I wasn't really anything except a disgruntled schoolboy), but that I needed a job and thought I could write. He asked to see some work. All I had was a longish essay on William Schwenk Gilbert, which I had written as a high school thesis. I proffered that and was told to return the next day.

That night I dreamed Brooks Atkinson, New York's leading drama critic, had fallen from the roof of the *Times* building and I had been offered his post, which for reasons I cannot remember, I declined. The next day, when I returned to Heider's office, I was told I would be taken on to the massive and imposing masthead of *International Theater* magazine and that my salary would be a massive $20 a week. I thanked Mr Heider, suppressing the knowledge that this was below the legal minimum wage, and told him I would try to be worthy of this, my first appointment. Whereupon he showed me the dummy of the new magazine and the cover which contained a poignant photo of a chalk-faced

Jean-Louis Barrault as the mime in *Children of Paradise*. 'This is Barrault,' I was told, noting down in my pad the letters B-A-R-O, 'and we are devoting most of our first issue to the French theatre.' I was shown stills from French plays, exhorted to read about Jacques Coupeau and Louis Jouvet, assured that the French theatre was the finest in the world and that *International Theater* (as it was to be titled) would be the first and foremost journal of the theatrical world, bringing together correspondents from theatre capitals throughout Europe and America.

When I got home that day, I conveyed my second-hand enthusiasms about Barrault, Jouvet and Coupeau to my mother, who was more concerned with the escalating price of butter at the Essex Street market. Her indifference to my reports suddenly made me aware that I had infiltrated some bright new world of culture beyond the comprehension of other mortals, and this knowledge preserved me through the rest of the week (a week, I might add, noticeably short on butter).

One morning after about three weeks of dutiful attendance at the offices of *International Theater*, I trudged up the stairs of the large brownstone building which housed the magazine and found the door locked. Heider, looking even more gaunt and hollow cheeked than usual, was sitting on the stairs. He always had a marked inclination towards the tragic demeanour and on this particular morning looked more woebegone than usual.

'We are locked out,' he said, 'and they have confiscated all the furniture, all the filing cabinets, all my manuscripts.'

It appeared that, although *International Theater* magazine was to be the first and foremost journal of its kind, the landlady of the house in which this cultural phenomenon was shaping itself refused to let offices without payment of rent.

'Don't be downhearted,' said Heider more to himself than me, 'I am sure we will be back in production within twenty-four hours.'

In fact, it was closer to twenty-four days, during which nothing was heard of Heider or the magazine. My family, advised of recent events, tongue-lashed me for wasting my time on '*ti-yater narishkeit*' (foolish playacting) and volunteered the information that the Essex Street market was looking for apprentice packers. My secret acquisition from Heider, that rich and efficacious world peopled with Jouvet, Barrault and all the other great artists who had now begun to populate my imagination, was impregnable against the onslaught of Yiddish sarcasm and so, when a few weeks later, Heider summoned me to the Beaux Arts Hotel in the East Forties, I quickly answered the call.

'*International Theater* magazine lives!' he announced with an unfortunate smile which revealed the hopelessly corroded state of his upper and lower incisors. 'I have managed to arrange credit. We will work, live and eat at the hotel and continue to prepare the first issue.'

By some alchemy, the secret of which only Heider knew, he had persuaded the hotel to extend an endless supply of credit. Salaries, of course, were not possible, but lunches in the vast dining-room were free and elegant work quarters in a suite of rooms generously laid on. I, and about five stalwarts, all working without salary, rejoined Heider and continued to prepare for the first issue. Every day each of us as penniless as the other and Heider more penniless than all trooped into the resplendent dining-room and ate like royalty. Wine flowed like a newly opened tributary of the nearby East River. On particularly buoyant days, champagne passed from hand to hand and total strangers from adjoining tables were invited to join the festivities. Then, one morning, after about three months of gastronomic jubilees, the hotel bounced Heider and his filing cabinets, informed him that court action would follow hard upon, and that they had recently discovered he was a notorious *persona non grata*, officially banned by the American Hotel Association.

'We are only weeks away from the first issue,' Heider said valiantly to a disgruntled staff stowing ham sandwiches into their briefcases. 'This misunderstanding will be cleared up in twenty-four hours. We must continue to work. Whose apartment is large enough to take the filing cabinets?'

To cut a long and event-filled story short, the first issue of *International Theater* magazine did eventually come out. Two years later it was followed by the second issue which, because Heider had become enamoured with her, featured Mai Zetterling both on the front and back covers, and then the magazine disappeared like the hobgoblin it surely was. Heider begged and borrowed his way to France, where he died of paralysis – very sick and very broke – but with a new set of teeth which a Swiss benefactor had provided during one of Heider's more brilliant sales pitches on the Continent.

I dwell on Wolfgang Heider and his ill-starred publication because, for me, it was an introduction into an almost fabled world of culture. Under his instigation, I read Wilde's *Critic as Artist* and went on to read Hazlitt, Pater, Arnold, Shaw, Beerbohm and Craig. Heider, who was not a charlatan, but one of those helpless aesthetes who cannot believe the world will not make a place for the artist, carried with him a long and well-sinewed European tradition. He was a serious, if not brilliant, critic and he infected all of us with the importance of criticism as an act, perhaps the highest act, of the civilized mind. 'You must respect what you profess to love,' he always used to say, and for him theatre was the great love, and writing about it with care and consideration the mark of respect. When I think back to the principles which gradually spawned my desire to write criticism, I find that, in almost every case, they stem from something I discussed with Heider or he had encouraged me to read.

In New York, in the mid-Fifties, it was that sense of 'trying to tell it how it is' that took me to the *Village Voice*, when that publication was just forming. Jerry Tallmer, its editor and leading critic, an astute, dialectical writer with a strong, independent viewpoint, threw a few off-Broadway tidbits my way and, before long, I was contributing regularly – climbing the backstairs of East side firetraps and refurbished West side cellars to chronicle the start of off-Broadway theatre. When I got to London, as mentioned, I made a bee-line to *Encore* magazine and found a kind of aesthetic euphoria in seeing my pieces printed in a magazine crackling with social and political concern, being read by a small, intellectual elite assiduously trying to change theatrical perceptions in England. Eventually, I wrote on a fairly regular basis for *Plays and Players* magazine, conscious always that my voice sounded too strident and insistent when directed to that more sedate, mainstream readership for whom the real harvest was the rich plums of Shaftesbury Avenue. Throughout the 1960s and 1970s, I was regularly lodging reviews from London for the *Village Voice* and the *New York Times*, feeling simultaneously like a war correspondent and a combatant pitching grenades at detestable enemy encampments, and then scurrying out in time to fire off dispatches about the course of the battle. Often I was using drama criticism to catch the overflow of the energy I was pumping into theatrical work in which I was now regularly involved.

When asked how I could reconcile directing plays with writing reviews, I always answered that they were two different expressions of the same creative impulse and I never experienced any conflict of interests. This never satisfied my professional colleagues, who staunchly believed that one was either in the kitchen or the dining-room, but not in both places at the same time. I concurred with Brendan Behan's observation that critics were often like eunuchs in a harem: 'They know how it's done, they've seen it done every day, but they're unable to do it themselves.' To avoid the pitfalls of that kind of voyeurism I believe a practical theatre-worker often makes the best critic. It certainly toned up the criticism of people like Harley Granville-Barker, Jacques Coupeau, George Bernard Shaw, Stark Young, Eric Bentley, Harold Clurman and Robert Brustein.

Wearing two hats often made it difficult to maintain professional relations with actors and other directors, although I never had any trouble with fellow critics – even when, as was often the case, I was subjected to their heavy fire in reviews of my own work. One directed plays, one invited critics, one's work was assessed; one then critically assessed the reviews – that was the nature of the hydra-headed beast the theatre was. Of course, it was more satisfying to be liked than disliked, but being disliked, even battered and bruised, was part of the contract to which one had agreed by working in the theatre in the first place. It wasn't masochism, but an acceptance of the fact that art triggers off powerful reactions pro and con, and so it was the most natural thing in the world to live in a climate of differing opinions. It wasn't until many years later that I came to realize that there was a profound distinction to be drawn between differences of opinion and contrasting world views. If everyone accepts the same criteria, being reviewed badly is something that one can live with, no matter how heavy the abuse. But, when one rejects the fundamental aesthetic principles behind certain people's taste, the philosophical framework in which they live their lives and view the world, it is necessary to shift ground or close up shop. That was to happen to me a couple of decades down the line.

Mingling with them in the same radio studios, often attending the same openings and finding oneself often lumped together with them in the public's mind, I came to know many of the English critics better than I would if only occasionally drawing their fire. And, of course, being fascinated with criticism, I tended to read them assiduously. Some of them, like Irving Wardle, for many years the critic of the London *Times* (now with *The Independent on Sunday*), even became good friends.

When I first met Irving, he was writing for the *Times Educational Supplement*, in which capacity he attended some of my early acting classes. We were thrown together again through *Encore* and the creation of the Open Space, whose productions he reviewed fairly regularly. In fact, when I was trying to conjure up autobiographical works from British writers, we managed to get a surprising little play out of him entitled *The Houseboy*, which I directed at the Space. It was fascinating to see Irving's critical equipment applied to his own work, that same sense of almost disinterested analytical integrity chopping, changing and rethinking material which, though strongly personal, was treated with almost surgical impersonality.

When you first meet Irving, you find a sheepish, shy, almost dithery person, fearful of giving offence, of being misunderstood, of hurting people's feelings, someone in a paroxysm of social tension. I have always thought of this as the Hugh Herbert version of Irving. (Herbert, you may recall, was a 1930s and 1940s American film comedian whose speciality was fluttery inconclusiveness and who was constantly pressing his fingertips together and nervously emitting, 'Woo, woos', to all and sundry.) But, behind this social guise is a steel-trap mind and the rigour of a Jacobean revenger, a Bogart, if you like, who is the very antithesis of a Hugh Herbert. It is as if the genteel Irving and the tough-minded cynic are constantly at odds with one another, and the review is the battleground which reconciles those opposing forces. There is a strong predisposition to avoid cruelty in Irving, which often manifests itself in those oblique and circuitous reviews where you feel the critic is trying to elude the snapping jaws of angry hounds yelping at his feet. Occasionally he becomes a set of snapping jaws himself, but, instead of drawing blood, he rounds you into a corner and immobilizes you by merely showing his fangs.

A poor critic is constantly blowing kisses or kicking your ass; a judicious critic knows that, after having been aloof and even withdrawn, the touch of his hand on your shoulder is stronger than a bear-hug or a wet kiss on the mouth. This, it seems to me, is Wardle's great strength: his ability to shuttle effortlessly between being glacially unimpressed and eloquently appreciative.

In the great critics, tone is everything. Beerbohm made a witty, aristocratically fluent noise that personified his dry, hierarchical attitude to art. Shaw grumbled, barked and occasionally spat fire, Tynan seduced you with a telling combination of acridity and passion – now canonizing, now excommunicating. Wardle maintains an evenness of tone which, because it is so delicately balanced, speaks volumes when it moves one decibel higher or lower. For some, it is a voice without flash or furbelow. I have heard him described as an 'anonymous critic', but for those who can appreciate the subtle accents of that probing diction, that unhurried motion which moves like a parabola from the play to its perception and then back again, there is no voice quite like it in British criticism.

I would often have him more pesky and less controlled, more prone to barometrical shifts, more given to spasms, but over the years, as many newer critics have fulminated and caterwauled, tap danced on the head of a pin or done somersaults over trivia, I've come to appreciate the steady warble of Wardle.

It is a tone of voice very different from Harold Hobson's, for instance, who was often a sucker for the exotic – whether in a baroque actress such as Edwige Feuillère or a flashy revival of a Shakespearian classic. Often hoodwinked and just as often reversing ill-considered judgements, Hobson was a constant aggravation during the 1960s and 1970s. Personally, he was an adorable man and I was sickened to hear that in his old age he has not been given the kind of comfort and consideration which his many years of faithful service entitle him to; but, intellectually, he did a great deal of harm to theatrical taste in the second half of the century and allowed many shoddy and insubstantial works to survive and flourish. In many ways it worked to his advantage to be regularly contrasted with Tynan in the *Observer*. It was probably useful to have a steady intelligence defending the traditional and the sentimental while, a few streets away, a petulant critic was forcibly casting those same beloved relics into the bonfire. Hobson's most remarkable review was his appreciation of Beckett's *Happy Days*, which he saw as an ecomium to the human spirit and its ability to persevere through the worst that life could inflict. Hobson, a Christian Scientist, had the ability to take Beckett's grim little essays on the futility of existence and turn them into valentines to the human race. Though misleading and misguided, it was nevertheless an impressive example of legerdemain.

Milton Shulman, who wrote (and still writes) for the *Evening Standard*, had a much lower cast of mind than Hobson and his reviews, written in a prose so pedestrian they felt like he dallied at every zebra crossing and never contemplated any means of locomotion faster than a Hansom cab, were suffused with the ordinariness of quotidien journalism. Michael Billington at the *Guardian* was one of the few critics who actually gave way to enthusiasm instead of making those grudging shrugs of tortured approval which so often pass for it among the more cerebral critics. Also, it was always reassuring to read a critic who could allude to a well-stocked frame of reference. Even when the reader lacks the evidence for all his examples, it inspires confidence to know that the writer has them. Like many critics, Billington occasionally writes himself into a set of beliefs that do not correspond with aesthetic realities – which is not simply a fancy way of saying I often disagree with him. There are critics who are often guided by their literary skills rather than by their artistic sensibilities and cannot quite jibe one with the other. Here, Wardle was always unique in that one felt his notices were the exact equivalent of the sensory truth the play had evoked in the man. I often disagreed with him, but could never fault that perfect correlation of reaction and expression which made his best columns gems of personal communication.

Of course, the trouble with almost all drama critics is that they tend to be spawned by the Fifth Estate and one feels the theatre is merely their 'beat'. In overestimating their responsibility to the readers and accepting the intellectual shortcuts enforced upon them by deadlines, they rarely delve very deeply into the aesthetic morass which is the artist's element. In being a kind of especially appointed Everyman for the general public, they eschew any responsibilities as specialists. Tipster, auctioneer, shopping guide, marker of scorecards, only one in a hundred ever transcends the reviewing stand mentality that distinguishes a Beerbohm or a Shaw, a Tynan or a Brustein.

When I left England, I more or less forsook criticism as a regular occupation, although I wrote occasional reviews for *The Times* and the *Guardian* from California, and always enjoyed the intellectual discipline of refining a jumble of often contradictory feelings into a prescribed square of reasoned equilibrium. The critic's voice, I've always felt, is what rounds out the theatrical experience and makes it whole. Sometimes, it is the crowning touch, especially where the critic's insights are superior to the artist's and are able to imply an artifact grander, deeper and more perfect than the flawed specimen under analysis.

Wearing two hats went further than doffing the director's beret and pulling on the first-nighter's topper. There was also a dichotomy in the kinds of theatre in which I was involved and in my own conception of what theatre should be, as opposed to what it was.

Like most New Yorkers who had grown up during the Thirties and Forties, I had been weaned on Broadway mythology. When I started work in the theatre, I fancied myself part of that band of fabled troupers that inhabited films such as *42nd Street, Ziegfeld Follies, Strike Up the Band, All About Eve* and others – films that glorified the traditions of show business which, from the very first moment the movies learned to talk, romanticized the ritual of putting on shows.

But in the Fifties, when a certain kind of new consciousness began to bud, when I had begun to inculcate the countermythologies of Stanislavsky, Brecht and Artaud, I was gradually seduced into a theatre which was the antithesis of show business: a theatre not setting out to reassure but to disconcert. But this was almost always a minority occupation, a rarefied refinement of what the theatre could be when it was most pure, most idealistic, most uncompromising. As time went on, I shuttled regularly between the viable commodities of show business and the unattainable goals of art, often rationalizing the time and energy I gave to the former for the sake of pursuing the latter. But it never became an either-or situation. One was continually to-ing and fro-ing between new plays, revivals, comedies, farces and the demands of strenuous experimental work which asked for one's finest perception and most imaginative efforts.

To the outside world, to friends and relatives, I was in the same business that produced the glittering wares of the West End or the somewhat more frugal commodities of the fringe – both essentially outposts of show business. In my own mind, I was committed to a much more demanding and abstruse Muse whose ideology was dead set against the notion of commodities for mass consumption and who encouraged an almost total immersion in process. But without subsidy, without permanence, without continuity, that Muse could only be served fitfully – in between efforts to survive – and so, work in the theatre meant constantly being yoked between two horses galloping in opposite directions.

As much as my temperament was drawn to the more demanding aesthetic, I must confess that the weakness for show business never entirely expired. Putting on a show, as opposed to dredging one's sensibility in order to express the inexpressible through new and unconventional means, remained a constant lure and when, in the Eighties the ground for experimental work was cut out from under me, I gravitated with alarming alacrity into the commission of conventionally crafted comedies. For me, comedy was always the highest and most unattainable goal. I firmly believed that one *Importance of Being Earnest* was worth half-a-dozen *Master Builders* and that there was nothing in Sophocles, Dryden, Webster or Tourneur which could not stand head and shoulders with Congreve, Wycherley, Kaufman or Hart. Purgation through pity and terror was a commendable aesthetic goal, but it could not begin to compare with the catharsis achieved by half a dozen really thundering belly-laughs.

To many, such a diversion seemed an appalling *volte-face*, but the fact is the two brigades, art and show business, are always marching in parallel ranks and it is the worst kind of snobbism to assume high-definition performance and creative ingenuity are the birthright of one and not the other. Ironically, there is more innovation in the American musical, for instance, than the work of most standardized experimental groups in England or the Continent, and when the tallies are in, it is very likely that Bob Fosse and Michael Bennett will be found to have advanced theatrical form further than Peter Brook or Peter Stein.

It was also hard to reconcile the contradiction that the most ambitious work was often being tried by the people least equipped to tackle it; a paradox addressed by Eric Bentley in the 1950s when he wrote: 'If the professional theatre fails because it is commercial, the non-commercial theatre fails because it is non-professional. A professional, by definition, has a trained talent, amateurs have ideals which are much less entertaining. Nor, for all the claptrap about simplicity and the dangers of too much scenery, is lack of money a recommendation.'

The commercial theatre, because it could afford it, employed the best talents, often in the commission of the most deplorable work. The non-commercial theatre, because it could not afford otherwise, regularly utilized inadequate talents to achieve aims which only the most skilful actors could accomplish. As one slogged away in the non-commercial theatre, it was always with an envy for the more resourceful artists who, for financial reasons, absented themselves from that arena. If embroiled in the commercial theatre, it was invariably with a disdain for the ephemera on which first class artists tended to squander their talents. As a result, my desire to work with the best often inclined me into that sphere which, on principle, I found the most contemptible – armed always with the rationalization that I could change the nature of the beast. The result of that was a schizoid attitude to my own status as an artist; experimentalist by instinct, traditionalist by necessity; advocate of the off-beat, the *avant-garde* and the untried – and yet a secret admirer of the best being produced within the established convention.

It was probably for this reason that criticism became an intellectual obsession – a way of defining not only one's own identity, but the changing identities of a theatre which indiscriminately commingled the elegant and the vulgar, the rarefied and the commonplace, the revolutionary and the tried-and-true.

There was a purity in criticism which was not to be found in the practical work of the theatre. It was a little like the difference between being a church theologian and a country parson.

Many thoughtful people believe the reflective life is superior to a life of action. Although retiring to a monastery and contemplating the mysteries of the universe would be alien to my character, I can easily visualize retiring from direction and spending my days reflecting on the work of the stage. It often happens in the history of theatre that, at certain periods, the exhortative voice of the visionary critic is more important and ultimately more influential, than the strident cries of the director trying to achieve pace or the whines of actors labouring to give birth to yet another banal offspring.

17   *Some literary encounters*

Peter Barnes, when I knew him, was a short, scowly man with a Cockney accent which refused to be camouflaged by the prissy academic tone forcibly imposed upon it. He wrote scorching little plays animated by malice and spite in which comedy and cruelty would regularly copulate. They revealed a palsied, Jonsonian view of humanity without a smidgen of sentimentality and were unredeemed by warmth or sympathy. They were often crudely funny, but, even when they weren't funny, the crudeness had a lively Rabelaisian zest about them which made you snicker even when it didn't make you laugh.

I directed the first of Peter's plays to see the light of day. It was called *Sclerosis* and provided a savage glimpse of the British Army torturing prisoners in Cyprus. It was premièred at the Traverse Theatre in Edinburgh and was brought down to the Aldwych for a special Sunday night performance, at which it was given a rough ride by some army veterans in the audience. In Edinburgh it was made memorable by the fact that one of the actors, a rough, portly Welshman, had developed an irrational *animus* against one of the London members of the cast, a wispy, physically slight, young Cockney, and regularly took swipes at him for no apparent reason – all of which charged the dressing-room with rather more drama than the stage.

For many months I had been touting *Clap Hands Here Comes Charlie*, a raucous comedy about a liberal couple that live to regret adopting an anarchic homeless vagrant, which got as far as discussions with Jason Robards for a Broadway production. When I started the Open Space, I staged *Leonardo's Last Supper*, a black comedy in which da Vinci, miraculously resuscitated, is again promptly put to death because the world is just not yet capable of living with him. This was followed by *Noonday Demons*, which bore a striking resemblance to a surrealist film by Buñuel. In between all of this, I honed and hawked Peter's 'big' play, *The Ruling Class*, trying to get it both cast and produced. It was finally accepted by Stuart Burge for the Nottingham Playhouse at precisely the same time that my production of *Fortune and Men's Eyes* was transferring from the Open Space to the Comedy Theatre in the West End. Despite the love and labour I had lavished on the play, I had to relinquish it for the sake of my own theatre – for which, I do not think, Peter ever forgave me. In 1980 I directed *Laughter* at the Royal Court, Peter's calculated affront to Jewish survivors, set in the bureaucratic environs of Auschwitz. After that, I never saw him again.

In those halcyon Sixties, however, Peter and I were what you might call 'an item'. We often double-dated: he with his scatty Viennese wife, Charlotte, and I with Gillian Watt, a resplendent English rose who, though we never tied any knot, was virtually 'the spouse' for the first seven years of my stay in London. Every opportunity I could find (and being a critic, journalist and broadcaster, they were numerous), I championed Peter as a coming playwright and tried to make people aware that he deserved attention and encouragement. We spent interminable hours in coffee shops around the British Museum, recollecting old movies and movie actors, discussing the parlous state of the British theatre and the pomposity of its leading lights and, with withering cynicism, mounted deadly critiques of politics, culture and art. We liked each other, saw a lot of each other, fostered each other's image of ourselves and, on those occasions when I could get them on, collaborated on his plays.

During the run of *Leonardo's Last Supper* and *Noonday Demons* at the Open Space, John Cater, one of the actors, after rehearsing the two-hander for several weeks (Joe Melia was the second actor), felt unable to continue. This created an immense problem for us, as we were just on the brink of opening, and in a two-character play, if you remove fifty per cent of the cast, you virtually dismantle the entire production. Although it was never made clear why, Cater left the show and we were obliged to replace him quickly with another actor. Once we had got into the previews and the show was about to open, some indefinable sea-change took place in Peter. He had become very angry with me. I never knew why and cannot explain it to this day. Suddenly, our relations became irremediably soured. Theatrical disasters, of course, have a way of positively dismantling relationships which, before openings, seem to be forged in hoops of steel, but the play's reception was good on the whole, so I don't think it could have been that. It didn't make future collaboration entirely untenable, because a few years later I directed *Laughter* at the Royal Court.

Given the number of bridges I have deliberately torched myself and the number of friendships I have dramatically flushed down the drain, it has always bothered me that I could not account for the severance of my relationship with Peter. No doubt I was guilty of some unforgivable transgression, but I cannot for the life of me tell you what it was. I know I spent many years proselytizing his work and gaining entrées for him which he couldn't effect himself – even to the extent of introducing him to managements that eventually staged his work – but I have philosophically accepted the fact that some dark and nullifying crime had been committed and that was that.

Harold Pinter was one of those writers put under protective custody by *Encore*. After the disastrous press reception of *The Birthday Party* at the Lyric, Hammersmith, in 1958, the magazine, unfazed by critical put-downs, published the play and for many issues thereafter insistently beat the drums for the new play-wright. *That* Harold, struggling, put upon, slightly paranoid, was a very different creature from the Pinter that emerged in the early and mid-1960s, when the entire critical establishment had begun to deify him and films like Joe Losey's *Accident* and *The Servant* had given him the kind of extra dimension that only film success can confer.

In those days I tended to think of him as the British counterpart to a lower East side *macher*, a bit of a wide boy from the working-class districts of Hackney (where his father had been a tailor) hacking his way out of the slums into a brighter, more socially lustrous world. (In one sense, the 'wide boy' always remained sequestered within him – like an unquenchable Mick from *The Caretaker*, shadowing the upward mobility of the bur-geoning cosmopolitan.) Like Beckett and many of the other mislabelled Absurdists, Harold was exploring that rich wilderness of suppressed desires and subterranean power drives which were barely touched upon in the works of the drawing-room playwrights who, in the 1950s, seemed to be wholly mesmerized by surface glitter. A few years later, while cosmonauts were pointlessly exploring outer space, Pinter, like Ionesco, Genet and Arrabal, was conducting fascinating archaeological expeditions into interior realities, and one knew instinctively that, in the long run, those discoveries would be vastly more significant.

In the late 1950s and early 1960s David Baron (Pinter's stage name) was still very much in evidence, although as we got further and further into the decade, he would recede almost to invisibility. (Even when Harold Pinter-Writer agreed to employ Harold Pinter-Actor, David Baron, barnstormer with Anew McMaster and zealous rep *tummler*, had been entirely deracinated.) He had many of the qualities one associated with the professional British actor of his period: attractive, well spoken, casual but forceful, even natty, in a kind of reserved Pop English fashion. When he spoke to you, his eyes would work over your face like an ophthalmoscope. It was a look that tacitly challenged you to be as honest and direct as he was. His dealings with people were free of the ambiguity which permeated his work. He set great store on 'the unrehearsed response' and had neither the knack nor the inclination to mince matters. One of his close acting associates said of him, 'Harold can't bear not to be confronted with the truth of an action', a trait that sometimes turned to bluntness and occasionally arrogance. He was very choosy about the assignments he accepted. Many of the things that came along, as he put it, 'just weren't me'. For Harold, all writing was part of a universal collective effort called 'the pursuit of literature' and he was zealously concerned with that at all times. He was frequently a behind-the-scenes booster of new talent: an early champion of Joe Orton (*Ruffian on the Stair* is, in many ways, unsalvageably Pinteresque) and Heathcote Williams, whose first play *The Local Stigmatic* was written as a piece of direct effrontery to *The Caretaker*.

Harold's terror of explicitness may have derived from Beckett, who was an early and centrifugal influence, as was his almost neurotic avoidance of interviews and reluctance to explain intentions, an attitude which seemed natural to Beckett, but somewhat put on by Harold. 'The desire for verification is understandable,' he wrote in an early programme note, but cannot always be satisfied. There are no hard distinctions between what is real and what is unreal, nor between what is true and what false. The assumption that to verify what has happened and what is happening presents few problems I take to be inaccurate. A character on the stage who can present no convincing argument or information as to his past experiences, his present behaviour or his aspirations, not give a comprehensive analysis of his motives, is as legitimate and as worthy of attention as one who, alarmingly, can do all these things. The more acute the experience, the less articulate its expression.

The tell-tale word here is 'alarmingly'. For Harold, to be wholly conscious of whys and wherefores was to create a finitude about life which ran against its very grain.

This was the early Pinter, the man for whom ambiguity and human mystery were something so sacrosanct that the writer had to respect those qualities in his characters by refusing to acknowledge even the little *he* knew about them. The other pitfall was, of course, sentimentality and this had to be avoided at all costs. 'I'm against all propaganda,' he once said, 'even propaganda for life.' At the height of the controversy about Britain entering the Common Market, Pinter, in replying to a questionnaire, wrote the shortest reply on record: 'I have no interest in the matter and do not care what happens.' Although, in the 1980s, with a new-found concern for political injustice and the practice of torture in totalitarian societies, he appeared to shift his position, it is disputable whether the work ever entirely did.

I remember a meeting with him shortly after he had finished *The Caretaker*. Speaking with the relish of an engineer who had drafted a faultless blueprint, he described to me the events of the play. Although I followed every word, I couldn't begin to understand what he was talking about and asked him to say very simply and in a few words what the play was about. A wounded look came over his face, as if I had asked him to betray some inviolable writer's trust. 'Well, it's about love ... about this house ... these people ... You'll have to read it!'

To his closest friends there was never anything arcane or forbidding about him. He enjoyed a pint in the local and had a keen appreciation of cricket, and when, in 1972, he was voted one of the ten best dressed men in England, was naïvely delighted. (Harold's meticulousness about male attire I always took to be an extension of his private obsession with reputation. It doesn't take much of a Freudian to see the connection between the two.) 'He's just a perfectly normal bloke,' said Henry Woolf, an actor friend of long standing. 'He's not one of these fellows who plays at being a writer. He just gets on with the job.' While Woolf was in New York acting in *The Marat/Sade*, Pinter paid for a private printing of his friend's poetry and had it sent to him. It is also characteristic that, being 3,000 miles away, he did not have to be on the receiving end of his friend's gratitude.

On the week in 1960 when *The Caretaker* opened in London everyone's attention was riveted upon the Royal Court where Ionesco's newest play *Rhinoceros* was about to be given a stellar production by Orson Welles with Laurence Olivier and Joan Plowright in the leads. If anyone thought of Pinter at all that week, it was with sympathy that he should be opening against such formidable competition. But one week later, while most reviewers were lamenting the fact that Ionesco had written himself into a cul-de-sac, words like 'masterpiece' were being showered on Harold's murky, three-character play about a victimized tramp who was trying to get to Sidcup.

By the early 1960s, after *The Collection*, *The Lover* and *A Night Out*, one gradually became aware of the Pinter technique, the art of creating maximum tension by providing minimum information. By the time he had produced *The Homecoming*, *Old Times* and *No Man's Land*, three of his most characteristic works, 'Pinterism' was beginning to feel like an adopted style – and it somehow didn't matter that it was being adopted by the man who invented it. The mature Pinter, perhaps too conscious of how he achieved his effects, ran the risk of being over-methodical and of repeating familiar patterns. Critics began to express a certain *ennui*. Just as one asked about Vivaldi, did he write a hundred different concerti or the same concerto a hundred times over, one began to wonder if Pinter wasn't simply making endless inversions of the same insights. In a piece for the *New York Times* in 1972, I wrote: 'One feels that in the shorter plays, before *The Homecoming*, he was scraping the bottom of his residual experience, that wealth of memory and sensation he had accumulated in his first twenty-five years of life. Now that his technique is at its highest point of perfection, one wonders if there will be content with enough urgency to keep it really occupied.' From the menaces of the lower-working-class bedsit underworld, Pinter began to concentrate on the 'high life', which was the milieu in which he now found himself. By then he had left his first wife, Vivien Merchant (who died a few years later), and had married Lady Antonia Fraser (which, in terms of its social impact, was like Mellors moving in with Lady Chatterley), and in plays like *Betrayal* one could hear the winch of the old techniques dredging up a new subject-matter in a different class setting. The old voice was still there, but, instead of croaking musical-hall ditties, it seemed to be, uncharacteristically, chirping operetta. There then followed a long fallow period out of which came new short works such as *One For The Road*, *Mountain Language* and *A Kind of Alaska*. Wondering whether the work of the new Pinter was merely a trend or an aberration, a journalist got this reply from Harold in 1985: 'I can't go on writing plays about torture, I wrote one sketch about the nuclear bureaucracy. [*Precisely* – less than two minutes' duration.] But still, I can't go on writing that kind of play either. They're very difficult to write. You can only write them if you can make them real . . . I don't see much of a future for me as a writer in this respect. It also makes it very difficult to write anything, however. I don't know what my future is as a writer . . .'

It may well be that, like many artists, Pinter is in transition to some other plane and his talent will re-emerge reinvigorated. One must fight the tendency to slough off playwrights just because, in the maturation of their talent, they become overfamiliar. But my suspicion is, the quality of Harold's life has become attenuated – which is perhaps a euphemism for complacent and unchallenged – and that is why he is finding it so hard to come up with new stimuli. Also, the ideological switch to more overt themes and specific political concerns may be dismantling his power to create. One cannot envisage Beckett writing about the evils of apartheid without his style suffering, and it is just as hard to imagine Pinter becoming socially direct and even agitational when his natural talent has been for indirection and obliquity.

My crush on William Saroyan dated back to my earliest high school days, when I had read and was transported by short stories such as 'Myself upon the Earth', 'Laughter' and 'The Daring Young Man on the Flying Trapeze'. When I arrived in London, I tried hard to get someone interested in his play *The Cave Dwellers* and eventually managed to mount a production of it at the St Pancras Arts Festival. I wrote a long, wet, sloppily sentimental letter to Saroyan requesting permission to stage the play and asking for whatever input he wished to make.

In 1960 Saroyan was very conscious of the fact that he was out of fashion. Round about this time he had come to London to collaborate with Joan Littlewood on a play hooched up in Joan's characteristic manner with actors, director and playwright all chipping in together. It didn't fare very well, but it was a lively jamboree for all concerned. Saroyan's overflowing humanism merged neatly with Joan's proletarian jauntiness and everyone enjoyed each other immensely.

Despite his descent into obscurity, Saroyan always harboured the notion he would one day be back in fashion. The modern theatre, as he saw it, was going through a phase that was alien to him and one day the virtues that made plays such as *Time of Your Life* and *The Beautiful People* popular in the 1930s and 1940s would be rediscovered, and then he would be restored to his rightful place in the pantheon. This was neither egotism nor sour grapes. Saroyan was simply standing to one side, noting an historical trend of which he accepted he was no longer a part.

In my talks with him I could feel the *angst* of a man who, though currently out of the picture, had once been the vortex of a popular literary whirl. He had become inured to current defeats, expected them, knew that in a sense they were inevitable, but knew just as well that no disaster, no matter how sweeping, could eradicate the thing he had been in the 1930s. At the time

I couldn't appreciate just how humiliating it must have been for him to approve a small-scale, semi-professional production of his play under the piddling circumstances I had devised. It was a far cry from the Theatre Guild, which had mounted *Time of Your Life* or the Group Theatre production of *My Heart's in the Highlands*. I was too callow to understand that what for me was a significant first production of the play in London was for him an agonizing form of slumming. Of course, the reason I never realized it is because he never made me aware of it. Throughout, he wrote and talked about the production as if it were the one that was going to bring off the reappearing act he was constantly anticipating.

Saroyan was burly, moustachioed and outgoing in a way that commanded the attentions and sympathies of everyone who met him. The kind of man who, when he walked into the office, caused everyone to stop what they were doing and gather round him to hear his anecdotes, laugh at his garrulousness and thrill to his common touch. It was in no sense a social façade, but merely a willed preference that life should be gregarious, affable and full of fellow feeling.

When, years later, I read about the wretchedness with which he had infected his family life and the callousness with which he treated his son, it wasn't entirely a surprise. I had always suspected that, behind that towering humanism, there might well be an imp of the perverse which whittled away at personal relationships in exchange for that irresistible, bear-hugging universal embrace. Tynan, too, was a great humanist in public and a shit in private. Was that perhaps an inevitable corollary? Were all the wells of public munificence spiked with the poisons of private spite and malevolence, and was it because of this that people made such an ostentatious grandstand play? In 1989 Paul Johnson wrote a book entitled *Intellectuals*, which more or less demolished the private moralities of artists such as Rousseau, Brecht, Sartre, Ibsen and Tynan. Reviewing it, I pointed out that there was no real corollary between an artist's achievement and his private persona – but, nevertheless, I was struck by the high incidence of Jekyll-and-Hydes chronicled by Johnson – a list I could easily supplement tenfold. My feeling then, as now, was that all one should be permitted to place on the scale was the work, that infernal machinations of the personality belonged to the psychologizing biographer, and that, no matter what judgements were finally made about private character, the character of the work was untouched by them.

The Cave Dwellers, like most of Saroyan's plays in the Sixties, received mixed notices and was largely dismissed as sentimental twaddle. It is a valentine to the human race in its struggle to survive, unquestionably soft centred and out of sync with the times. After I wrote him about the play's reception, he wrote back a resilient letter from France which, being highly characteristic, I reproduce in its entirety; the sections in square brackets are my inserts.

Rue Taitbout, Paris 9e, France. 29 March 1961
Dear Marowitz,
Well, you see, that's the way it is in the theatre:
it surely takes some plays a century (or even
two) to get themselves adequately understood,
directed, performed and ace accepted (enjoyed);
and I'm not even beginning to think that mine are
in that category. It's hard to get everything the
way it ought to be; in the meantime the best that's
possible under the circumstances has to do. I
saw opening night of *Roots* at the old Billy Rose
Diamond Horseshoe, where I had boozed long
ago, listening to Willie Solar the Abba Dabba Kid
(although I think he had it King, damned fool)
and other old-timers of vaudeville. Well, *Roots*
was boring, that's all – but I could see quite clearly
all the while that it could very well not be boring,
even if inside-the-sad-house plays tend to be
automatically boring. But you just can't get Joan
Plowright every time, that's all. *The Cave
Dwellers* probably turned out good enough, but
your critical observations about it surely stand [I'd
sent him a rather fierce *post mortem* of the work],
are surely valid in one degree or another, and
so there is no dispute on that account; but do you
think for a minute that any real playwright is ever

that expert? Only hacks and Hollywood writers are expert, but they just aren't anything else, and so their expertness doesn't help, does it? Your favorable review in the *Village Voice* kicks hell out of the pride I have been taking in a clean sweep. [An upbeat notice appeared in the *Voice* for which Saroyan thought I was responsible; I wasn't.] Surely you must have knocked it a little, so I can be proud again. If you have a copy of the review or of the whole issue, can you send it along. My 17-year son reads it fairly steadily, I believe; and catches all of the Off-Bway stuff: his favorite seems to be *The Connection*, which I didn't get around to seeing. I liked the Brecht, though, *In the Jungle* etcetera, *Three Japanese Plays*, and most of all Lonny Chapman's *Cry of the Raindrop*. *Sam is* very nearly flawless [this was the title of the work that grew out of the Joan Littlewood collaboration] and that fact hasn't got anything to do with dramatic form or the filling out of character with appropriate action, etc. (I have quoted, that is): it is to do with theatricality, period. The play has two characters, the playwright's, and the audience's. Who are we kidding about this character stuff? We get 'characters' when we cheat to drama by means of emotionality, and let's face it, it's great, it's right, it's easy, but it's childhood at its worst, and the time is coming when the greatest dramas will be laughable, parodies almost, to the human race in general. Now, the theatre belongs to a kind of specialist who is actually very backward. Tortured plays, tortured audiences; well, when the audiences aren't tortured, as we must presume they shall eventually become, a whole new order of drama has got to come along: Beckett, Ionesco, Adamov, Genet *et al* are serving that new order well by making the old as sick as it is possible to be an hour or two before death itself, which is next, most likely. Genius and trauma are the cliché partnership, but there are other partners for genius – but not now, maybe; and that's a little of the reason my stuff can annoy some people terribly. They see all in themselves and around them as sickness and impending death, and they have got to be impatient with anything else, or less, or more. I saw [Alan] Myerson for a minute, have an idea he may be a good playwright, although over there with the new mob; black and all, that is. Tell me about the Armpit Theatre [i.e. my newly formed In-Stage Company]: twenty seats, or six, or what? When I get to London, let's meet; I'll phone, most likely. All best.

William Saroyan

In the summer of 1965, when I was little more than a fledgling director myself, I was asked to 'enlighten' a group of up-and-coming British writers buoyed up by a Ford Foundation grant at a retreat in Wannsee, a suburb of Berlin best remembered as the site of the Wannsee Conference at which Hitler's final solution was casually ratified.

It was here that I first met Tom Stoppard and my most vivid memory of him is when, in conversation with other members of his group (which included Piers Paul Read, Derek Marlowe and Peter Bergman), he blithely and unselfconsciously referred to himself and his cohorts as 'the coming men'. How refreshingly conceited, I thought to myself, to know already with such certainty that one was 'a coming man'. But Tom was quite correct. He 'came on' very rapidly after that.

Towards the end of the seminar, each writer had to present an excerpt from some work in progress and I was expected informally to adjudicate. Tom's excerpt, unquestionably the weirdest of the lot, concerned two minor characters from *Hamlet* who spent a lot of time tossing coins in the air and receiving visits from a hoary, old, self-denigrating gent called King Lear. It struck me as piece of academic twaddle and I remember thinking that Stoppard, whom I knew as a sometime reviewer in

London, would probably be more gainfully employed knocking out copy on Fleet Street.

Two years later, rejigged and refined, Lear deleted and a slate of new material inserted, the play emerged on the stage of the National Theatre as *Rosencrantz and Guildenstern Are Dead*. It was like an idiot child making such a miraculous recovery that he was now ready to take up his duties as Dean of Linguistic Philosophy at Oxford or Cambridge. As I lacerated my palms expressing my enthusiasm, I had a disturbing little flashback to the tiny Berlin stage where I had seen the play gestate and, downgrading my powers of perception by several notches, marvelled at the transmutation of which art was capable.

In one of those curious flip-flops that often occur between members of the same generation, Tom wrote a review of one of In-Stage's earliest efforts, *The Trigon*, a black comedy by James Broom Lynne. It concluded with the words: 'After sitting in acres of plush watching the worst two-thirds of London theatre, it is slightly eerie to sit in that ridiculous little attic and watch something so polished.'

A few years later, I was reviewing *Travesties* and preparing a profile on him for the *New York Times*. Now enthroned in a vast house in Slough (that most un-Stoppardian of all London suburbs), we jockeyed around trying to determine the latitudes and longitudes of our altered relationship. Having known him in the grubby Fleet Street days, I thought I sensed a slight embarrassment as he showed me around the sumptuous garden of, what in my memory looms as, the baronial manor. He was as dry and witty as he had been when knocking out notices for his newspaper in Bristol, but his manner seemed to imply that both his property and his status were the result of some incredible spin of the wheel which he could not properly explain and which, in any case, would shortly be reversed.

His philosophical curiosity was as alive as ever, but the new acquisitions, both of property and status, had removed that nervy edge of questing which had made him both narky and ratty several years before. Some part of him suggested that he wasn't really entitled to his new-found prosperity, but that was aggressively countered by another part which defiantly asserted its claims in the teeth of all self-doubt. If I had just been a journalist on assignment, I am sure he'd have been able to muster exactly the right tone, but, being a director and critic with an indelible memory of his earliest days, I think he was slightly discommoded, as if my knowledge of his scroungier life in some way subverted the success he had now achieved.

What was always arresting about Tom's work was that outside-looking-in perspective, which enabled significant events – such as the Russian revolution, the rise of Dada and the travails of James Joyce in *Travesties* or the central action of Shakespeare's play *Hamlet* in *Rosencrantz and Guildenstern Are Dead* – to be glimpsed, as it were, through the wrong end of a telescope. Paradoxically, Stoppard, who in *Jumpers* larked his way through classical philosophy, seemed to be most airborne when carrying the heaviest freight, and the consequence of this paradox is that his deepest concerns often appeared trivial, a word that has become affixed to his lapel as gruesomely as the yellow star was to the death-camp Jews.

In 1975, in that *New York Times* piece, I asked whether it was true to say he had no strong political feelings. 'I'm not impressed by art *because* it is political,' he replied. 'I believe in art being good art or bad art, not relevant art or irrelevant art. The plain truth is that if you are angered or disgusted by a particular injustice or immorality and you want to do something about it, *now*, at once, then you can hardly do worse than write a play about it. That's what art is bad at.' However, in recent years, Stoppard, like Pinter, appears to have developed a Johnny-come-lately political awareness and in works such as *Professional Foul*, *Every Good Boy Deserves Favour* and *Night and Day*, has foisted a new aspect of his literary personality. For my money, most of these works fail to convince as political statements, but, in a romantic comedy like *The Real Thing*, Stoppard's talent and subject-matter magically coalesce. Treating subjects such as infidelity and the hunger for genuine (as opposed to delusional) experience, he appears to have found his truest voice. Heard in the fullness of its range, it is the voice of an incisive, sceptical, bemused observer of human foibles (more Marivaux than Molière) who uses comedy to agitate social and psychological insights.

In that same interview, he said: 'I think to be amusing and

entertaining about a serious subject is a reasonable objective.' Acting on this principle, Stoppard seems recently to have become the Bard of the Hampstead and Highgate Set, those upwardly mobile, slightly paunchy yuppies whose gospel is the Sunday colour supplements and who find in sexual promiscuity and political activism an antidote to social *ennui*. The wellspring of many of Stoppard's characters (here, too, he resembles Pinter) is boredom. One feels that they are not motivated by conviction so much as the need to amuse, divert or reanimate themselves. And the same observation could be applied to the playwright. Sizzling social and political issues are (if you'll pardon the mixing of metaphors) the meat of which Stoppard makes his cucumber sandwiches. To hear him address subjects such as the enslavement of East Europe or the brainwashing of political prisoners in the USSR is to hear Rudy Vallee belting out excerpts from *Götterdämmerung* through a megaphone.

In our time the compulsion of comic writers to deal with serious issues in a serious way has flattened out Woody Allen, hamstrung Neil Simon, attenuated Alan Ayckbourn and dehydrated Tom Stoppard. None have been done permanent harm and in some cases (as in the film *Manhattan* or the play *Henceforward*), a judicious balance has been struck. But, on the whole, the Pagliacci syndrome has gone against the grain of a talent whose natural tendency was flighty, capering and wholesomely trivial. As if comedy could not accommodate every idea consciously crammed into serious drama.

In the early Sixties, at In-Stage, a theatre situated in the attic of the British Drama League on Fitzroy Square, I had managed to acquire the British rights for Samuel Beckett's mime play *Act Without Words II* and journeyed over to Paris to meet with the author before launching into the production.

We had arranged to meet at the Closerie des Lilas, one of Beckett's favourite haunts not far from Notre Dame. When I wandered into the bar, Beckett, sitting on one side, was immediately apparent. He had the look of a nearsighted hawk; his hair appeared to be trying to escape from his head. I found myself trepidatious in his presence – not because he was an internationally renowned writer, but because I felt myself to be in the presence of a man who had come within a hair's breadth of death and miraculously survived. It was the trepidation of meeting someone who had actually been on the 'other side' and so made a terrestrial encounter spooky. The webs of other-worldliness clung to his skin, his eyes still clouded over with terrors he'd seen there.

Since he sat saying nothing, I engineered an opening gambit which sounded as contrived as it was. He gave no quarter. He refused to collaborate in any form of small talk. I whipped out the script and we immediately began to talk shop.

For Beckett, mime was not sufficient unto itself. And the term, as commonly used, did not refer to either of his mime plays for they were, quite rightly, as he had titled them, 'acts without words'.

'With Marceau,' said Beckett, 'I always feel the absence of words, the *need* for them.'

In his own mime works, actions were seen as a self-sustaining substitute for language. He felt that mime, over the years, had been stretched beyond its bounds – being asked to do things it cannot do by itself and which language can do more easily. (I disagreed, of course, but, as he spoke, found myself incarcerated, as it were, in a Beckettian pause.)

'Directors', he said, 'don't seem to have any sense of form in movement. The kind of form that one finds in music, for instance, where themes keep recurring.' (Years later, a close friend of Beckett's told me that, for him, chamber music achieved the kind of apotheosis that drama strove for, usually in vain.) 'When, in a text, actions are repeated, they ought to be made queer for the first time, so that when they happen again – in exactly the same way – an audience will recognize them from before. In the revival of *Godot* [in Paris] I tried to get at something of that stylized movement that's in the play.'

Beckett was unhappy with the way he had been treated by producers and, as time went on, greater and greater liberties were taken with his works, so much so that in France he actually interceded to stop a production of *Endgame* set in a Metro station. Of course, Beckett's problems date back to the first production of *Godot* in America, when, in a lead article in the *New York Times* one week before the show opened, producer Michael Myerberg sent out a call for 70,000 intellectuals to support the masterpiece he was valiantly bringing from the Continent. I vividly remember the balcony of that New York theatre as 70,000 intellectuals rallied to the call, a teeming mass of beards, jeans, wire glasses and myopic stares. It was as if all the trendier and more pretentious bars of Greenwich Village had been sucked out by a giant vacuum and discharged into the balcony of this Broadway house.

Beckett felt the original production at the Théâtre de la Huchette (directed by Roger Blin) came nearest to realizing the play. He was dissatisfied with Peter Hall's London production. 'The text asks for a bare stage – except for this tree – and there the stage was so cluttered the actors could hardly move.' Beckett tried unsuccessfully to stop a later London production billed as 'the most uproarious comedy of the century'.

He believed that there was an inevitable correspondence between words and movement, certain lines simply could not be delivered from certain positions without compatible actions.

'Isn't this a matter of each director's interpretation?' I asked.

'Yes and, within the limits of a specified text, the director has plenty of scope for interpretation. But in a lot of cases directors go directly contrary to what is needed.'

I was reminded of Bert Lahr's Estragon. When Vladimir (E. G. Marshall) asks: 'Which way did he go?' Estragon replies: 'That way.' In the original text, the stage direction specifies 'no gesture'. In the Lahr production the comedian put up two fingers indicating opposite directions, an old-hat vaudeville gag that went for and got the cheap laugh.

Over the years a tight-fisted Beckett cult of directors and protectors has sprung up around the playwright. All attempts to reinterpret the works or give them a different spin were fiercely resisted. As with Brecht, Beckett has promulgated an 'official' approach to the *oeuvre* – strong on textual fidelity and unwavering in terms of setting and costume. His works are the poorer for it. For if they are as rich and resourceful as I believe they are, they can withstand the permutations of experimental productions and unexpected imagery, but the Beckett cartel, out of a misguided sense of loyalty, has seen to it that they are revived, filmed and televised in strict accordance with the Beckettian letter of the law. As a result, we will have to wait some time to see the plays genuinely stretched and reinvigorated. It is not the first time an artist and his sycophantic stalwarts have rigidified work that should be elastic and open to alternative readings.

Beckett exuded a kind of clergyman's tolerance. When he was not talking, he was entirely turned off. His accent was an odd mixture of soft Dublin and indistinguishable Continental influences. He seemed wholly at home in Paris, spoke ruefully of his two years in London and spitefully of the one week that recent business compelled him to spend in Dublin. He had seemed thoroughly himself when sitting alone, cocooned in a shell of his own making, but became taut and wary when obliged to communicate with a stranger. One thinks of saints having an aura, well Beckett had one as well; not so much an aura, but a protective covering, an invisible magnetic field behind which he could contemplate the world without it getting at him.

When I left the Closerie des Lilas, I found myself bristling with indignation against myself. So much of my time was being spent trying to penetrate the minds of others instead of getting on with my own business. I became aware of that immense void that one stuffs with books, travel, controversy, criticism and other forms of preventive nonsense – all designed to divert time and energy from one own's own unique and supremely essential work. It was as if my own sense of purpose had been subverted by something radiating out of Beckett's nature – his sense of the futility of all human endeavour. How much of it was actually there and how much of it I simply read into him because of my knowledge of his work, I don't know, but, for whatever reason, I found myself walking away quickly from Samuel Beckett.

Round about the same time Trevor Griffiths was establishing his reputation with *Occupations* at the RSC (circa 1971), the Open Space was preparing a production of his play *Sam Sam*, a North country *Corsican Brothers*, which examined the British class system from the standpoint of two brothers, each named Sam. One remained rooted in his proletarian origins; the other gravitated up to the higher reaches of W1 and left his background behind him. In a sense, Griffiths was both.

A bow-legged, shambling, saturnine, black-haired Mancunian with (when I knew him) a Zapata moustache, Griffiths looked like a walking advertisement for Rent-a-Rebel. He had a snide, North Country wit and always made you feel that he could see through all your stratagems even when you didn't have any. I think he prided himself on his dialectical approach to life and it was very much in evidence when we worked together on *Sam Sam*. In all our discussions, he brought a calm, low intensity, thoroughly objective approach to the play. In his view, the piece, now freed from its chrysalis, had to flutter in its own right.

He had the North Countryman's no-nonsense approach to stage problems, examining carefully what might conceivably make an inert scene come alive – without automatically assuming the scene already *was* alive simply because he had written it. He assessed the qualities of actors in relation to what he had written and instinctively realized that sometimes one had to make concessions to the human factor, that is, the character had to bend in the direction of the actor when the actor could not naturally make it bend towards him. Of all the writers with whom I worked, Griffiths was best able to detach himself from original intentions and enter into the practical collaboration of rehearsals. It was a craftsmanlike approach which, though it wouldn't compromise on fundamentals, didn't become warped and attenuated by ego considerations. When we both agreed on the revealed inadequacy of one of the lead actors, it was not a cue for shrieks or breast-beating. It was one of the givens in the theatre: you didn't always get top players and, when forced to make do with the second eleven, you just did the best you could.

In *Sam Sam*, as in the later Griffiths plays (i.e. *Comedians*, *The Party*), sex and politics are often interwoven, and the playwright has acknowledged the influence of Reich in much of his work: the way in which sexual frustration and social repression often march hand in hand. His untrammelled vision about people also takes the form of unvarnished diction. Griffiths has recalled with pride that Olivier once told him he was the first writer to have the word 'cunt' spoken on the stage of the National Theatre, although he admitted 'the actors have said it under their breath often enough'.

Although one feels Griffiths's earliest political convictions are still knocking around deep inside him, one also feels, as with the more urbane and conformist protagonist in *Sam Sam*, that he has been diverted by films, mini series and assorted media deals. But the fire is unquestionably still in his belly and, unlike Osborne, who just got flaccid and lazy, or David Hare, who is openly voracious for commercial success, Griffiths may yet turn out a work lit by the fires of his earliest passions.

In 1972 or thereabouts, Sam Shepard looked me up in London. He'd been given my address by mutual friends in New York and was looking for a flat for himself, his wife and their small child – did I have any ideas? I suggested a few telephone numbers and made a few calls on his behalf. Throughout our talks, I dreaded the fact that he might brandish a playscript in front of me because, although we had staged *Red Cross* at the Open Space, I was not a fan of those poetical riffs and abstruse arabesques which constituted his early one-acters. They struck me as sub-standard Americanized versions of European Theatre of the Absurd and visions from a world so private that they defied intelligible discourse with the real world. Although, at that time, my admiration for Beckett and Genet was staunch, my tolerance for Ionesco, Adamov and their British imitators had begun to reach vanishing point.

It turned out he *had* brought a play – contained in two or three blue-lined children's ledgers – the kind of notebooks schoolkids still use for compositions. I agreed to read it, but explained that most of our season was already in place and American plays always had a rough ride in London (an argument sorely weakened by the fact that we had built a reputation at the Open Space introducing the work of contemporary American writers).

The work was titled *The Tooth of Crime*. It was written in an invented language derived from several American idioms such as pop, underworld slang, sports jargon and that slithery, constantly reformulating vernacular that musicians keep alive amongst themselves and which gradually filters into the national tongue. I read it at one sitting like a chocoholic gobbling up an ice-cream sundae and felt it was the most exciting play I had come across since Mike Weller's *Moonchildren*. I told him I would stage it at the Open Space as soon as humanly possible. (Curiously, Mike Weller wound up being cast in one of the roles.)

Several months elapsed while finance was sought – in vain. No one seemed to be able to make out the play and everyone advised against. Sam's patience began to get shredded. By summer he had had the London scene and was chasing remote serenities in Nova Scotia. Despite only securing a part of the financing, we decided to push ahead and let the British overdraft do its work.

As the director–writer collaboration began, our easy amity became threadworn. We each had a vision of the play and they didn't always tally. Shepard had a fierce dislike for 'flash' and tended to recoil from bold, 'outside' theatrical effects. I, on the other hand, have always had a fondness for artifice which, when properly employed, seems to me to get closer to inner truths than brow-beating, interior probes. Since I was a complete neophyte as far as rock music was concerned (and the play required a rock accompaniment), I let Sam get on with finding the band and assembling the music, hoping that would keep him off my back during the essential spadework.

The central fable of the play is that Hoss, an ageing pop hero, who is at the same time the leader of a futurist criminal gang, is threatened by the arrival of an ambitious rock upstart named Crow. When Crow actually arrives on the scene, it triggers a mortal combat between the two leaders which takes the form of a style duel (electric rock rhythms battling jazz-based, pop cadenzas; the kind of metaphorical contest that might have occurred between Elvis Presley and Mick Jagger, had they been exact contemporaries). Hoss is beaten hands down and Crow blandly appropriates his mansion, his standing in the charts and all the other accoutrements of his success. It is the traditional defeat of the old king by the new challenger and reinforces the notion that victory belongs to he who has the courage to break existing codes and impose a new one.

At the end of the first act, Shepard had written a long,

rallentando speech for Hoss, which, in my view, dissipated the energy of the act and contained no imperative or hook into the next act. Retaining the downward spiral of the speech, I added a tail-piece in which an incessant rock crescendo grows steadily behind the immobilized figure of Hoss while simultaneously, in the background, a spotlight picks up the shadowy figure of Crow, whose myth had been regularly promulgated throughout the first act. As the act comes to a close and the light fades on Hoss, it comes up brilliantly on the sinister figure of Crow, resplendent in leather and studs, materialized for the first time. As the crescendo reaches its climax, the lights fade on the static figure and we are into the interval.

Shepard was furious with the atmospheric change, the 'outside' effects, the substitution of a charged climax for a dying fall. That was neither what he had intended nor what he had written. What those moments *did* supply was the director's need to create an act curtain which mobilized interest in the next act for, having been introduced to this compulsively sinister figure, the audience (I argued) would become eager to find out what kind of confrontation would ensue between the clapped-out champion Hoss, and the newly arrived challenger, Crow.

It was not the first nor the last time that a director's interpretative preference would challenge an author's personal vision. In this instance, however, I was not only director of the play but also management of the theatre which was presenting it, and so could impose my own choices. I am sure Shepard never forgave me. He was used to calling the shots and, apart from anything else, construed this as a blow to his ego – which then, as now, was considerable.

The production caused widespread perplexity among the British press, which was unfamiliar with the American vernacular and could not really appreciate a social milieu terrorized by opposing street gangs. The fringe publications were obstreperously enthusiastic and we mustered good houses for the show – perhaps because of the musical content, perhaps because there were then two publics in London: the Shaftesbury Avenue crowd, who wanted the theatre to reassure, and the fringe lot, who expected it to startle and disturb. There was also the fact that it bore a genuine American stamp – both Shepard's and my own

– and that already pre-sold it to a certain number of *Time Out* readers and fringe regulars.

Shepard went on to become something of an American icon, a transformation which has yet to be appropriately analysed or explained. In the 1960s, his work was largely scorned by American critics, the critic of the *Village Voice* being the striking exception. It was a time when most American reviewers had not yet got the hang of the new drama. It was still being assimilated from Europe, but not sympathetically. In 1970 the tide turned for Shepard – mainly with the Lincoln Center production of *Operation Sidewinder*, which, although not a success, had the clear imprimatur of the American establishment upon it. By then, the newness of the new drama had sunk in and Shepard, having been there from the start, was hailed as a kind of cultural *arriviste*. It didn't matter any more that critics could not figure him out; the obscurity itself was a mark of distinction in an age that had come to revere Ionesco, Beckett and Genet. By the late 1970s, a *rapprochement* had taken place between the critics and Shepard. No longer the dispenser of *avant-garde* novelties for undiscriminating youth culture, Shepard was now turning out family dramas such as *Curse of the Starving Class*, *Buried Child*, *True West* and *A Lie of the Mind*. The style was recognizable, the language comprehensible and the tradition redolent of the domestic sagas found in works of Eugene O'Neill, Arthur Miller and William Inge, that's to say cosily familiar. There were still quirky characters and odd-ball settings, but it was now perceived as unfolding in the lost wasteland of the American West, the territory Shepard had carved out for himself.*

My own view is that much of Shepard's work is highly perishable and the social and intellectual structure so thin as to creak dangerously under the weight of serious analysis. The searing blond good looks that turned him into a movie star in the 1980s have in some way interfused with his reputation as a playwright. Like Gabriele d'Annunzio, his social charisma has tended to bolster his literary reputation and, as in d'Annunzio's case, one really has nothing to do with the other. For me, his

---

* I am indebted here to critic Helen Knode, whose analysis of Sam Shepard appeared in *Alarums & Excursions* in 1989.

works are quirky and unconvincing – extensions of his own personal confusions about life (his own and other people's) which, artistically undigested, are leavened into his works without causing them to rise. He is, to cite an Irish parallel, the Dion Boucicault of the *avant garde*, churning out expressionist melodramas which, because they contain an authentic American vernacular, falsely presume to crystallize certain obsessions in American society. There are some durable mid-period works – particularly among the 1970s plays and I think *The Tooth of Crime* has weathered well – but, by and large, the true quality of the writer has to be winnowed out of the media myth that has been created around him.

18   *Private lives*

It would be very misleading to suggest that for the twenty or so years I lived and worked in London the main current of my life was spent only with writers, actors and theatrical personalities. Like most people, I had a private life and, on the whole, it was lived with three women, the memory of whom is indelibly implanted on my mind. Because they were rooted in my experience, because they were psychically as well as physically part of my life, I want to try to define these women without retouching or romanticizing their memories.

Living with someone, no matter how impermanent the arrangement is thought to be, is, during the period of togetherness, an inescapable factor in the lives of both parties. Afterwards, as people drift off, move to other countries or marry others, it is the easiest thing in the world to allow those memories to become diffuse, to imply they were merely transient and not very significant periods in one's life which simply led to more permanent liaisons. But that is the present meanly downgrading the past and, in an honest recollection, the tendency should be resisted. At the time, certain people, the way they dressed, the way they smiled, the way they brushed their hair in the bathroom mirror were pivotal to one's life and it is contemptible to belittle that just because it happened a long time ago, in another country and therefore to assume 'the wench is dead'. For me, these women are luminously alive and to neglect them here would be to turn one's back on vital memories from my past.

I met Gillian Watt in 1957, when I was conducting a Method Workshop in London. She was a delicately boned, slightly pigeon-chested girl from Chiddingford, who looked as if she had been plucked out of a luxuriant English garden and presented to the world as a corsage. Her auburn hair was shoulder length, curly and groomed in such a way that the strong, intelligent face beneath it seemed to be sculpted in white Italian marble. Her sense of humour was such that it immediately caught the absurdity behind thinly veiled pretensions. She had begun as a pianist

(I can recall only ever hearing her play one piece and that endlessly) and then gravitated into acting. Once, we actually acted together in a musical revue I wrote for a Dublin Theatre Festival. The sketch, which concerned visiting American tourists, took place on the back of a bus and was full of barbed satirical humour as well as atrocious puns such as 'In which newspaper can I find Nelson's Column?' She appeared in a few films such as *The Captain's Table*, *The King in New York* and *The Great Train Robbery*, but, to her credit, was not temperamentally suited to being an actress. Always a voracious reader, she eventually became a story editor and literary scout for film companies and foreign publishers.

Being the first person with whom I entered into a long-standing relationship, I always think of Gillian as the person who introduced me to England and taught me its ways, not through any conscious instruction, but by simply being English in relation to my gauche and groping Americanness. Heaped into an unsteady and corroding Austin tourer or a decrepit, shambling Ford, we went on hair-raising journeys throughout the country. I remember the first time we ventured to Southend – the breathtaking gasp of joy as we turned from the main road into the town's approach and suddenly came upon the sea sparkling below us. Caesar encountering the Nile for the first time couldn't have known a more stirring sensation. Our journeys were more than weekend getaways; they were astonishing discoveries of paradisiacal towns like Hastings, Brighton, Bexhill and Dover, which seemed to me then to be the wonders of Europe.

Gillian's loyalty, which at the time I callously took for granted, I see now was one of the inbred virtues of the British character. Whatever I happened to be doing, be it the formation of an experimental theatre at the British Drama League or the promotion of a new magazine or merely a fleeting obsession destined to wither in a matter of weeks, was a crusade to which she devoted every ounce of her energy. This was a trait which I discovered in her over and over again, even when we were no longer together: soldiering valiantly for a London agent, with whom she had forged a relationship, or stoutly supporting a British publisher, with whom she had temporarily become enamoured or hulking LPs from one part of town to another to aid and abet the record company of a man she eventually married. To whomever she gave her sympathies, she would automatically commit her industry. It was an adorable trait and one, I fear, that led to her being shamelessly exploited more than once.

One day at Leamington Spa, we walked into the Pump Room – threading our way through a clutch of tables, at which a variety of ladies with blue-rinses sat spooning tea and balancing scones at the end of long, bejewelled fingers. On the dais, a scratchy little string orchestra was playing those deeply entrenched English tunes that still evoke dreamy reveries among members of the pre-war generation. It was like having climbed out of a space-ship and into a daintier, more genteel epoch, when the crunch of pastry and the tinkle of teacups was the sweetest music that anyone could ever hear, sweeter even than the string ensemble hacking away at excerpts from Gilbert and Sullivan and Percy Grainger. As we slithered into our seats and joined the dowagers and retired colonels, the beflowered matrons and corroding old-age pensioners, the absurdity of the situation totally enveloped us. What started as embarrassed smiles and suppressed giggles soon became uncontrollable cachinnations. Some irresistible imp of the perverse had scoured away our civility and sense of tact, and, try as we might, we could not keep ourselves from doubling up and detonating helpless laughter. We staggered out of the Pump Room, stuffing handkerchiefs into our mouths until we got to the outer doors, then released the full blast of our delirium. As we fled down the stone stairs and into the street, strangers gaped at us like the capering idiots we surely were.

There were several occasions when Gillian and I were united by a joint mania that in some way underscored the lunacy of the unventilated, buttoned-up society in which we always seemed to find ourselves. We were linked by laughter like Siamese twins stitched together at the lower vertebrae, constantly looking through the windows of an orderly world which, from our vantage point, seemed killingly hilarious.

We lived for a while in Notting Hill Gate and for a longer time at St Mark's Crescent, directly above Clive Jenkins and his wife Moira, in a flat where the Regent's Park canal threw shimmering diamonds on to our ceiling. When we looked out the back window, we could see, at regular intervals, Jason's Barge chugging its load of sightseers past our private lives, a tour guide announcing that this was the house of the notable Union leader Clive Jenkins, but neglecting to mention it was also the abode of a rollicking couple who were jointly discovering the marvels of each other and the pleasures of life in a frivolous and insouciant Britain. It was a time when we were both questing our way through the start of our careers; she as an actress, and I as a director. A time when it seemed as if the summers were unspeakably golden and the winters heated as cosily by gas fires as by the warmth of our mutual affection.

I was wretchedly unfaithful to her and round about the mid-1960s became hopelessly engulfed by a statuesque blonde named Liza Thomas, who, when she announced she was going to marry a top-flight agent, caused me to throw myself impulsively at Gillian's feet and suggest we too get married. By then we had only the fag end of a relationship and Gillian, to her credit, knew it. We parted amicably, saw each other on and off for several years afterwards, and, I think, cherished much of the time we had spent discovering each other, the marvels of the countryside and the *frisson* of being young and madcap in a world that seemed so much brighter and more roseate than what it became eight and ten years later.

A young Australian voice on the other end of the phone said she had read my book *The Method as Means* and found it stimulating. She had just arrived in London from Melbourne and, because the book led her to believe she knew me, sought me out. I was enchanted with the voice, flattered by the compliment and so we arranged to have tea in my flat in St John's Wood. When, a day or two later, I opened the front door for her, I was thrown for a loop. It was like being smacked in the face by a sackful of angel dust. The girl was dark, curvaceous, tremulously feminine and with eyes that seemed to be ignited by Catherine-wheels. She was simply the sexiest creature I had ever encountered on the face of the Earth and I could feel something shift inside me like the giant wheel of a bank vault which clangs shut securing precious goods from the probing eyes of an avaricious outside world.

At the time, I had been actively pursuing Sian Houston, a sanguine redhead whom I was determined to whisk away into the countryside for an Easter tryst, but when Gypsie hove into view, I immediately mustered all my heaviest artillery and directed all fire-power in her direction. It was she whom I wound up secreting out of London that Easter and eventually into the flat in St John's Wood, where she virtually remained for seven years, the essential seven years during which the Open Space was inaugurated and eventually established.

There were loving excursions into Wales and the New Forest, she discovering England as I had discovered it, but this time, with myself acting as guide and mentor. I had picked up for a song a disused old church hall in Burley, just outside Ringwood, and turned it into a retreat. There, on innumerable weekends, the back of the MG Midget bulging with provisions, we would mingle with ponies, trek through woodlands, munch scones in local tea-rooms and secrete ourselves in sheltering rusticity. For many years Burley was the oasis from the hurly-burly of London and despite the starchy conservatism of its residents and the haughty horsiness of our jodhpur'd neighbours, it provided a welcome antidote from plays, contracts and urban imbroglios.

We collaborated on a few theatrical projects at the Space and, before long, she was working for Donald Albery in the West End, playing a native girl in *Conduct Unbecoming* and appearing in occasional television spots for comedians like Benny Hill and Max Bygraves. The first phase of that relationship was idyllic – although that is too tranquil a word to describe Gypsie's effect. The drives and potentialities she awoke in me caused me to emit banshee howls of delight and sent me into stupors of exhaustion. For the first time, I began to understand what being a bond slave must have felt like. The intellectual gap between us was unbridgeable, but didn't in any way matter. I would have sacrificed a dozen intellectual soul-mates for the intensity of those highs. Even now, twenty years later, the memory of them starts pistons in my loins and engenders memories of euphoria that seem to belong to another creature who lived in another time. Is all of this a hyperbolic way of saying she was a magnificent turn-on? No, it was never as commonplace as that and, if it had been, it would never have rooted itself so irretrievably in my psyche. Something in her created inside of me metabolic changes so drastic that it altered my physiology. I came to understand the craving of addicts and why they were insatiable. It would be no exaggeration to say that Gypsie renatured something in me and added a dimension to my maleness which never existed before.

The layers of her personality were endless: onion skins wrapped around onion skins that never found a centre. It was two years before I learned that she had been married in Australia and several more years before she confessed she had a child there which the courts had taken away from her during a bitter custody battle with a conniving husband. Gypsie was wedded to 'dark secrets' and, whenever I managed to uproot one, it seemed incredible that something so potent could have been concealed so deeply, so well and for so long. Thelma attributed it to her Scorpio nature. It was a nature that I could not fathom. It was so full of side-windings and back alleys that it would have made a fascinating mystery novel and one in which no reader would have guessed the turn of events.

The satisfaction I derived from her was inestimable and yet, after a while, I found myself constantly pursuing other women and not covering my tracks very well. The impact of those infidelities on her must have been agonizing. Although I never admitted to them, the hearsay evidence was overwhelming and London then, as now, was too small a city in which to conduct a double life effectively. The irony for me, thinking back to that surreptitious period, was that in no instance did I find any satisfaction greater than what I had with Gypsie. The impulse to reconnoitre, pursue and appropriate a wide variety of women was entirely out of proportion to the happiness it brought. At home I had an inexhaustible fount which quenched my every thirst and yet I loped around the streets like a man parched for drink. In retrospect, it is clear that motivations of the *ego* rather than the *id* were behind all those endless forays, but I was so out of touch with my own nature that I was unable to appreciate the joys I possessed nor relate them to those I was neurotically pursuing.

Ultimately, the attenuation of her own career and the escalation of my own became a constant aggravation. I tried to include her wherever I could, but, since the motive for doing so was largely altruistic, it produced an unspoken resentment – not only on her part, but on the part of others too. Eventually, the threads, worn down to a frazzle, came apart in 1976, when she opened a letter (the tendency to appropriate personal mail having by then become a self-justified defence against betrayal) written by a Danish *amorata* which seemed, to Gypsie, to foreshadow my imminent departure to Denmark. Of course, nothing of the sort was ever contemplated and what she read was merely the dreamy meanderings of a moony girl, but, of course, when the decision to bolt has been emotionally made, it needs only the slightest pretext to trigger it into action.

Gypsie forsook St John's Wood and moved in with a friend. The actual rupture hit me like a ton of bricks. The physiology as well as the psyche screeched out the truth I had conveniently ignored for several years – that, whatever disparities existed in our relationship, the emotive reality on which it was predicated was irreplaceable. I could have other women, as I had been having them for some time, but I could no longer have that gratification for which others provided only inadequate substitutes.

I mounted a frantic campaign to salvage what I had foolishly undervalued and heedlessly lost. I set her up in a flat that I had acquired in Swiss Cottage and, from within that monitored domicile, tried to repair matters, but they were irreparable. The particular infidelities were secondary to the major infidelity, which was that I had violated my own appreciation of what had been so precious for so long. Ethically, I didn't have a leg to stand on. I had clearly brought this down on my own head. But sexual gratification notwithstanding, I had to acknowledge the social incompatibilities which had caused me to act in the way I had. With painful objectivity, I realized that this was a relationship which no longer had a foundation nor a *raison d'être*, but, though self-evident, I could not persuade my biology to relinquish what it had learned to feed on.

In the last desultory stages of the affair, Gypsie, without warning, suddenly moved out of the Swiss Cottage flat, which she recognized was the last tangible hold I had over her. When I walked into the place, it was stripped bare, its undecorated white walls taunting me with the final retreat. Only one item had been left in the flat: a copy of *Confessions of a Counterfeit Critic*, which I had dedicated to her. On the frontispiece I had had printed: 'To Gypsie Kemp, without whom . . .' Now, had I wished to, I would have been able to complete that fragmented sentence in a thousand different ways – all of them poignant.

All that happened in 1976. Within a month I met Julia Crosthwaite, model, actress, goddess, demon, Vargas girl *extraordinaire*, and within weeks of that encounter was married to her and living in the same St John's Wood flat I had shared with Gypsie. From Gypsie's standpoint, it would have had to have seemed that this liaison was started during the period she and I were together. The fact that it hadn't, the fact that it was a sudden and unforeseen development was probably never bought by Gypsie, who, by that time, was prepared to believe only the worst of me. In fact, I had fallen from a kind of heavenly limbo into a heavenly hell, but was not to feel the singe of the sulphur until two years down the line. Ironically, when the marriage came falling about my ears, I had the temerity to seek out Gypsie again and she the indiscretion to countenance a reunion. It was a dead man and a disembodied wraith who came together in Stratford-upon-Avon in 1979, stoking the dead coals of contrition and recrimination. In a curious way, the demise of my first marriage was also the final resting-place of the turbulent seven years I had shared with Gypsie. It was a kind of double funeral.

Within the compass of these relationships and in the interims between them, there were several memorable encounters. Lesley Ward was a kindred spirit whose maniacal humour was almost an offshoot of my own. We met only months after she had married. Had we met months before, the graph of both our lives might have been dramatically altered. Thin, dark, sultry with astounding cheekbones and a dead ringer for the young Loretta Young, Lesley was a capering sprite in Edinburgh, where she played the young daughter in David Pinner's *Fanghorn*. 'The reason we get on so well,' I told her, 'is that I am you. You merely a feminized offshoot of myself.' The symbiosis between us sustained something rich and invigorating for many years. The kind of affinity that can be picked up intact even after the passage of decades.

Before Gypsie became lodged in my gut, I had a short, swirly liaison with Rachel Stewart, a long, slim, red-haired vicar's daughter whose graciousness of spirit was almost angelic. Bred in the higher reaches of upper-middle-class gentility, she was an incongruous combination of spotless respectability and primitive urges. Articulate, cerebral, an insatiable reader, a cellist, she moved successfully into publishing and into a late and, as far as I know, happy marriage. When I was with her, I was acutely conscious of sinning, of suborning her Church of England rectitude into nefarious perversions, but I was also aware of the devil inside her enthusiastically co-operating. There is something heady and intoxicating about the mix of a rabid, lower East side Jewish youth and the wilful abandon of a church-going *shiksa*, a fusion of Heaven and Hell to which only William Blake could do justice.

At the end of relationships one is in the clutches of despair and indignation, and it is easy to believe that everything was just a long preamble to dust and ashes. But, with the passage of time, the glowing lineaments of what brought people together and sustained them for many years gradually becomes clear. Ultimately, it doesn't matter that one was tempest toss't by rows, delusions and incompatibilities. What does matter was the voyage itself and that, in retrospect, it had an abundance of fair days and clear skies; a passage, perhaps more turbulent than smooth, but one that progressed from knot to knot, from island to inlet, while a lot of other heady and routine business was being conducted. Both Gillian and Gypsie were seven-year voyages. Julia's foundered after only two. Amazingly, the bark remained intact, the vessel still seaworthy, the sense of adventure still alive to hazardous new journeys.

19   A *Closed Space*

In 1976, the Tottenham Court Road basement being threatened with redevelopment, I found a new set of theatre premises a couple of blocks away – an old post office building on Euston Road. This was also the year in which Julia and I, after a whirlwind courtship of six weeks, impetuously married. The rumour of our nuptials was scoffingly dismissed at the Open Space and, when our box office manager circulated copies of the evening papers pictorially proclaiming the event, the effect was pulverizing, the incredulity being based on the fact that, over the years, I had so dramatically perpetrated the image of the footloose bachelor and 'gay buckaroo' that its sudden dissolution was hard to assimilate. The incredulity was enhanced by the fact that a slouchy, dishevelled, Jewish *avant-garde* director seemed to have captured the very incarnation of the *shiksa* goddess.

While Thelma supervised the reconstruction of the new theatre, the incongruous newly-weds went off for a long jaunt to America. When we returned, we experienced the first tremors of the quake which eventually was to pull down everything. In an attempt to involve herself in my work, Julia had offered to design a snack bar at the new theatre. Although at first received with enthusiasm, once the project got under way and had to be budgeted and financed, it began to cause friction between Julia and Thelma. Suddenly the insinuation of a fresh taste which was neither Thelma's nor my own was manifesting itself – and it took some adjusting to – particularly on Thelma's part for, from the beginning, she always assumed that, using a certain amount of feminine obliquity and tactful circumnavigation, I could always be swayed on crucial issues. There were odd tensions, bitches and broodings and the gradual development of 'atmospheres' between Thelma and Julia, but I was too besotted and 'out of it' to pay any real attention. After forty years of insouciant profligacy, the phenomenon of marriage was all absorbing. But the storm clouds continued to gather and eventually I had to face the fact that there was something in the garden that wasn't roses.

Immediately after the marriage Thelma's behaviour had become inexplicable. She carried on like a jilted woman and made me feel that the marriage was somehow a betrayal of everything we had built up together. Our relationship, as I have said, was deep and emotional, but never romantic or intimate. Thelma had once said: 'There's no such thing as a relationship between a man and a woman which isn't sexual – in some way or other.' I now recalled the observation ruefully. What I had failed to take into account was the delicate strands of feeling that had been woven between us for almost fifteen years and what those represented in her mind. It was probably callous and stupid not to have informed her of the marriage beforehand. As I say, it was decided on a whim, barely eight weeks after Julia and I had met. With only one day's warning, I had asked Thelma to come to St Pancras Town Hall and be a witness at the civil ceremony. I was too engrossed in what was happening to me to realize that, at the same time, emotional repercussions were going on inside her. I could not understand why there should be any sense of betrayal. I was not 'betraying' one woman for another; one was my partner and the other my wife. But, eventually, it became clear to me that there were bonds there which defied rational analysis.

When, at the very start of the Open Space, Thelma had married an American actor named Lawrence Pressman and gone to the States for a honeymoon, I was almost immediately on the telephone summoning her back to London, where she was needed to help manage the Space. This was, no doubt, high handed, but she understood the priorities that made me ask her to return and responded to them. When that marriage began to go on the rocks, only months after being consummated, I was told I was being cited as a co-respondent in the divorce proceedings because of that peremptory return. Since nothing intimate had ever gone on between us, I found that preposterous, although it was certainly true I had urged Thelma to return to the theatre 'where she belonged' and equally true that she forsook her newly minted husband to do so. Perhaps some vestige of that memory was in her head when I suddenly married and then launched a three-month honeymoon in America. The labyrinth of emotions through which we both stumbled during this period can only be unravelled by in-depth analysis. At the time, I found her behaviour sullen, irrational and infuriating, but, with the passing of time, thoroughly understandable and to a large extent even justified. In any case, it marked the beginning of the end – not only of the Space but of our partnership.

Then came the pink bathtub scandal.

During the same period that the new theatre was being fitted out on Euston Road, Julia and I were furnishing our new flat in Hampstead and, having access to furnishers and builders, I arranged the purchase of certain items at trade prices from many of these same firms, one of these being a pink bathroom suite. One of the labourers helping to convert the new theatre, it turned out, was also a would-be actor whom we had routinely auditioned for our opening production, *Variations on The Merchant of Venice*. Being in many ways a better carpenter than he was a mummer, he never received a call back and, by devious means, found an uncomplimentary comment scrawled beside his name on the audition sheet.

This ambitious thespian and part-time builder, as it turned out, was living with a feature writer on the *Evening Standard* and, when part of the pink bathroom suite arrived at the theatre (to which it was diverted because the lease on the flat had not yet been completed), the umbrage he had taken at being rejected found a suitable outlet for revenge. The bathroom fixtures (he deduced and presumably reported to his journalist girlfriend) were goods intended for the theatre but appropriated for personal use and, as more and more of these 'items' began to appear at the building site, it seemed to him that a giant rip-off was in progress.

A few weeks later in Hampstead a reporter pried his way into the flat to ascertain that, indeed, a pink bathroom suite had been installed there and, while I was off at a conference in Stockholm, the storm broke in London: articles appeared implying misappropriation of funds on the part of the Artistic Director in regard to the newly furnished Hampstead flat in which his 'glamorous cover-girl bride' was to be ensconced. My own notoriety at the time was restricted to artistic and theatrical circles, but Julia being a top model (and highly photogenic) fanned the flames of the story for two or three days.

As one of the theatre's inaugural events, I had been planning a theatre event entitled *Bridal Suite*, based vaguely on my own nuptials, but dealing more essentially with the contradictions of the marital state and so, at the same time, was exploring the possibility of obtaining items for that production. This, coming as it did in the midst of the personal acquisitions, tended to complicate the issue further and raise even more doubts about my veracity.

Thelma feigned ignorance of the whole matter (although fully aware I had acquired various items at trade prices) and before long the Advisory Board, harried no doubt by the Arts Council, met to demand a full explanation.

With a great deal of umbrage and not a great deal of tact, I provided it. Yes, I had acquired the items in question and yes, I had them delivered to the theatre until the flat was ready for occupancy, and no I had not spent a penny of the theatre's money for these items – although it was certainly true I had acquired them at below-the-counter prices which, as far as I could see, was not a crime since everyone furnishing a new home sought to acquire goods at the lowest possible cost. But had I, in certain instances, negotiated them on Open Space stationery? Yes, I had, but clearly specifying that they were for personal use and not for the theatre. The brunt of my crime seemed to be that, in mixing up the acquisition of these items with the business of the theatre, I had put myself in a compromising position. The real point was that the odour of wrongdoing was in the air and so, according to the moral imperatives unleashed by the press, I had to counteract suspicions of guilt by heavily verifying my innocence, although the media's concern was neither my guilt nor my innocence, but how long they could protract what for them had become a 'hot story'.

With a variety of vouchers, receipts and letters, I made it abundantly clear that these were personal dealings and that no money from the company had been used – although the firms in question had been obtained through theatre contacts. Once the implication of misappropriation of funds was clearly ruled out, I asked for and received a letter from the Advisory Board removing the stigma of any shady dealings and declaring that 'the board were satisfied that there had been no misappropriation of Open Space funds by the Artistic Director' – a motion carried without dissent.

That done, I proceeded to push for a libel action against the *Evening Standard*. My solicitors roughly estimated the expense and advised that the most I could hope for was a retraction, but virtually no financial settlement, since I had suffered no financial damages. Knowing that a retraction many months, possibly years, after the initial story would be only a pyrrhic victory and reeling from the estimated costs of a protracted legal action which would unquestionably be defended by top-flight lawyers at the *Standard*, I let the whole thing drop – which was a gigantic error on my part, because forever after the incident remained nebulous, the most memorable part being the original allegations. As often happens, the pseudo-scandal had happened in public, the vindication in private.

Thelma made tracks shortly after that and, although she had been threatening to do so for many months before, to the outside world it appeared as if her disaffiliation was the result of the newspaper stories, whereas, in fact, it was because of a growing disenchantment with my new marital status and the introduction of an insupportable third party into a relationship which, for sixteen years, had been impregnably mutual.

Ironically, the marriage itself began to go to pot around the same time and, with it, my enthusiasm for the Open Space. No doubt, this was reflected in our work and the dilatory nature of our seasons. (We mounted a highly successful production of Strindberg's *The Father* with Denholm Elliot and Diane Cilento in the leads, and an off-beat musical entitled *Censored Scenes From King Kong* by Howard Schuman, co-author of a highly successful television series called *Rock Follies*, but the spark simply was not there.) Coupled with the squeeze from the Arts Council and a general disenchantment with Britain (which had been growing since 1976), it all wound down to an inevitable halt around 1980 – fulfilling my own prediction that most theatre-companies, if lucky, have about ten years of life.

We had eked out twelve. During those years, we had introduced the work of playwrights such as Peter Barnes, Howard Barker, David Rudkin, Trevor Griffiths, Howard Brenton, Mike Leigh and John Hopkins – and a whole roster of Americans including Sam Shepard, Terence McNally, Michael Weller, Lawrence Melfi, Jean Claude van Italie and Charles Ludlam. Many of our company actors wound up in the National Theatre or the RSC; our resident designers, particularly John Napier and Robin Don, made sizeable dents in the British theatre of the Seventies and Eighties. We had taken a flying kick at about two dozen classics, particularly Shakespeare, and gone further into theatrical experimentation than any other London company bar none. The impetus of the Sixties, which had brought us to life, had imperceptibly segued into the scintillating Seventies, and, by the time the next decade had begun, our fires were beginning to wane.

But, more important, the theatre in Britain was beginning to shed the skin of the past fifteen years and turn into something safe, less raunchy and considerably less charged. I do not mean to imply that *après moi* came the deluge. Far from it; many of the artists whom we had spawned went on to some of their best work – as actors, writers and directors – in the large subsidized companies, in the regions and in the West End. Whatever it was that made those twelve years of the Open Space unique – the off-the-wallness, the risk-taking, the wild cards – all that was beginning to peter out as the *Zeitgeist* which had brought it into being changed direction.

More pertinently perhaps, *I* was beginning to peter out. The ruinous marriage, the split with Thelma, the depressing liquidation of the company, the disaffiliation with everything British – all that brought about a sea-change in my personality and outlook. The British experience had begun to hollow me out. Putting on plays simply wasn't any fun any more. The actors took on their roles grudgingly, looking over their shoulder to television and film possibilities that would free them from the treadmill of low-paid theatrical chores. The audiences seemed to be made up of the same faces – dull, glazed, intellectually snide gapers who hungered only for novelty and seemed to be drawn almost exclusively from the ranks of the profession. Producing a show was like laying on a gigantic party for a roomful of guests one detested and then having one's home invaded by some of the most obnoxious people in London. After the plays were on, no matter what their critical reception, there was a terrible sense of desolation – a kind of post-coital depression from which all memory of any satisfying coitus was absent.

Shortly after the theatre's demise, I had an illuminating flash about myself and my 'career' – although to be honest, I'd never thought of it as a 'career' – it was just the course my obsessions happened to be taking at any given time. The realization was that, over the years, I had acquired a rather disagreeable public persona.

My theatre criticism, my public pronouncements, the nature of the plays I staged and the opinions publicly and privately expressed had combined to create a dark, cynical, pugnacious and abrasive personality which, by and large, tended to rub people up the wrong way. I had never gone out of my way consciously to cultivate friends and contacts. Over the years, I had written a multitude of personal letters in which I expressed my contempt for people's values, opinions or behaviour and blindly assumed that, after reading those insulting missives, they would be sufficiently chastened to mend their ways or at least reflect upon their shortcomings. At public meetings or in private discussions, I didn't mitigate my feelings about politics, art, commerce or personal assessments of people's character. I heed-lessly 'put down' actors, writers and artists in the hearing of people with whom they probably had close personal relations – not taking into account that in so doing I might be wounding sensitivities or bruising egos. I secretly prided myself on the fact that unadorned honesty was a kind of personal trademark without realizing that for others it was a sign of crude, rude and insolent behaviour.

Although brimful of prejudices, it never struck me that people actually took them personally or could possibly respond with genuine loathing. In a wholly irrational way, I assumed they would see that, despite my strong critical judgements, I never intended personal malice and it was genuinely shocking to discover that they should believe I disliked them *personally* for the ideas they espoused or the shortcomings they revealed. No matter how much I may have disliked certain actors or writers, it would never occur to me to boycott persons who were 'right' for certain roles or appropriate for certain projects. Was this naïveté or obtuseness or just plain stupidity? Probably all three.

In addition, I discovered that I had an unfortunate sense of humour, one that was often described as 'sick' or 'perverse', inventing outlandish details about people and/or myself with a perfectly straight face and then finding it incredible that people took these things seriously. It made them feel foolish, and the more abstruse the comic invention, the angrier they seemed to be. What for me was an innate and all-embracing sense of absurdity was for them a misplaced show of levity, often on grave matters where levity was clearly out of place. The fact that it was apparently serious, though in fact ludicrous, made many question my sense of propriety and many others my sense of balance. When people got to know me, they blithely accepted this comic perversity as part of my natural persona, but in most cases it was a deterrent against further familiarity and people conscientiously did *not* get to know me. For those who experienced it briefly and only in passing, it was further proof of my daemonic and disagreeable side.

As a director, I had introduced unorthodox rehearsal methods spawned from my reading of Artaud, Meyerhold, Stanislavsky and Michael Chekhov. For British actors, improvisation was terrifying enough, but I had got them to improvise using sounds and movement, forsaking the sacrosanct text and playing out their intentions in assorted rhythms, sometimes in gibberish, sometimes in whispers, singing their text, dancing their sub-text, sometimes marooned in different corners of a darkened auditorium, sometimes playing with bags over their heads or curled up in the foetal position. On occasion, I would transfer rehearsals into corresponding social situations – a pub, a community centre, a dance-hall – and ask them to interact with strangers. At other times, we would rehearse silently, expressing intentions only with our eyes or through hand signals. In final run-throughs, they would be asked to adopt foreign dialects, speech impediments or a bombastic nineteenth-century style of delivery which encouraged them to 'ham' unconscionably and to act as badly as they could.

Over the years reports of these practices began to circulate throughout the profession, inducing terror and alarm in the more vulnerable and faint hearted. A fierce resistance developed among those who knew of my work only from rumour or hearsay, who were not privy to the reasons behind these practices. 'All that stuff', they would convince each other, 'had nothing to do with acting', was disruptive, undignified, idiotic.

The irony was that, when actors terrified of these techniques were actually exposed to them, they not only came to understand the method behind the madness but to enjoy the artistic release that such work induced. But for every actor who experienced me as a director, there were a hundred who knew of me only from hearsay and so the theatre was awash with distorted anecdotes and ludicrous exaggerations. Today many of those techniques are widespread in the theatre and improvisation is not only an acknowledged tool but has also become an art form in its own right. But, in the mid-Sixties, it all felt like insidious subversion washed up on British shores by that most detested enemy of the British way of life, 'a bloody foreigner'.

So, when the Open Space shut its doors and I was thrown on to the marketplace, I discovered that there was a vast horde of people out there who wanted nothing to do with me and would never for a moment consider my directing a play for them or engaging in a collaborative project. A commercial agent, explaining why he wouldn't take me on, tactfully said: 'You see, you have this reputation of being well – volatile – and that tends to make people wary.' I don't want to overstate the case nor play the martyr. I wasn't exactly a pariah and certainly I had my share of advocates and champions, but by and large I was *persona non grata* in the British theatre and the reason for this disaffection seemed to be the 'style' I had cultivated for some twenty years and the connotation I had acquired as a critic, director and 'public figure'.

During the last three or four years of my stay in England, most of my theatre work was on the Continent, in Germany or Scandinavia. Almost all attempts to initiate independent projects in London came to nothing. Thelma, who was by then Director of the Round House, was instrumental in my mounting a free-styled adaptation of *Hedda Gabler* with Jenny Agutter in the lead, but even this project was badmouthed by a number of people in her own organization and roundly abused by critics when it opened. (The original *Hedda* had been a tearaway success in Norway, but this was because Ibsen's play, played in its original language, was ingrained in the Norwegian culture and audiences in Oslo and Bergen could appreciate the deviations and juxtapositions of a 'collage' treatment. Translated into English, it looked like a freaky exercise in cut-ups and had none of its original impact. Its reception was not due to the shortsightedness of British critics, but a serious case of misjudgement on my part.) Matters were further strained by the fact that I was now working on Thelma's turf – rather than our own – and so was conscious of the fact that, to the outside world, the production may have appeared to be the result of cronyism. In any case, it flopped badly and, coming after the fiasco of the Spike Milligan version of Jarry's *Ubu Roi* with Charlie Drake in the lead, it felt as if I had been set adrift on a flimsy raft rapidly going down stream.

Belatedly, I learned a number of political truths. In the theatre, it appeared, you did favours for certain people on the clear understanding that they would, at some point in the future, return them. You cultivated people in key positions either by flattering their egos or providing upbeat responses to their work on the assumption that they would reciprocate in kind. You maintained good relations by suppressing or diverting your true feelings so that, when the time came, you could call upon them to help realize your own aims and intentions. You kept 'in' with influential managers and producers because 'you never knew when they would come in handy'. You socialized in pubs and at parties in order to ingratiate yourself with people to whom you might have to turn for professional advantage. In short, you 'played the game' and, as a result, stood the chance of winning certain innings, perhaps even 'scoring big'.

For close on fifteen years as the director of my own company and immersed in my own artistic agenda, I had not 'played the game'. I had played my own, and according to rules, it now appeared, not shared by others. Although in superficial contact with the rest of my profession, it suddenly appeared that I was actually alone. My assumptions were not theirs, nor theirs mine. We had never had to confront one another and tally up the differences in our world views. Ostensibly, we were all 'in the theatre', all 'doing our own thing', but this was an illusion.

As 1980 rolled around, I had to accept a number of grim truths. The kind of theatre I had been espousing for twenty-five years

– experimental, continuous, based on a permanent company and exploring areas which were intrinsically non-commercial – was never going to acquire a subsidy in Britain and, without subsidy, could not exist. At best, I could mount a one-off production illustrating the kinds of concerns I had and the sorts of areas I wished to explore, but because it *was* one off and not the product of a finitely researched continuing process, it would never convince. I was placed in the position of a man who, more than anything else, wished to be a scientist but was denied a laboratory, instruments, the ability to conduct research or monitor his experiments. On occasions, I was given an ancient microscope, some cracked test tubes and a Bunsen burner, relegated to a small alcove behind a large kitchen and told to see what I could come up with – although as soon as meals started to be served I must expect to be dispossessed. Gradually, I had persuaded myself that writing meant more to me than directing – or was this an enforced rationalization because the much-touted permanent company never came about?

Throughout these years I had realized that the single greatest stumbling block in directing had been people. Although I experienced a great rush of adrenalin transforming my ideas into concrete theatrical images, I had become progressively more impatient with the people upon whose work I depended. I had concocted a kind of shibboleth that said: 'I wish to make contact with my actors' talent – not their personalities. It is what they can creatively conjure up that concerns me, not who or what they are.' It was a way of by-passing the obvious fact that I could not (or did not wish to) deal with them as individuals. I wanted the fruits of collaborative labour without the irritations of personal interplay. Or is this merely a circuitious way of saying I just didn't like people? Although that is rather sweeping, I have to admit to a certain surge of misanthropy in my nature and particularly in regard to actors and actresses, whom I had come to see as narrowly circumscribed individuals with limited interests and vaunting egos, the smaller the talent, the greater the ego. One of the attractions of writing was that it rescued me from the quicksand and potholes of social contact which, by 1980, I had come to loathe.

Another part of this general perception was that, certainly in

Britain, mediocrity would always be enthroned. Glen Byam Shaw, Michael Langham, 'Binkie' Beaumont, Lord Goodman, Bernard Delfont, Lew Grade, Bernard Miles, Lord Chandos, Peter Hall, Stuart Burge, John Clements – these were the tiny titans of my times. On the second tier, one could find somewhat upgraded specimens such as George Devine, Laurence Olivier, Trevor Nunn, Max Stafford Clark, Richard Eyre. But, as a general rule, it was the sludge that rose to the surface and those who were callow, cautious and unenterprising who made their way into the top posts to preserve the *status quo* and ensure that, even if boats were rocked, waves would never be made.

Ultimately, I came to realize that the forces that were gradually asphyxiating me had more to do with the social and intellectual climate of Britain than anything else. My enemy was the society which, some twenty years before, I had fervently embraced as civilized, literate, intellectually challenging and culturally stimulating. Whether the result of a massive introjection, I cannot say, but it was clear that something was coming to a close in Britain and, if I was to survive that closure, I had to make tracks. I was starting to do what I never dreamed I would ever do: re-confront my Americanness and my bond with a country I had resolutely left some twenty years before. I was, in fact, shrugging off the mortal coil of my British self and preparing the rebirth of my American persona.

Within a year, I would be living in California and watching the links of over two decades in Europe gradually loosen and fall away.

20   *Escape from Wonderland*

The meltdown of the theatre and the bust-up of the marriage opened a 'slough of despond' which was only the first stop in a progressive cycle of descent which, when it finally came to a halt, found me in some pit far to the south of Dante's seventh circle of Hell. Shrinks, I found, were useless. I was never able to buy the premise upon which their psychic interrogations were based and, as a result, could abide neither their manner nor the obviousness of their methods. I declined the 'little green pills' because I didn't see how a chemical capsule could possibly affect a crisis of circumstance.

I declined all offers to direct abroad. I didn't return phone calls about television appearances or attendance at symposia and conferences. I cut, offended or overtly insulted people who had been helpful, encouraging and genuinely useful in the creation of the theatre. I avoided certain restaurants where I knew I would find 'colleagues' or ex-collaborators. I stopped trying to reach people on the telephone. I stopped listening to music. I stopped reading newspapers. After a frustrating and aimless meeting with the Advisory Board of the Open Space, Thelma now ensconced in her new job at the Round House, my natural juices as dry as an old sow's dugs, I decided to liquidate the Open Space. This was done in 1980 and, in the wretched and irrational morass which was then my mind, I saw it as a sacrifice made on the altar of the dead marriage.

During these doldrums, the only activity I found myself able to pursue was sex, believing that the possibility of new sensations could be found only in some magical partner who might have the power to re-charge me, turn on what circumstance and my own sloth had so resolutely turned off. The search was unflagging; the rewards, when not paltry, contemptible. There was a myriad of one-night stands, followed by a cluster of short-term relationships in which I became expert at fabricating nonexistent qualities in people who, when they lost those false attributions, vanished in the smoke of my own self-delusions. There was a long sequence of regular frustrations as I found myself bowling outside my league, and even greater ones when scoring easily within it. The social chain of being, I discovered, consisted of men lusting after desirable women they could not obtain whilst undesirable women lusted after them.

There was one oasis, one watering-hole where the possibility of reanimating myself became just barely possible. Her name was Susan Kyd: a bright, wide-eyed actress with a strong, chiselled face reminiscent of the early Ann Sheridan, whose natural incandescence managed to light up the impenetrable darkness in which I seemed to be shrouded. By then, I had made up my mind to return to America. But Susan's commitment to England was deep-rooted and unshakeable. For her, it was a bright land with tantalizing possibilities which consistently keyed up her enthusiasm and kindled her hopes. In the mist of all that brimming optimism, I felt like a devil trying to corrupt an angel. I heard myself watering down her praise for plays and players, putting forward my devil's advocacy for people and movements she would instinctively champion, squirting my insidious cynicism like so many dollops of poison into her bubbling wells of optimism. Although I felt a kind of desperate fervour in regard to Susan – that is, I came to believe she could save my life – it became clear that the redemption couldn't happen at the scene of my spiritual demise, and there was no way of prying her out of England.

At about the same time, to ward off penury and to force me to interact with living persons as opposed to wraiths, I took on a teaching position at Trent Park College in Middlesex. There, twice a week I found myself bleating about the theatre to a small aggregation of pimply youths whose unswervable aims were passing exams and securing jobs. It was like lecturing serried ranks of shop window mannequins, never really expecting any response because one knew from the outset that their heads were fitted into place by a five-inch screw in their necks. Only one of these expressionless wads of moulded plaster actually had a face. It was the face of a cherub, blonde, blue-eyed and with a luminescence that clearly indicated there was spirituality behind that delicately sculpted mass of living tissue. Being the helpless moth I was, I flew immediately to that light. Her name was Jane Allsop.

Here, I encapsulate events.

We began arranging trysts nearby the school, but obviously our stratagems weren't very subtle as an item appeared in the Diary column of the *Evening Standard* alluding to the 'special attentions' instructor Marowitz was paying to one of his more nubile students. On a sudden impulse, we went to New York for Christmas. When we got back, I went to do a show in Seattle. Jane followed. I then went to do a show in Oslo. Jane followed again. I had by then resolved that I was going to pack up England and move to California. I put this to her, sensing the absurdity of proposing that, at the age of twenty and still a schoolgirl, she leave England and join me in a part of America of which I knew nothing and which likewise knew nothing of me, and which therefore might not be able to sustain either of us in any form of employment. Without blinking, she opted to join me. We arrived in Los Angeles in 1981 amd checked into the Breakers Motel; from there we moved to a small apartment in Santa Monica, then to a one-room pad on Ocean Avenue, eventually to a two-bedroomed apartment, and finally to a three-storey house in Malibu overlooking the Pacific and beyond the reach of all the heinous succubi which had tried to drain me dry in England. Slowly, I recovered something of the cultural patina I'd had when I was living in America. For Jane, the identity transformations involved the invention of a stage name, i.e. Windsor, which, to my whimsical imagination, conjured up exactly the right regal associations to impress the gullible American hordes which would shortly be assessing her qualities as an actress.

In a sense, we both became other people. I had put a great torch to England once and for all and, when I looked back, it was as if every bridge I had ever crossed was smoking in the distance, belching up great, big, dirty flames and declaring themselves permanently impassable. That was the way I wanted it. I threw the firebrand from my hand, watched it fizzle out in the Pacific, then turned to what would doubtless be the last third of my life in an American city which, for me, was as far from New York as London was for Jane.

As we sat on that plane winging us towards California, I felt the time distancing me from Heathrow to LAX was not ten or eleven hours, but two and a half decades, and that, when I stepped off the plane, it would be like disembarking a space-ship that had sped me from one life to another, that the person who walked down the gangplank in Los Angeles would bear no resemblance whatsoever to the one who had hauled his cases through the London traffic only hours before.

In California I experienced the liberating sensation of starting from scratch. Some of my British reputation had made it over to New York, but, by and large. I was an unknown quantity in California. For Jane, bred in Felixstowe and domiciled in Enfield, it was the epitome of the 'brave new world', a world peopled with tanned and burnished sun-worshippers in sawn-off shorts and T-shirts, a world whose blue skies and incessant sunshine made a mockery of the decades we had spent in the ubiquitously pissing rain of England.

Soon after arriving in Los Angeles I was drawn into one of the two professional theatres in the city, where I directed a number of classics and new plays, adapting myself to an intellectual climate and a public very different from the one I had known in London, maintaining a tenuous link with Old Sod by lodging reviews for publications such as the *Guardian* and *The Times*, and beginning to write plays in a vein very different from the classical adaptations I had fashioned in Europe. One of these, which I have already described, *Sherlock's Last Case*, leapfrogged from Los Angeles to Broadway, where it had a run of about six months. Other plays were performed in Seattle, Houston, Chicago and New York. That part of me which had edited, cut and reviewed the work of dozens of British and American writers suddenly came to the fore, and I found myself being considered by others, and grudgingly by myself, as a playwright as well as a director.

After a time, I found my natural instincts being blunted by the Los Angeles Theater Center, a theatre which espoused innovation but was essentially tame and timorous, ground down in my opinion by a tasteless management and an inbred lack of style, and so, though situated snugly under its central arch, I set fire to that bridge as well, leaping quickly free of the flames. With all those fuliginous fumes still permeating my nostrils, I landed the post of drama critic on the *Los Angeles Herald Examiner* which, nine months after I joined them, came crashing into ruins – whether through my aegis or its own massive deficits I could never be certain. Theatres I had savaged in print and artistic directors on whose good graces I depended began to distance themselves from my overtures. Letters did not get answered and phone calls were not returned. That wariness which had hounded me in England gradually began to surface again. It seemed to some that I was invisibly mined, that if some untoward move were made, it would detonate an invisible explosive and send shrapnel flying everywhere. The acerbic, goading, hectoring and admonishing side of my nature which found it impossible to bed down with mediocrity or slither into the embraces of cosy compromise had gradually reasserted itself.

In a blinding flash of satori-like recognition I saw that I was staring again into the face of my own wilfulness. All the work I had ever done that had ever amounted to anything I had conjured up for myself – almost always in the face of daunting odds: my very first off-Broadway group in New York when I was eighteen years old; In-Stage in London in 1958; the Open Space ten years later. The only collaborator I could ever count on whole-heartedly was myself and, if I was going to continue to work in the theatre, I had to banish all idea of easing myself into someone else's context – no matter how *simpatico*. I was, for better or worse, one of those truly damned people who could only maintain what he himself engendered. I was, as I had always been, congenitally unemployable – except by myself in tandem with my own vision and my own idiosyncratic preferences. I was writing plays. They were being produced – not only in California and in regional theatres but also on Broadway and in Europe. I was functioning as a writer and as a director, as a critic and as a teacher. Despite the wariness, despite the apprehensions, when I looked about, there always seemed to be a number of willing ears and helping hands, actors who wanted me to direct them, writers who wished me to stage their works, editors who wanted to publish my opinions.

I suddenly thought to myself: all those bridges! – I hadn't burnt them. They had conflagrated themselves – gone up in smoke as if to verify the fact that they were spanning distances

I had never meant to negotiate. I was not, as I had believed, a burner of bridges, but a builder of bridges – and the real point was not that they had collapsed but that I had managed to rebuild them one after the other. With my impulsive departure from the L.A. Theater Center, the most recent one had crumbled, and so another had to be constructed in its place. Metaphorically assembling my pylons and cables, my mortar and steel, I took a long hard look around me.

I was living in Malibu, California – a fast-growing, leisure-laden community without a theatre. I began to envisage another theatrical entity – no different in essence from the one I'd envisaged when I was eighteen, when I was twenty-five, when I was thirty-four. All the old clay was at hand waiting to be re-cast: an ensemble, a training ground, a clutch of classics, a wadge of new plays, an embryonic audience, money to be raised, letters to be written, a dogma to be espoused, a certain stance to be adopted – another bridge! And, if this one were also to be burnt behind me, it no longer mattered. I was now the proud possessor of bridge-building equipment and, as long as I had that, all I really needed was space and time and will.

Appendix

Marowitz/Tynan correspondence in
Transatlantic Review 16.

Dear Sir,
I've just read Charles Marowitz' interview with
himself in *Transatlantic Review 16.* It's a
remarkable piece of narcissistic bravura (one
pictures Marowitz, the fastest gun in the West
End, practising his draw in front of a mirror), but
it contains a few comments on the National
Theatre that really ought to be tempered or
corrected.

Marowitz derides the N.T. because its company
'lacks any semblance of style'. As I write, the
company is just eight months old. If it had evolved
a 'style' as rapidly as that I would be ashamed
of it, although trendseeking journalists might well
have been impressed. Later in the article
Marowitz triumphantly declares that the theatre
of the future will have 'no patience with stylistic
consistency'. So where does this get us? For
lacking 'style', the N.T. is condemned and the
theatre of the future applauded. I long to hear this
contradiction resolved.

Nor is it the only one. Having singled out Jack
Richardson as the most promising off-Broadway
playwright precisely because he is a
'language-man and a true parodist', Marowitz goes
on to acclaim improvised 'happenings' and the
anti-literary theatre of Artaud as the brightest
hopes for the future. Citing the Theatre of Cruelty
season at LAMDA to prove his point, Marowitz
says that the Royal Shakespeare Company is

'more important' than the National Theatre. He might have added that he is employed by the Royal Shakespeare Company and that he co-directed the LAMDA season.

A word or two on the tangled question of 'style'. Most of the great companies who have created recognizable 'styles' have confined themselves to a more or less limited repertoire – e.g. the Comédie Française specializes in the French seventeenth-century classics, the Moscow Arts Theatre specializes in late nineteenth-century plays, the Berliner Ensemble specializes in Brecht. Moreover, when the Royal Shakespeare Company itself ventures outside the works of its eponymous bard, it habitually (and quite naturally) invites the help of guest performers. If you restrict the range of your repertoire, it is much easier to build a permanent company and evolve a consistent production style.

What Marowitz ignores is that the National Theatre works from a wider brief. It is called on to cover the whole theatrical waterfront from Sophocles and Shakespeare to Coward and Beckett. I can't off hand think of a production style that would be equally appropriate to *Philoctetes* and *Hay Fever*. Perhaps Marowitz can.

Perhaps, on the other hand, he wouldn't want to. I detect in his prophecies, with their enthusiasm for action painting, 'happenings' and 'booting Ibsen and his whole school solidly up the ass', the familiar provocations of the professional outcast who loves to be hated, who needs an audience to reject him, who wants experimental theatre to get back to the minority cellars where it began, who resents the idea that minority theatre should ever become popular, and who fails to realize (and this is the crucial, deplorable failure) that the purpose of a true *avant-garde* is not to be an end in itself but a beach-head from which to conquer the majority. For Marowitz, theatre ceases to be art as soon as people like it. I don't think majority theatre, however good, would ever have much appeal for him. It's significant that he should have chosen to interview himself. The kind of theatre he prefers could easily end up 'talking to itself'.

Yours sincerely,

Kenneth Tynan

Charles Marowitz: A Reply:

The spectacle of Ken Tynan turned PR man is quite rattling. As a critic one could both admire and oppose him, but as National Theatre apologist one just shakes one's head in dismay. Even his style seems to have suffered: the brilliant punster of the late 1950s would never have stooped to something as laboured as 'the fastest gun in the West End'.

As for his confusion over company style and 'stylistic consistency', they are quite patently two different things. The style of a company is clearly the product of social and aesthetic attitudes: how actors and directors feel about their craft and the world. Being impatient with 'stylistic inconsistency', as is quite clear from the context, refers to hard-and-fast uniformity of style within the same play rather than abrupt stylistic switches – i.e. naturalistic drama suddenly turning into black comedy, farcical situations played in dead earnest. My point was that the former was a prerequisite of a permanent company, and the latter a rigidity of the drama that the theatre of the future might well discard.

Considering the amount of publicity the LAMDA season received, I would have to be boneheaded to pretend I wasn't associated with it and, in fact, the biographical note in the last issue of *Transatlantic Review* directly acknowledges that association. But if Tynan wants evidence of personal drumbeating, he might be interested to learn that I am staging a Jack Richardson play at the Edinburgh Festival, and the *Hamlet* experiment I mentioned in my piece was devised by myself. This raises the very interesting question as to what comes first, the enthusiasm or the commitment? I don't admire Richardson because I am staging him; I am staging him because I admire him. I don't respect the Royal Shakespeare Company because I happen to work there, I happen to work there because I respect its policies. If affirming one's enthusiasms is also blowing one's own trumpet, I suppose I am guilty of some pretty hot licks. (However, if testimonials to my objectivity were required, I could provide Tynan with at least half a dozen highly critical pieces of the Royal Shakespeare Company written while in its employ.)

Tynan's third point is a scaling down of the truth for his own polemical purposes. Although the companies he mentions do 'specialize' in certain plays of certain periods, nevertheless, they do stage works which are completely uncharacteristic. When the Moscow Arts play Wilde or Sheridan, the style of the company is still in evidence – obviously adapting itself to the stylistic needs of each particular play. The TNP under Jean Vilar, which could never be accused of 'restricting its repertoire', manages in every production to retain an unmistakable ensemble character. This is not, as Tynan suggests, an external production style which gives a company its character, but the interaction of shared technique and social beliefs. My criticism of the National Theatre Company was that I could not discern any such technique or beliefs from its work, and that criticism still stands.

Tynan's last point is the most shattering in its obtuseness. 'The purpose of a true *avant-garde*', he writes, 'is not to be an end in itself but a beach-head from which to conquer the majority.' Tynan's conception of the *avant-garde* is seen – like everything else – in Marxist battle terms. On the one hand, the established theatre (Batista) and on the other, the insurgent army (Castro) who wants to wrest control. This is not my definition.

The true *avant-garde* is a *running alternative* to the boulevard theatre, which is too necessary and entrenched ever to be 'conquered'. Experimental theatre does not mean showcase productions through which new writers and directors are picked up by commercial managements and thereby infiltrate the 'big time', but the establishment of little clans of artistic dissent which attract their own audience and do their own work. This work may or may not seep through to the majority theatre. It is certainly not directed to it. Some groups like the Living Theatre in New York and the Actors Workshop in San Francisco throw down roots on their 'beach-head' and operate there for people who prefer beach-heads to bastions. If Tynan thinks the secret ambition of the *avant-garde* is to set up shop in Shaftesbury Avenue, he has very little understanding of the kind of people involved in such activity.

If one has been brought up with stars in one's eyes (as Tynan has), the greatest theatre is the place where the most celebrated actors work. But it is this majority theatre – whether on Broadway, the Paris boulevards or Shaftesbury Avenue – which is in such a dire state today. One has to be godawfully blinkered to theatrical dilemma to subscribe to Tynan's Panglossian view of 'popular theatre'. And it is a view that can be held only by people for whom everything is already taped. For Tynan, the theatre is Marxist–Humanist–intellectual and star-studded. The idea that its forms might be radically overhauled sends him into quiet paroxysms. He is offended that anyone should 'hate' it and certain that the 'hater' must be a 'professional outcast' or a secret masochist. (Offended, perhaps, in an almost personal way by those people who don't think the New Wave and warmed up Brecht is the avatar of theatrical achievement.) He is nonplussed by the possibility that the modern theatre with its nineteenth-century hangover, its Ibsen–Shaw axis, is in fact very *unpopular* with a whole new generation of theatre artists who find it woefully effete next to the modern film or the modern sculpture.

The kind of theatre I was writing about (point conceded) *does* 'end up by talking to itself' or, to put it more accurately, to a minority audience that prefers the accents and inflections of a small theatre to the often predictable hoopla of the established playhouses. The Moscow Arts Theatre started by talking to itself; so did the Vieux Colombier and the Group Theatre. How else does one assemble one's own thoughts? Talking to oneself, it seems to me, is certainly preferable to addressing multitudes and having nothing to say.

Charles Marowitz

Index

Index